DIVIDED
LIVES

DIVIDED LIVES

American Women in the Twentieth Century

ROSALIND ROSENBERG

CONSULTING EDITOR: ERIC FONER

HILL AND WANG

A division of Farrar, Straus and Giroux

New York

For Helen, Thomas, Doris, and Irwin

CONTENTS

PREFACE ix

1. *The Family Claim: 1900* 3

2. *Domesticating the State: 1901–12* 36

3. *Claiming the Rights of Men: 1912–29* 63

4. *Crisis Years: 1929–45* 102

5. *Cold War Fears: 1945–61* 138

6. *Feminism Reborn: 1961–73* 180

7. *The Family Claim Revisited: 1973–91* 220

Epilogue: Toward the Year 2000 245

BIBLIOGRAPHICAL ESSAY 257

INDEX 279

PREFACE

Since 1900 American women have made extraordinary strides toward achieving personal autonomy, sexual freedom, economic independence, and legal rights. And yet even today they remain lesser members of the family, the economy, and the polity. The purpose of this book is to explain both the extent and the limits of women's achievements in this century, by examining women's lives within the larger context of the social and political history of which they have been an integral part. Ironically, the very conditions that have most encouraged women's movement away from Victorian dependency have often hindered their achieving full equality. The American tradition of federalism, racial and ethnic diversity, geographic mobility, and relative abundance has fostered a politics of individual liberty that has been critical to women's winning such legal guarantees as the right to vote, the right to equal employment, and the right to control their reproductive lives. Yet, largely because of these same conditions, women have been far less successful in overcoming inequality within the family and in winning the kinds of social services that might make private inequality less burdensome. Women have won the formal right to equal employment, but the domestic service that men continue to expect from them puts women at a competitive disadvantage in the economic world. Women have won the right to vote, but divisions of class, religion, race, and ethnicity often prevent them from speaking with one voice on women's behalf. As a consequence, women have led divided lives—divided between domestic and paid labor, and divided from one another.

The modern history of American women dates from the 1960s and reflects the influence of the civil rights movement. Just as civil rights leaders were emphasizing the essential sameness of blacks and whites, so, too, did women's historians stress the fundamental identity of women and men. Working from this assumption, historians tended to portray women as victims of discrimination and faulty socialization, and to explain change as something that happened to them—as when World War II pulled large numbers of women into the labor force, changing their behavior and, eventually, their attitudes. By the middle of the 1970s, however, a new approach was emerging. Rather than emphasizing the sameness of men and women, historians began to stress their differences. In this view women no longer served primarily as symbols of disadvantage but instead represented agents of change who openly criticized the dominant political system on the basis of values forged in a separate female culture. Historians who emphasized women's differences from men were not as ready as earlier scholars to regard male achievement as the measure of female emancipation. Instead, they tried to see the world as women saw it and to identify the ways in which women's distinctive values altered the course of history. In the process, the study of housework, mothering, sexuality, and women's organizations all took on added significance.

By the mid-1980s a new concern complicated this historical debate. Historians of working women, African-Americans, Latinas, and Native Americans began to argue that differences between men and women were often inconsequential compared to differences among women of different class, race, and religious backgrounds. Sexuality had different meanings for poor, rural women than it did for privileged urban women. To black women the feminist preoccupation with rape often sounded like a veiled attack on black men. To the middle-class career woman, equal rights had an allure it did not hold for the daughter of Zuni Indians, whose culture respected maternal authority. Increasingly, historians came to stress that race and class are sometimes more powerful forces than gender in shaping women's lives and in claiming women's loyalty.

This book argues that none of the approaches described above can alone explain the history of American women in the twentieth century. The first, in emphasizing women's identity with men, fails fully to explore women's distinctive contributions and experiences. The second, in stressing women's differences from men, neglects the dramatic changes in self-conception that have taken place among women in this century. The third, in focusing on the diversity of women's lives, has failed to recognize the extent to which women from varied backgrounds have shared common experiences. And none tells us as much as we need to know about the larger political, economic, and cultural context in which change has taken place.

This book does not attempt to tell one story; there is no one story of American women's past. But it brings together the differing perspectives outlined above, traces their roots back to the beginning of the twentieth century, and explores their interaction over time. It begins with an explanation of the domestic sources of the belief in women's distinctive, nurturing power. It examines the emergence of the countervailing faith that women and men are essentially the same. And it sets the story of these competing beliefs within the larger context of economic change and cultural and political conflict. At times women's lives seem to have changed with stunning swiftness, as they did in the years around 1912 when the first feminists began challenging the conventional view that women and men were fundamentally different. At times all change seems to have ground to a halt, as it often appeared to do from the 1930s through the 1950s, when the Depression, then World War II, and finally the Cold War branded women's concerns as selfish, except to the extent that they served men's needs. Even in periods of seeming stasis, however, long-term trends prepared the way for new departures. Women's growing control over their own fertility, their increasing educational achievements, their growing work-force experience all laid the foundation for a new burst of change in the 1960s. And then in the 70s and 80s a conservative backlash threatened to bring the country full circle to the domestic concerns of the century's start.

Throughout the century these fundamental changes have been complicated by the diversity of American women's experiences.

While middle-class white women campaigned for individual rights early in the century, immigrant women struggled to maintain their cultural traditions. While Northern working-class and middle-class activists worked to include women within the New Deal, Southerners fought any extension of federal power. While Southern black women struggled for individual rights in the 1950s, middle-class white women professed a renewed belief in self-abnegation. While Chicana farm workers found new pride in their struggle to win better lives for their children in the 1960s, middle-class white women were declaring motherhood to be a trap. And while a few professional women climbed to the very pinnacle of corporate success in the 1980s, the majority shouldered a double burden of domestic responsibilities and wage labor. This is not, therefore, a tidy story of steadily increasing freedom for all, but rather a complex tale in which the very concepts of freedom and progress, commonality and difference, have been the subject of continuing debate.

This book could not have been written but for the work of hundreds of other scholars who have been exploring the history of American women in the twentieth century over the past two decades. I owe them all a great debt. I owe much as well to the librarians at Barnard College, the Columbia University Oral History Collection, the Schlesinger Library, and the National Archives for guiding me through their collections; to Dean Robert McCaughey and History Department Chair William McNeil of Barnard College for granting me time to write; and to Catherine Clinton, Nancy Woloch, Ellen Chesler, Clarence Walker, Elizabeth Capelle, Herbert Sloan, Beth Bailey, David Farber, Mark Carnes, Caroline Niemczyk, Kenneth Jackson, and Gina Morantz-Sanchez for offering suggestions along the way. I am especially grateful to my editor, Eric Foner, and my publisher, Arthur Wang. This book has been much improved by their advice. Finally, I wish to thank my sons, Cliff and Nick, and my husband, Gerry, who, as always, encouraged and sustained me.

DIVIDED
LIVES

1

The Family Claim
1900

"It has always been difficult for the family to regard the daughter otherwise than as a family possession," wrote Jane Addams in 1898. Addams was thinking of women like herself, educated daughters of well-to-do parents. But few women of her time escaped what she called "the family claim." Whether a daughter was a rural sharecropper, a small-town schoolgirl, or a big-city factory worker, her family expected that she devote herself to her husband and children if she married, or to her parents and other relatives if through some misfortune she did not. Even women like Addams, who left home to establish a career, found that the family claim affected their lives. It set limits on their independence, reinforced any impulse toward self-denial, and shaped their expectations about power and powerlessness both in the home and beyond.

For their brothers the situation was different. As Addams observed, "The grown-up son has so long been considered a citizen with well-defined duties and a need of 'making his own way in the world' that the family claim is urged much less strenuously in his case, and as a matter of authority, it ceases gradually to be made at all." The weakening of the family's claim upon the son derived both from the democratization of American politics after the American Revolution and the growth of the country's economy over the course of the nineteenth century. Once the Revolution declared all men (that is, all white men) to be equal, neither the state, the church, nor even their fathers could exercise the same power over sons as had been common in colonial America. Economic growth eroded that power still further by removing production from the patriarchal household to shops and factories. Women joined in this removal; in fact, by 1900 they made up 21.2 percent of the work force. But most conceived their work outside the home to be temporary, to be interrupted after a few years by marriage and a return to the hearth. As men spent more time away from home, household burdens fell exclusively to women. In 1900, wherever they might live, women fed and clothed the family, nursed the sick, taught the young, and fostered communal ties.

Within this common experience, however, the family claim took many forms, depending on where a woman lived and the work the men in her family performed. At the turn of the century only 20 percent of all males were employed in the white-collar or professional occupations that qualified a man and his dependents for middle-class status. Another 40 percent of all men worked in the expanding industrial sector. Because industrial wages were typically too low to support a family, most women added sewing and the care of boarders to their other duties to make ends meet. The remaining 40 percent of all male workers continued to work on farms, where the burdens on women weighed most heavily of all. As farm prices fell at the end of the nineteenth century, many women found themselves sharing the work of the men, while, in the words of one black woman, "doing a woman's part at home."

A Southern Sharecropper

When Lucy Hurston's water broke, she could find no one to help. Her husband, John, had not been seen for months. A carpenter and self-taught minister, he was often away building houses and preaching, or so he said. All of the other "grown folks" in the all-black town of Eatonville, Florida, were off butchering hogs, either for themselves or some other family. Lucy sent one of the younger children to find Aunt Judy, the midwife. Most rural women relied on midwives to help them through their labor; doctors were for well-off city women. But Aunt Judy had gone to a hog-butchering party a couple of miles away. Lucy, having given birth six times in ten years, worried that this baby would not wait for Aunt Judy's return. How was she going to manage alone? Ninety pounds and frail, she might not be able to push without help. But she did, and then lay motionless, too weak to do anything more. Listening to the baby's wails, she worried what would become of them both.

When help finally arrived, it did so in an unlikely form. A family friend, a white man, had butchered the day before, and, knowing that John Hurston was gone, he decided to drive the five miles to Eatonville to bring Lucy and her children some fresh meat. He arrived a few minutes after the baby, heard its cries, and ran to help. He cut the umbilical cord, put water on to boil, and cleaned up as best he could. But when Aunt Judy finally appeared, she gave him no thanks. Indeed, she grumbled for years that the cord had not been well cut, nor the bellyband put on tight enough. The baby would probably have a weak back, and not be able to hold its water. According to Aunt Judy, birthing couldn't be trusted to menfolk.

The attention of a midwife in a birthing mother's own home gave women a sense of security and control over their lives that they later lost as hospital deliveries became more common, but the primitive state of obstetrical knowledge cost women dearly. At the turn of the century, one in seven babies died at birth, as did one in thirty mothers over the course of their childbearing years. The poverty of city slums and isolated rural areas, plus the failure to license midwives, gave America the dubious distinction of having one of the highest rates of infant and maternal mortality among all industrialized countries. Only tuberculosis posed a greater hazard to the lives of women of childbearing age. Fortunately, both Lucy and her new daughter, Zora Neale, survived their first ordeal together, despite the odds against them.

Lucy Hurston was still a young woman, twenty-six years old, when she gave birth to her seventh child. Born in 1875 to the landowning Potts family of Macon County, Alabama, she had met her husband when she was only fourteen. Singing in the choir of the Macedonia Baptist Church one Sunday, young Lucy noticed a tall, strongly built, light-skinned man staring up at her. She learned he was one of those "niggers from over de creek" who lived from one white man's plantation to another. "Regular hand-to-mouth folks. Didn't own pots to pee in, nor beds to push 'em under," as Zora later reported.

Lucy Potts's mother was none too happy about a man like John Hurston paying attention to her daughter. Mrs. Richard Potts had no intention of allowing Lucy, the prettiest black girl in Macon County, to throw herself away on a poor sharecropper, and a bastard at that, allegedly a certain white man's son. Mrs. Potts hated the Southern racial-caste system and what it had done to blacks. White men in the South idealized the purity of white women, while casting blacks of both sexes in the role of sexual libertines. They set white women on pedestals in the name of female virtue, lynched black men as a threat to that virtue, and preyed on black women on the grounds that they had no virtue. To Mrs. Potts, John Hurston's pale skin represented everything she despised—sexual immorality, violence, poverty—and she had no intention of allowing her daughter to be touched by these malign forces.

Not all black women shared Mrs. Potts's moral views. Indeed, many embraced a much freer acceptance of sexuality. Sociologist Hortense Powdermaker, studying rural Mississippi in the 1930s, observed that among poor blacks premarital "chastity is neither very common nor very highly prized," and that among older people "there is a fairly complete acceptance of illegitimate children, with no feeling that they are branded or disgraced."

An easy acceptance of sexuality was not confined to blacks. Among rural whites in backwoods areas removed from the tensions of the interracial South, sexual practices would have shocked Mrs. Potts and many of the other ladies of the Macedonia Baptist Church. In the Ozarks, for instance, couples regularly copulated amid their newly planted fields, a practice meant to ensure a good crop. This bawdy approach to life carried over into local square dances, where fiddlers sawed out such tunes as "Grease My Pecker, Sally Ann" and "Fucking in the Goober Patch." One Missouri fiddler later recalled that these dances remained popular until "the folks that knowed 'em . . . got religion" in the evangelical revivals of the early twentieth century.

Whatever their view of sexuality, most rural people regarded marriage as an essential goal for all young people. Indeed, marital rates in the South stood well above the 90 percent average for the country at large. Lucy Potts's mother may have been more puritanical than most, but she was not alone in wanting her daughter to strike as sound a bargain as she could when it came to choosing a husband. Lucy's daughter Zora grew up to write poignantly of this aspiration in *Their Eyes Were Watching God* (1937), the story of a black girl named Janie coming of age in the South at the turn of the century. Janie's elderly grandmother Nanny wants desperately to secure her granddaughter's future by marrying her to a landowning farmer the young girl barely knows and does not like. Trying to reconcile Janie to this arranged marriage, Nanny counts the blessings of the economic security this marriage would provide. A landed farmer could offer his wife "protection," which would allow her to "sit on high," not be "kicked around from pillar tuh post," nor made vulnerable to "de menfolks white or black" who might make "a spit cup outa you." In Hurston's story Janie did as Nanny told her, but in real life Lucy Potts went her own way. One night, she put on the silk dress she had made from goods paid for out of her egg money and slipped off to the Baptist church to marry John Hurston.

The average age at marriage at the turn of the century was twenty-two for women and twenty-four for men, but in rural areas, especially among blacks, fourteen-year-old Lucy and twenty-year-old John were not unusual. Maturity meant a woman's being old enough to give birth and a man's being strong enough to push a plow; by that measure they were both full grown. So Lucy "said her words and took her stand for life, and went off to a cabin on a plantation with him," Zora later remembered. "She never forgot how the moon shone that night as his two hundred pounds of bone and muscle shoved open the door and lifted her in his arms over the doorsill."

Though people like the Pottses looked down on sharecroppers, the economic woes that beset the post–Civil War South were making the economic plight of John Hurston the norm. By the end of the century, half of all farmers had lost whatever land they had ever owned to the bank or the furnishing merchant. With the cost of seed and clothing so high, the pressure to turn all land, even the vegetable garden, over to high-paying cotton was enormous. But with cotton prices falling, most families finished out the year deeper in debt and with less to eat.

Sharecroppers were not the only rural people to suffer privation in the depression years of the late nineteenth century. In the West, a tiny remnant of the millions of Native Americans who had once populated the continent struggled to preserve tribal life on government-sponsored reservations; women followed the "primitive" traditions of their foremothers, grinding corn, herding sheep, and gathering wild foods—according to their particular tribal customs. Among other rural families, including recent immigrants from Europe, Asia, and Mexico, extreme poverty forced many women to violate the sexual division of labor adhered to in more prosperous families by joining their husbands in the fields, while still continuing to care for their households. In the South, however, decades of soil depletion and an exploitative credit and marketing system made life for the sharecropper especially difficult.

Many sharecropper wives spent almost all of their time in the fields during planting and picking seasons, leaving only to prepare meals. Their diet typically consisted of corn bread, molasses, salt pork, and, if they were lucky, collard greens and peas from the garden. Some families were able to keep a cow, chickens, a few pigs, but hunting and fishing took too much time away from cultivating the cash crop. Sharecroppers subsisted on a diet so poor that many children were bent with rickets or weak with pellagra, and few adults had all their teeth. Even fertility was affected. While the birthrate in America had been falling for a century as couples increasingly resorted to using some form of birth control, among rural blacks like Lucy Hurston the birthrate declined less because of conscious effort than because of disease and malnutrition. Whereas rural white women bore an average of eight children, black women averaged only five.

By the middle of the 1890s John Hurston could face the discouragement of sharecropping no longer. Leaving Lucy and three young children, he headed south in search of a better life. He discovered it in the black town of Eatonville, Florida. Eatonville was not the "backside" of the typical white Southern town, but a completely independent enterprise, with its own laws and mayor, a place where a hard worker could make a better life for his family. Lucy arrived a year later with the children, some quilts, a featherbed, and a bedstead. Working as a carpenter and minister, John saved some money, bought some land, built a house, and Lucy planted a huge garden. Never again did the Hurstons go hungry.

John Hurston took particular pride in his house "full of young 'uns" and the fact that he had never allowed his wife to go out and "hit a lick of work for anybody a day in her life." In 1900 black husbands struggled to protect their wives from working for others, but with work for black males being so uncertain and paying so little, many wives ended up in the labor force for at least part of their lives. While only 3 percent of all white wives worked outside the home for wages in 1900, 25 percent of black wives had to do so.

In Lucy's case, the babies, the house, and the garden filled her days. As the children grew older, she sent them to school, a luxury that many sharecroppers could not afford. John had picked up reading and writing between cotton chopping and cotton picking, but he had never enjoyed any formal education. Lucy, in contrast, had spent several years in one of Booker T. Washington's schools, and each evening she helped her children with their lessons, turning the younger ones over to the older ones as they passed long division and parsing sentences.

Lucy was luckier than most black women she knew, but she had her share of misery. John drank too much, and his philandering plagued her mightily. At least she was spared the violence that seemed the lot of many women, including her sister-in-law, Caroline Potts. Wife-beating was illegal in most states and deplored in all, but it was a chronic problem, especially among the poor of all races. Cramped quarters and unexpected setbacks could provoke the most even-tempered husband, and when alcohol fueled discontent the mix could be explosive. Since water was frequently unsafe, liquor provided an important beverage. Moreover, many used it as an anesthetic. In 1900 Americans spent well over $1 billion on alcohol, about what they spent on all food products and nonalcoholic beverages combined. Both

men and women drank, but hard drinking was considered a
male prerogative. Those who exercised this right by drinking
up their wages at the local saloon often returned home to wives
who were angry over the loss of money for food, resentful at
having been left home alone, and furious at the prospect of
being forced into sexual relations with a drunken spouse. When
violence followed, wives and children usually got the worst of
it.

John Hurston used to shake his head and say, "What's the
use of me taking my fist to a poor weakly woman? Anyhow,
you got to submit yourself to 'em, so there ain't no use in beating
on 'em and then have to go back and beg 'em pardon." How
would he survive without a wife to tend the garden, gather the
eggs, prepare the food, wash and iron the clothes, care for the
"young 'uns," and nurse the sick? He found to his sorrow how
difficult it would be, when Lucy died in 1910, aged thirty-five
and the mother of eight. Her daughter Zora, only nine at the
time, was never sure of the cause, but she later remembered a
terrible cough that lasted a long time, suggesting that death may
have come from tuberculosis, aggravated by too many pregnancies.

Lucy died at home, surrounded by family and friends who
removed the pillow from under her head, turned her bed to the
east, and covered the mirror and clock to prepare for her spirit's
safe passage to the next world. Few people died in hospitals in
those days, but even if Lucy had wished to do so, no white
hospital would have admitted a black woman. Jim Crow reigned
supreme in the early twentieth-century South, even over death.

A Small-Town Housewife

About the time Lucy Hurston gave birth to Zora, Margaret
Grierson Thompson moved to Hamburg Village, ten miles outside of Buffalo, New York. The wife of Reverend Peter Thompson and the mother of three young children, Margaret was
presiding over the Methodist parsonage on Union Street as the
new century began. The parsonage was a white, green-edged,
wooden building of two stories, identical in appearance to doz-

ens of others in the neighborhood. Set in the middle of the village, it stood directly opposite the schoolhouse and across a wide lawn from the church where Peter Thompson preached each Sunday. There were two parlors downstairs, one cold and formal for guests, the other comfortable and shabby, with a round cast-iron stove. In the latter room Margaret gathered her children to read, pray, stitch, darn, rest, play games, converse, or simply wait for the reverend to come back from the rounds of his ministry.

Margaret Grierson, born in 1874 to a Scotch-Irish immigrant family in Pittsburgh, Pennsylvania, had married Englishman Peter Thompson in 1892 at the age of eighteen over the objections of both their families. The Thompsons were "gentle," the Griersons not, and both families shared Mrs. Richard Potts's reservations about marrying outside one's class. But the marriage had flourished, in no small measure because Margaret made it revolve around Peter's needs and aspirations. Not that she occupied a degraded position in the home. On the contrary, as the wife of a minister she worked as long and as hard as her husband to set the example and tone of right living in a Christian society, and she was widely respected for her contribution.

Margaret's oldest child, Dorothy, who would one day achieve fame as a journalist, later remembered her mother as immensely hardworking. She had to be, given the uncertainty of the reverend's income. In good years, the family, dependent on the contributions of parishioners, could count on as much as $1,000, which was better than most families but allowed for no luxuries. In bad years, they had to subsist for months at a time on nothing more than rice and apples. When there was little money coming in, Margaret Thompson's skills as a housewife could mean the difference between extreme want and modest comfort.

Like most women, Margaret Thompson rarely stayed in bed past daybreak, even when she was sick. She ran the house, made the clothes, cared for the sick, and grew and processed much of what the family ate. A few middle-class families in urban areas were beginning to install indoor plumbing and electrical wiring, but the Thompsons could not dream of such extravagance. Margaret's sole laborsaving devices were her treadle sewing machine, the mechanical wringer she used to do the wash, and the great cast-iron stove she fired up each morning to cook the meals and boil the water.

A week's washing alone required more than a full day's labor. Clothes had to be boiled in a big tub on top of the kitchen stove, washed on a scrubboard, and rinsed before they could be wrung and hung out to dry. The whole operation required about fifty gallons of water, all of which she had to haul from the kitchen pump. The following day the clothes had to be pressed with heavy irons heated on the stove. With the week's washing completed she could turn to her sewing. As in most families she purchased her husband's clothes and some of the children's and her own. But sewing still required at least a day each week and often several evenings. Another day had to be set aside for cleaning house, still another for baking, and, somehow, in between, meals had to be prepared and children tended.

Although her days were long, she broke them up with visits to neighbors, attendance at church, and simple forms of recreation. Dorothy later recalled a constant round of church suppers, sleigh-ride parties, ice-cream socials, and charitable societies, canning and quilting, choir singing and berry picking, candymaking and chestnut roasting.

There was a seasonal rhythm to Margaret's tasks. Spring meant cleaning the house top to bottom, beating rugs, turning mattresses, and washing down walls blackened from the winter's accumulation of soot from stoves and kerosene lamps. Spring was also planting time in the garden behind the house. In the summer there was the garden to care for, and in the fall the harvest of fruit and vegetables had to be canned and root vegetables had to be stored in bins and barrels in the cellar. These canned goods—the pickles, relishes, jams, and jellies—helped liven the monotonous winter fare of rice, potatoes, and, in good times, meat.

In addition, at unpredictable times throughout the year she had to abandon some part of her housework to care for someone who was sick. In villages like Hamburg women rarely called a doctor unless the patient was critically ill; instead, they provided most medical care by themselves. It was hard, often frightening work. Most mothers suffered the strain of nursing each of their children through a severe illness, and the still greater trauma of burying one or more of them.

As well as routine illness and accidents like colds, stomach upsets, chicken pox, mumps, cuts, sprains, and broken bones, women confronted a daunting array of life-threatening illnesses. The major killer, then as now, was heart disease, but tuberculosis, pneumonia, influenza, gastritis, cancer, typhoid fever, diphtheria, and measles took a heavy toll, killing many hundreds of thousands annually. In Southern regions malaria recurred each year as spring gave way to summer; polio could strike any community as summer gave way to fall. Moreover, men's practice of visiting prostitutes (as an estimated 70 percent of all white men did at some point in their lives) meant that venereal disease was a common affliction. The absence of central heating aggravated illness, and the absence of modern drugs made them more difficult to treat. These health conditions kept life expectancy rates low. A white man born at the turn of the century could expect to live only to the age of forty-seven, a white woman two years longer. Among blacks, poverty depressed life expectancy rates still further, to thirty-three years for men and thirty-four for women.

Margaret's children were reasonably healthy, but her husband was physically frail, suffering from pleurisy and, later, heart trouble. It was for this reason, Dorothy remembered, quite apart from the agreed-upon value of his work, that her father was "so tenderly treated."

Well-to-do housewives employed cooks, maids, nurses, and laundresses to free them from many of these tasks, but like most middle-class housewives Margaret could afford at most to hire a laundress or cleaning woman once a week. For the great majority of American women, especially those in rural areas and in the poorer districts of towns and cities, household help was an unattainable luxury. Indeed, among the poor, women were more likely to work as servants at some point in their lives than ever to employ one themselves. Since the Civil War, population growth had steadily outstripped the supply of domestic servants, so that by 1900 there was only one available for every ten families.

Legal tradition guaranteed that Margaret Thompson would

continue to serve her family in the event that the honor attached
to her position as the reverend's wife proved an inadequate
recompense. The marriage contract into which she had entered
at eighteen resembled an indenture agreement between master
and servant. Indeed, economically speaking, wives might be
viewed as the last large class of indentured servants in America.
Under the terms of the marriage contract, a husband promised
to support his wife in return for her promise to serve and obey
him.

Men's legal responsibility to support their families added
weight to labor leaders' demand that male workers be granted
a "family wage," that is, an income sufficient to support both
themselves and their dependents. By 1900, men in strong
unions, those successful in business, and those in the professions
could usually support families by themselves; but the majority
of all men fell outside these categories. In bad years, Margaret
had to stretch what little there was from her garden to keep her
family fed. Countless other wives were forced to contribute to
the family income by caring for boarders, raising chickens,
churning butter, or doing piecework for the garment industry.
If they were desperate, wives might even take a job outside the
home, but such a step was rare, except for black women.

No matter how difficult a marriage might be, few women ever
contemplated divorce, and those who did encountered great
difficulty. At the end of the nineteenth century, as legislators
became aware of a modest but nonetheless unsettling rise in the
divorce rate to one in ten marriages, they reduced the statutory
grounds for divorce from four hundred to fewer than twenty.
Only three states continued to allow courts to grant divorces on
any grounds the courts thought reasonable. New Jersey allowed
divorce only for adultery and desertion; New York, only in cases
of adultery; and South Carolina prohibited divorce altogether.
Even where divorce was possible, men's strong advantage under
the law discouraged women from ending their marriages. In
thirty-seven states women possessed no rights to their children,
and even in those states where they did, fathers could usually
win custody of their children if they sought it.

The law added force to the traditions that bound women to
the family in other ways as well. Women's efforts to control

their fertility met with especially severe legal resistance. Since the middle of the nineteenth century a movement of middle-class men, led by doctors but also including such prominent political figures as Theodore Roosevelt, had sought to inhibit what they believed to be an immoral trend among white, middle-class women to restrict childbearing. Warning of "race suicide," by which they meant the extinction of white Anglo-Saxon Protestants, these crusaders sought to make contraception and abortion illegal. By 1900 doctors and their sympathizers had persuaded Congress to outlaw the dissemination of birth control information through the mails; many states restricted the sale or advertising of contraceptive devices; and the Society for the Suppression of Vice, headed by Anthony Comstock, was waging a campaign to enforce these laws. In addition, every state in the country banned abortion except to save the life of the mother. Authors offering marital advice avoided all discussion of contraception and abortion out of fear of imprisonment, and many doctors denounced the use of artificial methods to limit fertility. When Margaret Sanger, the future leader of the birth control movement in America, was still working as a nurse on the Lower East Side of New York, she once witnessed a young Jewish wife begging her doctor for advice on how to avoid future pregnancies. His reply: "Tell Jake to sleep on the roof."

It was in public affairs, however, that women suffered most. Although the United States Constitution begins "We, the people," the framers did not intend that "people" be understood to include women in any direct sense. For all their opposition to the absolute patriarchal rule of the king of England, the Founding Fathers thought it natural and inevitable that men be dominant in the home and represent the family in politics. That view persisted. Even in 1900 a woman was viewed as merely a supportive assistant, not an independent person. She therefore had no right to participate in politics in any formal way. For the most part, she could not serve on juries; she could not hold elective office; and, except in four sparsely populated Western states—Wyoming, Colorado, Idaho, and Utah—she could not vote. Thus did the law bind women to the domestic sphere.

Not that Margaret Thompson felt especially bound, either by the law or anything else, except, perhaps, by sex. "I 'always

knew' that my father and mother loved each other," Dorothy
later remembered, but she also recalled her mother's careful
observance of Victorian propriety. Margaret Thompson hardly
ever allowed her children to see her in a nightgown with her
hair down, "because going around practically undressed was
immodest."

In a culture that emphasized hard work and discipline, im-
modesty was only one step away from loss of control. Loss of
control could lead to large families, which though advantageous
on farms where extra hands were always needed, spelled economic ruin in an urbanizing economy where good jobs required
long years of training. Families like the Thompsons could not
hope to maintain their middle-class status, much less ensure it
for the next generation, if they had too many mouths to feed.

The sexual views of middle-class housewives like Margaret
Thompson are difficult to reconstruct today, given their reti-
cence on the subject and the primitive level of survey research
at the time. But historians do have one interesting source. Between 1890 and 1910, Dr. Clelia Mosher, of Palo Alto, California, interviewed several dozen middle-class wives about their
sexual beliefs and practices. Mosher found many who thought
expressing love and attaining intimacy between spouses were
important and legitimate purposes of intercourse. Two-thirds
of her respondents, however, agreed with the conventional Victorian belief that reproduction was the primary purpose of sex
and that unrestrained passion between husband and wife could
only "degrade their best feelings toward each other." Most
women reported less sexual desire than their husbands, and
many described the "ideal habit" as involving less sex than they
had.

Most women in urban areas sought to control their fertility
in some way, despite laws discouraging their efforts. Some favored abstinence to limit the number of children they bore.
Many more favored withdrawal, the rhythm method, or one of
a wide range of contraceptive devices then available, including
condoms, sponges, douches, and cervical caps. Unfortunately,
none of these methods was very effective, and some posed special problems. Abstinence required utter self-denial, withdrawal
considerable self-control. Many men objected to using con-

doms. Douching proved difficult for the great majority who had no bathroom. And the rhythm method often failed because medical texts disagreed about the timing of ovulation. (Many couples carefully restricted intercourse to the "safe" period midway between the menses, only to find the wife pregnant nonetheless.) When contraception failed, one in five pregnancies ended in abortion, despite the laws against it. Poor women, in particular, relied on this most drastic means of birth control. Author Kate Simon's mother, a Jewish immigrant in early twentieth-century New York, recalled having thirteen abortions in addition to three children, "and that was by no means the neighborhood record."

The success of these combined efforts is obvious in the data on birthrates. In 1800 the average number of births per white woman was 7; by 1900 that figure had dropped to 3.5. While many rural women continued to have large families (except where hindered by malnutrition), small-town and urban women were giving birth to fewer children than at any time in American history. The effort had its costs.

In 1901 Margaret Thompson's mother arrived for a visit and did not like what she found. Margaret was working too hard; Peter's income would not support a church mouse; and Margaret was pregnant again. Something had to be done. Administering "such herbs and potions as old wives knew about and used for such purposes," Dorothy subsequently learned, Grandma Grierson induced an abortion. But it did not proceed as planned. Margaret began to hemorrhage and the doctor was called, though Grandma Grierson was afraid to confess what she had done. The doctor "plugged the flow, sealing in the poison," and Margaret died of septicemia within forty-eight hours. Twenty-seven years old, she left three children under the age of eight.

A "Working Girl" in the Big City

Death struck adults between the ages of twenty-four and forty-four so often at the turn of the century that children were ten times more likely to be orphaned then than now. Indeed, the loss of a parent was so prevalent an occurrence that orphans appeared regularly in the childhood literature of the day. In

1900, for instance, L. Frank Baum published the first of many
stories about Dorothy Gale, the little Kansas orphan swept away
by a cyclone to the land of Oz. In the center of that magical
land rose Emerald City, a place, Dorothy discovered, where no
one grew old from the wind, the sun, or the backbreaking toil
of prairie farming; food and clothing appeared by magic; no
one was ever sick; and girls became princesses, revered for their
wisdom and power.

These tales must have given particular comfort to girls like
Zora Neale Hurston and Dorothy Thompson, for in their fan-
ciful way the Oz stories suggested the allure of the growing cities
that would soon attract them both. In the city new inventions
glittered—electric lights, telephones, streetcars, skyscrapers,
and more. For millions of young women the city promised re-
lease from a life of drudgery, the chance to buy pretty dresses
with their own earnings and to enter a world of glamour and
excitement. The nineteenth-century frontier, the mythic symbol
of American opportunity, had always appealed to men more
than women. The twentieth-century city was women's frontier.

It certainly was for Sadie Frowne, a fifteen-year-old Jewish
immigrant who in 1900 was supporting herself in Brooklyn, New
York. Sadie's father had died in Poland when she was ten, and
her mother had not been able to pay the $6-a-month rent on
the family's small grocery store by herself. An aunt in New
York had offered to help, sending money for mother and daughter to emigrate. In New York Sadie's mother found a job in the
garment industry, while Sadie took a position as a domestic
servant. Together they formed part of the 80 percent of all New
Yorkers (and the one-third of all Americans) who were either
immigrants or the children of immigrants. All went well at first,
but within a year, Sadie's mother had died of tuberculosis, leaving Sadie on her own. That Sadie survived had much to do with
the changes then taking place in America's economic life. Improved technology, an expanding transportation network, and
burgeoning cities were creating hundreds of thousands of new
jobs each year in factories, offices, stores, and schools—too
many for the male work force to fill. Sadie earned more in one
week in New York City than her mother had earned in a month
in rural Poland.

The economic gain in moving to the city was real, but rarely enough to bring real comfort. At least half of all urban families earned less than they needed to maintain a minimum standard of health. They were "the other half," as reformer Jacob Riis called them, unskilled migrants like Sadie, whose move to the town or city was a step up, but only to the bottom rung of the urban ladder. They were less well educated and skilled than those who came before; in the case of the immigrants, they were often unable to speak English. They all led hard-pressed lives.

The men of the "other half" worked as unskilled laborers in jobs vulnerable to seasonal fluctuations and the ups and downs of the business cycle. In places like the steel town of Homestead, Pennsylvania, where wages were high and the mills ran seven days a week year-round, only the least-skilled men could not support their families at a modest level. But for most of the men who worked in construction, on the railroads, in the mines, or in the factories, work was both irregular and poorly paid. Male breadwinners never knew when they would next be laid off, making family income uncertain. Moreover, industrial accidents and disease took a heavy toll, crippling and killing thousands of men each year. Many families relied heavily on the wages of unmarried children to make ends meet.

In 1900 roughly 40 percent of all unmarried daughters over the age of fourteen worked for wages. The majority were either black or from immigrant families. What a daughter did depended on her ethnic group and the opportunities available. In the North the Irish and Scandinavians dominated domestic work, while Jews and Italians were concentrated in the garment industry. Native-born whites gravitated to teaching, nursing, stenography, and other officework, positions generally barred to immigrants. In the South, whites took jobs denied to blacks in the textile plants that were coming to dot the Southern hills, while blacks worked as domestics, laundresses, and in those factory jobs that whites would not take. In the farming, ranching, and mining regions of the West, and in the steel towns of the North and South, few daughters worked outside the home, except as domestics or agricultural workers.

Rarely did women perform the same work as men. As investigator Elizabeth Butler observed of employment patterns in Pittsburgh in 1907, those few jobs held by both men and women were almost always on their way to being held only by women. Employers could pay women half of what they paid men, because, according to popular belief, women did not have to support themselves, while men were responsible for the support of their families. Employers eagerly took advantage of this convention, hiring women for jobs that required little strength and that could be easily learned. Many men feared the rapid influx of young women workers as a threat to their status and the idea of the "family wage," but for the most part women did not compete directly with men in the work force, and thus had little immediate effect on their wages.

The most common employment for women in 1900 was domestic service, accounting for a third of all women workers. As Sadie Frowne could attest, domestic service had certain advantages. The work was familiar and widely available in large cities. When she arrived in New York, her aunt Fanny found her a position "living in" almost immediately. She was able to work at her own pace, and at $2.25 per week, plus room and board, she could save more money than most other women workers could. These advantages did not compensate, however, for the lack of freedom. Domestics worked an average of two more hours each day and one and a half more days each week than other workers. They could expect only one evening a week and every other Sunday off. "Aunt Fanny had always been anxious for me to get an education, as I did not know how to read and write," Sadie recalled. But servants had no time for school. "So when mother died I thought I would try to learn a trade and then I could go to school at night. . . ."

In 1900 Sadie joined the growing number of young women (slightly less than a third of all women workers) who were choosing the factory over life as a servant. Like Sadie, the typical female factory worker tended to be young, single, and an immigrant or the daughter of immigrants. About half were employed in the manufacture of cloth and clothing, including shoes, gloves, hats, stockings, and collars, making them a majority of all garment workers. But many held jobs in tobacco factories, packing plants, and commercial laundries. Sadie showed off her night-school education by describing her experiences as a garment worker in *The Independent* in 1902. Unable to live alone on her $4 earnings for a six-day week (a worker needed about $7 to live), she shared a room in a Brooklyn boarding house with another girl and cooked on an oil stove in their room. She worked in a small garment factory alongside male workers, many of whom harassed her, and she sewed at a frantic pace. "The machines go like mad all day," she wrote, "because the faster you work the more money you get. Sometimes in my haste I get my finger caught and the needle goes right through it. It goes so quick tho, that it does not hurt much." Garment workers generally labored eleven hours a day, six days a week. During the busy season, the workday could stretch even longer.

If a family could afford to keep a daughter in school through the eighth grade and if she could speak good English, the road would be opened to a position as a salesclerk. The job of clerk carried high status, even though the wages were often lower than those in manufacturing. Rose Schneiderman, later to become a Women's Trade Union League president, reported that when she quit her job as a department-store clerk to become a sewing-machine operator at twice her former salary, her mother was "far from happy. She thought working in a store much more genteel than working in a factory."

The hiring of young women as salesclerks marked a new departure in retailing. In the early days clerks had typically been men. They had bargained with and sold to customers, and even purchased merchandise. The department store, however, with its specialized buying staff turned the clerk's job into a menial position, similar to that of a servant. As one manager proudly declared, "Salespersons do not urge the customer to buy and dilate upon the beauties of his wares. They simply ask the customer what he or she wants, and make the record of the sale." The stores did not generally pay a commission on sales, but rather offered a set wage. Men preferred to look elsewhere for jobs, to places that valued initiative or allowed more responsibility or prospects for a greater income.

Several rapidly expanding occupations offered the possibility of modest independence to white, native-born women with some education. The first was teaching, a field that women had come to dominate after the Civil War when the establishment of compulsory education greatly accelerated the demand for instructors. By 1900 women constituted 98 percent of grade-school teachers and earned an average wage of $325 for a seven-month school year. Second was clerical work, where by 1900 expanding opportunities led secretaries to outnumber teachers. Female clerical workers earned an average of $450 for a full year's work. Finally, nursing, which until the 1870s had been regarded as little different from domestic service, was rapidly expanding. As the efforts of a small group of women to improve the training of nurses led to higher standards, wages leapt upward. In Cleveland, a private-duty nurse working thirty weeks a year could make $600.

The educational background of white-collar workers varied greatly. Agnes Smedley taught grade school in New Mexico in 1908 without ever having graduated from grade school herself and without being able to "remember one rule of grammar." She later became a secretary in Denver without further schooling. But most white-collar workers had at least a grade-school education by 1900, and increasingly they had finished high school. Today a high-school degree is commonplace, but in 1900 only 6 percent of the population finished twelve years of schooling. Significantly, 60 percent were female, since boys tended to leave earlier for the work force. As new white-collar jobs opened up in schools, offices, and hospitals, women's educational advantage worked to their benefit. By 1910 female white-collar workers outnumbered domestic servants.

Most young women went to work to help their families, but labor proved liberating in small, but important, ways. On downtown sidewalks and streetcars, in offices, department stores, restaurants, and factories, and in parks at lunch hour young men and women flirted with one another and made dates. After work, they took advantage of the commercialized amusements sprouting up everywhere. Sadie Frowne loved to go to the dance halls at Coney Island with her boyfriend, Henry, a fellow worker who had won her favor by protecting her from the fondling and rude remarks of other male workers. "I am very fond of dancing," Sadie confessed, "and, in fact, all sorts of pleasures." At dance halls, young couples began to gyrate to music by black entertainers, whose styles had originated in the brothels of New

Orleans and Memphis. Willie Smith, a jazz pianist in Harlem, described some of the dances favored by the young as "pretty wild." They were called "hug me close," "the shiver," "hump back rag," and "the lovers' walk." Quickly imitated by white youth these "tough dances" required the suggestive motion of "the pelvic portion of the body." Nighttime dance halls were but one of a variety of amusements that sprang up. Coney Island also boasted the Cannon Coaster and Barrel of Love, while vaudeville theaters were beginning to show motion pictures.

Working women, especially the 10 to 20 percent like Sadie who were supporting themselves, could not afford the entertainments of the city. They therefore accepted "treats" from men in the form of drinks, theater tickets, and other incidentals in conscious exchange for attentions ranging from flirtatious companionship to sexual intercourse. While they were not promiscuous, neither did they adhere strictly to the Victorian code of feminine decorum.

Adults often viewed young women's behavior with alarm. An Irish mother in New York reported with dismay that her daughter "stands up and answers me back. An' she's coming in at 2 o'clock, me not knowin' where she has been. Folks will talk, you know, an' it ain't right for a girl." In Chicago an immigrant father, a shopkeeper, told Jane Addams that he dared not withhold money for the theater from his daughters for fear that "they would steal it from the till." Parents worried that daughters might become pregnant, or worse, turn to prostitution to finance innocent pleasures.

Some women, perhaps as many as 200,000 according to a 1910 U.S. Department of Justice estimate, did turn to prostitution. Contemporaries usually blamed women's low wages for the problem, but other factors were often more important. Among Chinese immigrants lived many prostitutes who had been kidnapped in China and brought to the United States to live in virtual slavery. Lack of education, trouble at home, unscrupulous seducers, disreputable employment agencies, or a desire for "easy money" often played a part. For most prostitutes the first sexual encounter was not associated with prostitution but with a boyfriend, family member, or stranger. One or two years after their first sexual contact, usually between seventeen and twenty-one years of age, they began practicing prostitution, having realized the money-making possibilities in the sexual favors they were giving away. A young woman making $5 a week in a store could make $35 as a prostitute. For some women prostitution led to venereal disease, drugs, and crime. But for most it seems to have been temporary, lasting no more than five years and ending in a return to menial work at low wages or marriage.

It is difficult to know how big an impact the urban environment had on the sexual experiences of young working women at the turn of the century. Studies of the incidence of pregnancy at marriage, however, offer a clue. In the middle of the nineteenth century only 10 percent of all women were pregnant when they wed, but in the decades from 1880 to 1910 that rate more than doubled. Since surveys of middle-class white women for the turn of the century suggest a rate of premarital intercourse of only 7 percent, it is likely that the increase occurred among working-class women.

The significance of working women's greater sexual experience before marriage is not clear. Much of it may have been forced upon them by suitors or supervisors. For others premarital sex may have been welcomed as a prelude to marriage, with pregnancy a way of ensuring the woman's marital choice. But whatever the reasons, it seems clear that young working-class women were engaging in more premarital sex than their parents had, as well as more than the middle-class women of their own generation.

It would be a mistake to suggest that either economic independence or premarital sex became the norm for young women workers. Most daughters turned over their pay envelope to their mothers each Saturday night unopened, and most daughters, especially the daughters of immigrants, continued to be closely chaperoned by their families until they married. But the heterogeneity of the city led women to question traditional values. Mixing daily with men on the streets and at work, violating by their very presence the Victorian ideal of separate sexual spheres, they set a new standard of female assertiveness. At seventeen, Sadie Frowne reported that her Henry "has been urging me more and more to get married." She thought that eventually she would like to, but unlike Lucy Hurston and Margaret Thompson, Sadie had some options apart from domesticity. For the moment, she concluded, "I think I'll wait."

The New Woman

By 1900 Jane Addams had long since decided not to marry at all. Since 1889 she had been running Hull House, a settlement house in the slums of Chicago where privileged women like herself could take up meaningful work among people in need. Those who came to Hull House were exemplars of what was coming to be called the "new woman." Independent, energetic, well educated, and generally well-to-do, the new woman found herself freed by technological change and increasing affluence from many household chores. Some privileged women took advantage of this new leisure to shop, join a club, or learn a sport. Working out in gyms, riding bicycles, playing tennis and even golf were all popular activities that a generation before no refined woman could have imagined engaging in. The women who came to Hull House, however, wanted the more demanding life that Addams offered. Most stayed a couple of years before leaving to marry; a few, like Addams, stayed a lifetime.

Born in 1860 in Cedarville, Illinois, Addams had grown up in a prominent family. Her father was a businessman, banker, and Republican state senator. Her mother, Sarah, died when she was two, and she was raised by her stepmother, Anna Haldeman, along with three older sisters, an older brother, and two new stepbrothers. Jane dreamed of going East to college, but barred by her father from venturing so far away, she settled for nearby Rockford Seminary, where she graduated in 1881 at the head of her class. The following year Rockford was accredited as a college.

Addams was part of the first generation of American women to attend college in large numbers. For decades most colleges and universities had resisted admitting women, but in the years after the Civil War this resistance proved increasingly difficult to maintain. As proliferating business opportunities diverted men for whom colleges and universities were competing, women promised to fill empty classroom seats. Moreover, the exploding

demand for teachers placed great pressure on colleges to admit
women to be trained for high-school teaching.

Open doors did not, women soon discovered, ensure a warm
reception. Convinced that the admission of women represented
a downgrading of their institutions, many male faculty and students were hostile to the "coeds," often refusing to acknowledge
their presence. A sudden outpouring of polemical literature
about the dangers of intellectual work for women's health underscored this hostility. The strain of a college education, pun-
dits alleged, would drain energy from women's reproductive
organs and make them unfit for motherhood. As late as 1904,
one of the country's leading psychologists, G. Stanley Hall, was
warning that higher education threatened to produce women
who were "functionally castrated . . . deplore the necessity of
childbearing . . . and abhor the limitations of married life."
Such warnings failed to halt the steady increase of women students. In 1870 1 percent of Americans attended college, of
whom 20 percent were women. By 1900 4 percent did so, and
36 percent were women. In the liberal arts women outnumbered
men.

The majority of these women attended coeducational colleges
and universities. But a significant minority entered women's
colleges. Vassar, which opened in 1865, was soon followed by
dozens of other women's colleges, which exercised an influence
over women's lives that greatly exceeded the number of their
students. Whereas coeducational institutions often ignored
women students, in women's colleges, as Bryn Mawr president
M. Carey Thomas declared, "Everything exists for women students and is theirs by right not by favor."

Wherever they pursued higher education, women gained what
no generation of women had ever been privileged to experience,
an education once reserved for men. Not that college educators
intended to turn women into men. Most believed that women
were different from men, wiser, more sympathetic, more nurturing. At Smith the purpose was to "ennoble women as
women," at Vassar "to fill every womanly duty at home and in
society." The vagueness of these aspirations obscured a fundamental ambivalence among educators, who were capable of
asserting, almost in the same breath, that women were the in-

tellectual equals of men, that women needed special programs to enable them to survive the rigors of higher education, and that women should be trained to serve both their families and the world.

As long as women were in college, they rarely had to confront these contradictions, but graduation inevitably brought a period of crisis. Having enjoyed four years of self-improvement, the graduate was expected to return to her family, "to stay at home," as Jane Addams put it, "help one's mother entertain, perhaps take a course in domestic science." Roughly half of all college graduates resolved the tensions evident in this shift by burying the personal ambitions that college had fostered and marrying.

But only to marry struck many as a terrible waste of the education they had won, and even those who eventually married often pursued a career until they wed. About 60 percent of all college graduates entered teaching, at least for a few years. Most taught high school, unless they were black, in which case they counted themselves lucky to teach in rural, segregated, one-room schoolhouses, where salaries were less than half those offered to whites and the school year rarely exceeded three months. White women, however, had come to take teaching for granted, and even to find it an inadequate goal for an ambitious woman. Grace Abbott, who tried it, later reflected: "A boy can come home from college, begin the practice of his profession, and advance rapidly in his home town. But when a girl comes back, what can she do? She can teach, but after she's done that she finds that she has reached the top, that there is nothing more for her."

Abbott followed her older sister Edith to graduate school in search of greater opportunity. A small number of women, less than 10 percent of all graduates, did the same. A handful found professorships in women's colleges; others took jobs in the dean's offices, physical education departments, and departments of home economics of the state universities. But most had to look for work outside academia. Women students provided much-needed tuition to colleges that had expanded too rapidly, but as prospective faculty they posed unwelcome competition for scarce jobs.

Less than 3 percent of women college graduates entered business in 1900, principally as highly skilled clerical workers, while
even fewer won access to most male professions. The ministry
and engineering recruited negligible numbers of women, while
law and medicine only a few. Women had long read law in the
offices of sympathetic male relatives, and by the end of the
century a handful were beginning to attend law school. Many
law schools, however, refused to admit women students. Moreover, attracting clients and making one's way in a hostile courthouse environment proved daunting tasks. Only the saloon
rivaled the courthouse in the belligerence of its masculine character. Not surprisingly, women comprised less than 1 percent
of all lawyers in 1900.

Medicine, where 5 percent of all doctors were women, provided a slightly more hospitable environment, but one that was
becoming steadily less so. Most women doctors at the turn of
the century had trained in women's medical colleges, but the
rise of scientific medicine with its greater demands for training
in the basic sciences transformed medical education. Though
increasing numbers of women students sought and gained admission to the better coeducational medical schools at the turn
of the century, most small medical colleges either closed or were
absorbed by large universities. Overall, the number of women
students declined.

Limited by convention, discrimination, and family pressure
in their pursuit of the careers that attracted their brothers, educated women began forging their own. Statistics suggest that
many of the women who might have become lawyers or doctors
became writers and journalists (usually writing for the women's
page of a local newspaper), or turned to the new helping professions of librarianship and clinical psychology. The most inspi-
rational career of all, however, was the one that Jane Addams
made famous.

For eight years following graduation from college in 1881
Addams suffered recurring bouts of back pain and depression
as she tried to decide what to do with her life. The summer
after graduation her father died suddenly of appendicitis, leaving her grief-stricken. She enrolled that fall in the Philadelphia
Woman's Medical College, but withdrew a month later because

of her back and the realization that she did not like medicine. Her anxious family sent her to Dr. S. Weir Mitchell, a famous Philadelphia neurologist. He prescribed complete bed rest, nourishing food, and no reading on the grounds that his patients must settle their nerves so that they could resume their domestic roles. Addams preferred surgery to Dr. Mitchell's regime, and after a six-month convalescence she embarked with her stepmother on a tour of Europe. In 1885 she returned to the United States, and for the next two years lived in Baltimore with her stepmother and her stepbrother John Haldeman, who was studying at Johns Hopkins. During this period Jane reached the "nadir of my nervous depression," as Jane Haldeman tried to pressure her into marriage with John. Still aimless and unhappy, Addams returned to Europe in 1887 and visited Toynbee Hall in London, where a group of young university men were trying to remedy the problems of urban poverty. Inspired by their work, she discovered her calling at long last. In 1889 Addams founded Hull House. At that time less than 3 percent of all social workers were women. By 1910 women were a majority, due largely to Addams's efforts, and more college graduates were entering social work than any other occupation besides teaching.

Social work shared one feature with other careers in which women made rapid strides—men were not much interested in it. As Dr. Alice Hamilton put it, "The American man gives over to the woman all the things he is profoundly disinterested in, and keeps business and politics to himself." Men might not be interested, but to women seeking a career, social work, especially at a settlement house, offered an exciting challenge. For Grace Abbott it guaranteed an escape from teaching; for Sophinisba Breckenridge it offered an alternative to a faltering legal practice in Kentucky; and for Alice Hamilton it presented a welcome alternative to the "remote and useless" life of a medical researcher. Hamilton spoke for many when she wrote that settlement life "satisfied every longing—for companionship, for the excitement of new experiences, for constant intellectual stimulation and for the sense of being caught up in a big movement which enlisted my enthusiastic loyalty."

The house that Addams selected had once been the country

home of Charles J. Hull, but by the 1880s it had been engulfed by the tenements and factories of the West Side's Nineteenth Ward. All around lived a tightly packed united nations of immigrants—Italians, Greeks, Germans, Russian and Polish Jews, Bohemians, Irish, and French Canadians—most of them desperately poor. The infant mortality rate was twice that of the city as a whole, cocaine addiction plagued the young, and prostitution flourished in nearby tenements. Neighboring families crowded into tiny, unventilated apartments. Women cooked on stoves in the main room, and hauled water for cooking and laundry from a pump in the hallway. Stinking basement privies were shared by an average of eight people, and bathtubs were a luxury available in only 3 percent of all tenements. Under such conditions, women fought an unending battle against dirt and disease.

The very extremity of the problems besetting the neighborhood, together with Addams's success in publicizing them, attracted residents and donations. Addams visited the wealthy families of Chicago and wrote articles in national magazines in which she argued that a settlement could help bridge the growing gulf between rich and poor that threatened democracy. She found cautious but growing support in the women's club movement. The General Federation of Women's Clubs (GFWC), founded in 1890, claimed 150,000 members by 1900, and though many clubs focused on literary activities, an increasing number were becoming interested in work on behalf of needy women and children. Among Addams's most reliable supporters were the middle-class wives and professional women of the National Association of Colored Women (NACW), which was founded in 1896 as an answer to the GFWC, which refused to admit blacks. The racism of American culture made these women much readier than most middle-class whites to press for social reform. As Oberlin graduate and NACW president Mary Church Terrell declared: "Self-preservation demands that [black women] go among the lowly, illiterate and even the vicious, to whom they are bound by ties of race and sex . . . to reclaim them." With clubwomen's support, Hull House gradually expanded until it included a dozen buildings sprawled over more than a city block. By 1911 it had grown to include fifty residents, of whom twenty were men, and its success had encouraged the founding of another four hundred settlements around the country, including a number organized by black women.

Settlement workers began with the belief that art, music, and lectures would lift the impoverished from their degradation, but they were soon offering more practical help. They built kindergartens, playgrounds, gyms, public baths, public kitchens, and even boardinghouses for single women. They established "information bureaus" for new immigrants; helped neighbors deal with hospitals, courts, and county agencies; provided refuge for homeless people; campaigned for safer conditions in local factories; and showed battered wives how to take their husbands to court.

Most settlement-house workers had learned as children that poverty stemmed from moral weakness, but as they lived among the poor they came to conclude that moral weakness was more often the product of poverty than the other way around. Sophinisba Breckenridge and Edith Abbott, who worked with juvenile delinquents in Chicago, recorded hundreds of cases of children who ran afoul of the law simply because they lacked supervision. One nine-year-old Irish boy, for instance, whose father had died when he was four and whose mother supported herself and five children by washing, ended up in court because his mother could not work and "at the same time take care of her three boys and keep them off the railroad tracks."

Poverty put people under pressure that most middle-class Americans could not comprehend. In *Democracy and Social Ethics* (1902) Addams noted the remarkable contrast she found between the generous attitude of her poor neighbors, who freely gave to those still less fortunate than themselves in the belief that poverty could strike anyone, with the approach of the typical charity worker, who insisted that money be given only after the moral worthiness of the recipient was confirmed. "They investigated me for three weeks, and in the end gave me nothing but a black character," complained one Nineteenth Ward resident. The longer settlement workers worked with the poor, the more settlements shifted from being organizations that tried to comfort and aid the unfortunate to agencies of reform.

Settlement workers never wholly escaped the prejudices of their upbringing—their disapproval of alcohol and their belief in the superiority of the white Anglo-Saxon Protestant tradition in which most had been bred; nor did their poor neighbors ever completely accept them. Immigrant men rarely visited the settlements, and though women and children came more often, they, too, viewed the settlement workers as outsiders. Immigrant women often resented settlement workers' efforts to substitute "thrifty" ingredients for the eggs and butter they preferred; they were horrified by the frank way that settlement workers discussed sex; and they found slightly improper the settlement workers' call for female garbage inspectors, policemen, and judges. And yet the settlements flourished, and as settlement workers described their neighbors in hundreds of articles and thousands of lectures, they did much to counter the xenophobic tendencies of many native-born Americans, to build sympathy for the plight of the poor, and to foster respect for differing cultural heritages.

Those who made a career of settlement-house work typically chose not to marry. Often this decision coincided with doubts about the institution of marriage, doubts that no one articulated more forcefully than Charlotte Perkins Gilman, a frequent Hull House visitor. Gilman had suffered a nervous breakdown following an unhappy marriage and the arrival of her first child in 1885. Her anxious family had sent her to Dr. S. Weir Mitchell's Philadelphia clinic, where she made no more progress than had Addams a few years earlier. Divorce and a career as writer and lecturer brought her back to health, however, and she achieved fame for her trenchant writing on the "woman problem." In her 1898 best-seller *Women and Economics*, she denounced marriage as a crude "sexuo-economic" exchange in which men paid money for the personal services performed by women. Ironically, Gilman observed, men paid in inverse relation to the work performed. Thus the poor man's wife, lacking servants and conveniences, had to work the hardest and was paid the least, while the rich man's wife worked only at being a parasitical consumer who, "in her unintelligent and ceaseless demands, hinders and perverts the economic development of the whole world." Barred by marriage from economic activity, Gilman continued, the human female "deteriorates in racial development and naturally transmits that deterioration to her offspring." In Gilman's opinion, as long as women were confined to the home, they would do more harm than good. Progress would come only when society freed women to pursue work outside the home by providing socialized child care, housekeeping services, laundries, and kitchens.

To others the problem was not so much marriage as men. Jessie Taft, trained in philosophy at the University of Chicago, believed that many of the educated young women of her generation longed for the companionship of marriage but could find no men with the qualities they sought in a husband. "The man who comes within her circle of possibilities is too often a man who has no form of self expression beyond his business and who therefore fails to meet her ideal of companionship in marriage." Only other women like themselves seemed able to provide the companionship they longed for. "Everywhere," she wrote,

> we find the unmarried woman turning to other women, building up with them a real home, finding in them the sympathy and understanding, the bond of similar standards and values, as well as the same aesthetic and intellectual interests, that are often difficult of realization in a husband, especially here in America where business crowds out culture.

Remaining unmarried, as Taft implied, did not necessarily mean being alone. Among women college graduates were many who were passionately attached to one another throughout their lives. Jessie Taft, for one, found a lifelong companion in Virginia Robinson while they were both students at the University of Chicago, forming what came to be known as a "Boston marriage." So, too, did Jane Addams, who formed a lifelong partnership with Mary Rozet Smith of Hull House. Like their mothers, these women spent most of their time in a separate, female sphere. In choosing not to marry, however, they created a new experience for women, that of living and working independently of men.

How sexual these relationships were is an open question. Probably, as in the heterosexual marriages of the time, the level

of sexual enthusiasm varied. Professor Vida Scudder of Wellesley College, who enjoyed decades of loving partnership with
the writer Florence Converse, commented, "A woman's life in
which sex interests have never visited, is a life neither dull nor
empty nor devoid of romance." And yet sex clearly did visit
the lives of many female couples. Katharine Bement Davis, who
studied twenty-two thousand mostly college-educated women
who had completed their education, on average, in 1900, found
that homoerotic relationships had been common among them
both in coeducational and women's colleges. Fifty percent of
unmarried women and 30 percent of those who married admitted to having intense emotional relationships with other
women. For half of each group the relationship included "mutual masturbation, contact of genital organs or other physical
expressions recognized as sexual in nature."

When compared to the thousands of women who were graduating from colleges and universities at the turn of the century,
the number of women who spent their lives together remained
small. Yet their ability to sustain each other emotionally enabled
them to act as leaders in the movement that brought women
out of the home into public life. Entering careers long barred
to women, or creating new careers, these pioneers not only
encouraged other women to take a larger part in the world
beyond the home, they also challenged them to transform that
world according to the ideals of nurturance and cooperation
that home life had taught them to value most.

The success of the "new women" bent on social reform rested
in large part on their ability to overcome the deep divisions of
region, race, ethnicity, religion, and class that divided women
like Lucy Hurston, Margaret Thompson, Sadie Frowne, and
Jane Addams. Ironically, the family claim, which limited women
in so many ways, also provided a key to that effort by ensuring
the common basis of experience essential to transcending those
divisions. The family claim guaranteed that the vast majority of
all women would marry and become mothers and that those
few who did not would nevertheless share in the female rituals
of cleaning, cooking, washing, sewing, and caring for family and
friends that linked all women. This shared experience created

a shared identity, however fractured it might be by other forces. As women gained more work-force experience, as they won greater educational opportunities, and as they came to enjoy more leisure time, the possibilities for acting on that shared identity to improve the lives of all women began to grow.

2

Domesticating the State
1901–12

The Progressive Spirit

One of the lessons that settlement-house residents had learned by 1900 was that the problems facing the poor—inadequate sanitation, disease, overcrowding, low wages, unemployment—could not be overcome through settlement services alone. These problems were too large to be solved privately, or even locally. In a country with a highly interdependent, national economy, change would have to take place on a national stage. Through their writings, their lecturing, and their contacts in women's groups around the country, settlement-house leaders began venturing far from the urban slums they called home to build a national movement for social reform centered on the needs of women and children.

Women did not champion national reform lightly, for doing so threatened to increase federal power and thereby subvert political tradition. Ever since the Founding Fathers had rejected the rule of the British Crown, most Americans had harbored a deep suspicion of centralized governmental authority. In the nineteenth century that suspicion spread to state and even local governments. Gradually these polities relinquished to the marketplace the task of regulating the economy, while abandoning to voluntary groups the care of dependents and the enforcement of moral norms. The fact that these privatized tasks tended to divide along gender lines, with men predominating in the marketplace and women in charitable societies, merely served to underscore the apparent "naturalness" of the antigovernment trend. Belief in governmental responsibility for the public good never disappeared entirely. In fact, the federal government's effort to reconstruct the South following the Civil War and the campaigns in favor of state activism of blacks, Grangers, and Populists thereafter represented important exceptions to the prevailing pattern of governmental laissez-faire. So, too, to a lesser degree, did the land grants and subsidies offered by Congress to encourage nascent industry, the government agencies established to gather information on the economy, and the courtroom judgments that occasionally condemned corporate misconduct. The conviction remained widespread, however, that the country's greatness depended on private initiative, impeded as little as possible by public interference.

Private initiative had, in fact, proven fabulously successful. By the twentieth century America had become the world's most innovative industrial power and boasted the greatest steel output of any developed country. But the cost of that success was enormous. Meat from the stockyards was often tainted; disease was rife; maternal and infant mortality were the highest of any industrialized country; schools were overcrowded; and air and rivers were polluted. Moreover, wealthy corporations were corrupting the political process. Powerful businessmen offered stock and cash to public officials in return for support, which the grateful recipients routinely gave. In Ohio, John D. Rockefeller exercised so much influence that cynics claimed Standard Oil had done everything to the state legislature except refine it. Even wholesale bribery, however, could not protect either business tycoons or the public from the most terrifying consequence of industrial growth—periodic, massive depressions.

Two events in 1901 underscored the need for federal action. The first was the creation in April of United States Steel, the world's first billion-dollar corporation. The second was the shooting in September of President William McKinley by a man rumored to be an anarchist. A week later McKinley died and Theodore Roosevelt became President of the United States. The new President quickly assured the public that he intended to carry on in the conservative steps of his predecessor, but the combination of a feared anarchist threat and the creation of the

largest corporation in the history of the world raised new alarm
in the country over what appeared to be growing divisions between the very rich, who wielded unprecedented power, and
the very poor, who had nothing to lose.

These episodes inaugurated the Progressive Era, the period
between 1901 and the first World War, which witnessed the
birth of the modern American state. That birth owed much to
businessmen and reform politicians, convinced by the violence
of the business cycle and the corruption of machine politics that
government must assume greater power in order to protect the
public from the excesses of the "robber baron." But it owed
more than has been commonly conceded to the women who,
entering upon the national arena, called for a very different kind
of state than that envisioned by most male reformers.

Middle-class women reformers like Jane Addams generally
shared the view of their male counterparts that the time had
come to use governmental power to remedy the ills brought by
private power, but they went beyond that. Observing that the
problems faced by modern society stemmed largely from male,
self-interested political and economic behavior, women activists
demanded a larger role for themselves in the modern state to
correct those ills. But that was not all. They insisted that society
recognize that the problems generated by industrial growth were
not confined to business and politics alone but had spread to
the most pressing matters of family life. As a consequence, the
state would have to exert greater power than most men would
like. It would, in particular, have to assume a much broader
responsibility for the health and economic well-being of its citizens, especially its women and children.

Women activists routinely explained women's new political
demands as the inevitable consequence of industrial and urban
growth. As Jane Addams observed in 1910:

> Women who live in the country sweep their own dooryards and
> may either feed the refuse of the table to a flock of chickens or
> allow it innocently to decay in the open air and sunshine. In a
> crowded city quarter, however, if the street is not cleaned by the
> city authorities no amount of private sweeping will keep the ten-
> ement free from grime; if the garbage is not properly collected

and destroyed a tenement house mother may see' her children sicken and die of diseases from which she alone is powerless to shield them. . . . In short, if woman would keep on with her old business of caring for her house and rearing her children she will have to have some conscience in regard to public affairs lying quite outside her immediate household.

As industry increasingly had drawn work from the home into factories, and as urban growth had made people more inter-dependent, the separation between private and public life had become ever more difficult to sustain and the inevitability of women's participation in the political order ever more obvious.

The women who sought to join the progressive reform move-ment came disproportionately from the ranks of white middle-class career women, but in urging women to participate in the political process they sought to incorporate the voices of all women and routinely stressed Woman's common needs. For them Woman was a universal category, a group whose shared qualities transcended ethnic, racial, and class divisions. More-over, since most women shared the experience of motherhood, reformers further assumed that the needs of women encom-passed the needs of children as well. Given this commonality of interest, any policy that helped one group would inevitably benefit all. In a period of growing public concern over selfish individualism and class divisions, women reformers promised a new integration of American society.

Organizing the Women

Florence Kelley, a resident of Hull House for almost a decade, played a particularly important role in building a national movement of women committed to reform. The daughter of Pennsylvania Congressman and prominent anti-slavery leader William D. Kelley, Florence had studied at the University of Zurich after graduating from Cornell. There she had translated Engels, married a socialist doctor, and become a socialist her-self. Moving with her three children to Hull House in 1891 when her marriage ended in divorce, she "galvanized other residents," Addams later recalled, "into a more intelligent interest in the

industrial conditions all about us." In 1899, Kelley accepted an
invitation to become general secretary of the newly formed
National Consumers' League (NCL). Moving with her children
to Henry Street Settlement House in New York, she undertook
the work of forming a national organization of consumers.

In trying to organize consumers, Kelley simply built on an
age-old women's tradition of banding together to protest un-
conscionable business practices that affected their families. An
example of that tradition played itself out on the crowded streets
of the Lower East Side in 1902, as Kelley's campaign got under
way. There a group of Jewish housewives organized a successful
boycott of kosher butchers who had just raised their meat prices.
Taking advantage of women's willingness to use their power as
consumers to work for causes they deemed important, Kelley
traveled thousands of miles to speak to women's clubs, labor
unions, legislative committees, colleges, indeed, any group that
would listen to her message that reasonable working conditions
and good wages were not just the right of all workers but a
necessary goal for a decent society. A democratic republic, she
argued, could not long flourish in which children were denied
their childhood and future mothers were robbed of their health.
In time, she organized sixty consumers' leagues in twenty states.
These leagues compiled lists of stores that paid decent wages,
limited work to ten hours a day, provided safe working conditions, and refused to hire children under the age of fourteen.
They then encouraged shoppers to patronize the employers on
their "white list." In addition, Kelley sponsored a "white label"
campaign in which manufacturers who met the league's standards could use NCL labels on their clothes, and she lobbied
for maximum-hours and minimum-wage laws.

Not everyone agreed that pressure from consumers was the
best way to help women workers. Many activists, especially
socialists and others with working-class backgrounds, believed
that the only way to ensure that women would not be exploited
in the work force was to see that they were integrated into the
labor movement of the day. No one thought this would be easy,
because labor organizers in America had long faced enormous
resistance. Ethnic and racial diversity in the work force enabled
employers to play one group off against another. In addition,

the conservative court system hampered unionizing efforts by making it easy for employers to win injunctions against strikers. The only labor groups strong enough to withstand these pressures were the craft unions of the American Federation of Labor (AFL) that protected their power by refusing to organize unskilled, largely immigrant workers.

The difficulties faced by labor organizers multiplied for those intent on organizing women. Hired to perform the least skilled, most poorly paid work, women were rarely eligible for membership in AFL unions. Moreover, male unionists did not take them seriously, viewing them as sisters, daughters, and future wives, not fellow workers. Men intent on securing a "family wage" for themselves had no interest in organizing women, whose very presence in the work force cast doubt on the need for the "family wage." Given no encouragement, women manifested little interest. They tended to view their work as a temporary experience from which they would one day be liberated by marriage. Besides, union meetings took place at night, when women workers had domestic responsibilities, and they were often held in saloons, where "nice girls" did not go. These obstacles contributed to the low number of organized women workers. At the turn of the century, one in every five men in the industrial labor force belonged to a union, but only one in every fifteen women did so.

The most important group to take up the challenge of organizing women workers was the Women's Trade Union League (WTUL), founded in 1903 at the AFL convention by Mary Kenney, one of only four women trade unionists at the convention. A friend of Jane Addams since the day Kenney first visited Hull House and Addams offered to work with her to improve conditions of labor, Kenney appealed to settlement-house workers to lend strength to the new organization. Kenney hoped to achieve an alliance between working- and middle-class women, first, to overcome the opposition of male union leaders to organizing women, and second, to overcome the timidity and inertia of women wage earners. Her idea was to train women workers in leadership and eventually to turn the organization over to them entirely. The WTUL, with its headquarters in Chicago, established chapters in Boston, New York, and a

dozen other cities. In the years between 1903 and World War
I it provided experience for a generation of women labor lead-
ers, like Mary Anderson of the Boot and Shoe Workers' Union,
Agnes Nestor of the International Glove Workers Union, Bessie
Abramowitz of the Amalgamated Clothing Workers of Amer-
ica, Leonora O'Reilly of the United Garment Workers' Union,
and Rose Schneiderman of the Jewish Socialist United Cloth
Hat and Cap Makers' Union.

Between 1909 and 1912 the WTUL helped tens of thousands
of women mobilize to protest their working conditions. A 25
percent reduction in wages, following the business downturn of
1907–8, sparked the first walkouts in the New York garment
industry in the summer of 1909. Other grievances, however,
contributed to a growing discontent. The hours were long—
especially during the rush season—workers were charged by
their employers for needles, thread, electricity, chairs, and lock-
ers; and they were regularly subject to sexual harassment by
foremen. Most disturbingly, safety hazards threatened. At the
Triangle Shirtwaist Factory, for example, which occupied the
top three floors of a ten-story building, the doors to stairways
were typically locked to prevent employees from leaving with
pieces of fabric.

As workers joined the walkout, the WTUL came to their aid.
Wealthy "allies" walked picket lines to give the women strikers
courage, to serve as witnesses in the case of arrest, and to
discourage violence. When violence occurred anyway they complained loudly to the police and the press. There was nothing
new in the arrest of striking workers, but when police hauled
wealthy WTUL president Mary Dreier off to court, reporters
from throughout New York began covering the story. They drew
attention to the determined young women who marched through
the cold and snowy winter, the thugs who tried to break up the
picket lines, the prostitutes who cheered on the disrupters, and
the police who pushed the strikers into patrol wagons as the
thugs ran off.

The publicity given the strikes generated new interest in the
city's garment union, Local 25 of the AFL. In the summer of
1909 it had fewer than one hundred members, but by October
its membership had passed one thousand. This growing mem-

bership owed much to two changes that had recently taken place in New York garment production. First, in contrast to the isolated conditions of tenement sweatshops, which had prevailed before 1900, most garment workers by 1909 worked with others in shops and factories. Factory expansion paralleled the growing shirtwaist business, which produced the high-neck shirts (worn with long dark skirts) that had become the uniform of the new women office workers. By 1909 this new business had produced six hundred waist- and dressmaking shops, employing thirty-five thousand to forty thousand workers in New York City alone. Four out of five workers were women, most of them under twenty-five years of age. The second factor contributing to the growing interest in unions was the changing ethnic composition of the workers. By the early twentieth century two-thirds of the New York garment workers were Russian Jews, many of whom came from a politically radical background, one very different from the elite craft tradition of most American labor leaders.

Infused with new, militant members Local 25 began talking with the WTUL about the possibility of a general strike. A meeting was called at Cooper Union for November 23 to present the proposal to the workers. As late as the evening of the meeting, however, the leaders were still not sure what to do. General strikes rarely succeeded, and Local 25 had no funds, though support seemed strong. It was left to Clara Lemlich, a young striker from the Lieserson shop, to speak for the thousands of workers who jammed the hall. "I have listened to all the speeches," she cried in Yiddish. "I am tired of talking. I move that we go on general strike." As the cheering that greeted her proposal subsided, the chairman of the meeting asked the crowd, "Will you take the old Jewish oath?" and the waist-makers replied, "If I turn traitor to the cause I now pledge, may this hand wither from the arm I now raise." The next day more than twenty thousand workers walked off their jobs.

Not all workers joined in the strike. Most Italian and black women ignored the protest, the Italians out of the conviction that such activity was not appropriate for women, the blacks because they felt no special solidarity with whites. In addition to these internal divisions, the strikers suffered a desperate shortage of cash. Determined to help, the WTUL began solic-

iting funds from wealthy sympathizers. Anne Morgan, sister of
J. P. Morgan, told *The New York Times*, "When you hear of
a woman who presses forty dozen skirts for eight dollars a week,
something must be wrong." The fabulously wealthy Alva Belmont, ex-wife of railroad heir William Vanderbilt and widow
of banking heir Oliver Belmont, added her support as well. The
owner of a mansion in Newport and a $3 million chateau on
Fifth Avenue, Belmont had little in common with immigrant
factory workers, but she had carried with her a deep sense of
all women's oppression ever since the discovery of her first
husband's adultery. Contributing her own cars she organized a
motorcade to galvanize support, and she sponsored an enormous rally at the Hippodrome, gathering together thousands of
suffragists, unionists, socialists, and other sympathizers. Socialist strikers complained of the publicity Belmont attracted
while poor women strikers marched unrecognized through the
bitter cold, but no one did more to bring attention to the workers' plight, to demonstrate the possibilities for cross-class alliance, and to raise money for the cause.

By December most of the small shops had settled with Local
25, and the Manufacturers Association, which represented the
larger companies, had agreed to negotiate. The association
acceded to demands that their members reduce hours, raise
wage rates, abolish fines, and improve sanitary conditions, but
it would not recognize the union. To the strikers, all the association's concessions were worthless without a union to enforce
them, and they voted to refuse a contract. Many of their wealthy
supporters could not understand the primacy workers attached
to the union and withdrew their support, but the strikers per-
severed. In the winter months that followed a few more companies settled with the union. The strongest ones, however,
resisted, and in mid-February the strike ended, with 150 firms
still holding out.

One of the largest nonunion shops was the Triangle Shirtwaist
Company. There on a late March afternoon in 1911 a cigarette
dropped in a remnant drawer ignited one of the large workrooms
and the fire spread quickly. Doors, locked from the outside,
offered no escape, so frantic workers flung themselves out of
windows. Some landed on sidewalks eight to ten stories below.

Others were impaled on the iron spikes of the fence that surrounded the building. By early evening 146 workers were dead.

Rose Schneiderman, distraught by the carnage and the failure of strikes to win more gains, gave an impassioned speech a few days later at the Metropolitan Opera House that expressed the rage of WTUL members and workers. "This is not the first time girls have been burned alive in the city," she told the audience of mourners. "Every week I must learn of the untimely death of one of my sister workers. Every year thousands are maimed. The life of men and women is so cheap and property is so sacred." She went on to say,

> We have tried you good people of the public and we have found you wanting. . . . Every time the workers come out in the only way they know how to protest against conditions which are unbearable, the strong hand of the law is allowed to press down heavily upon us. . . . I know from my experience it is up to the working people to save themselves . . . by a strong working-class movement.

The possibility of such a movement seemed to heighten as women workers struck across the Northeast and Midwest—in Philadelphia; Brooklyn; Boston; Chicago; Cleveland; Muscatine, Iowa; Kalamazoo, Michigan; Paterson, New Jersey; and Lawrence, Massachusetts. It was a pay cut of thirty cents a week (the cost of five loaves of bread) that sparked the Lawrence strike in the winter of 1911. So low were wages in the Lawrence textile mills that entire families had to work to survive, and children were chronically malnourished. "Better to starve fighting than to starve working," cried one worker as twenty thousand textile-mill operatives, half of them women and children, left their machines. In response to some minor violence the governor called in the National Guard, but despite this display of force the strikers maintained a staunch unity.

As in New York the common experience of working side-by-side in a factory setting contributed to their willingness to stand together. Unlike the New York strikers, however, those at Lawrence could not draw on a common militant heritage; they hailed from twenty-five different countries. They nevertheless held firm against their employers, demanding that their old wages be reinstated. Support from a coalition of outside labor leaders helped for a time—the AFL, the WTUL, and the Industrial Workers of the World (IWW; the Wobblies—a radical labor movement devoted to organizing unskilled workers). Wobbly leaders Big Bill Haywood and Elizabeth Gurley Flynn galvanized the crowds with their passionate speeches in simple direct language demanding justice for all workers. The workers won the strike, but when the AFL settled separately with the mill owners, unskilled workers, including the women and children, were set adrift. The WTUL felt betrayed. Few of its members were ready for the radicalism of the Wobblies, who alone seemed willing to organize the unskilled, but neither could they trust the AFL to stand by them. Their commitment to unionism began to founder.

Turning to the State

The failure of male trade unionists to support the efforts of women workers dealt a crushing blow. Though women continued to work, especially in the garment trades, to organize women, to educate them, and to provide services for them, the great period of women's unionizing was over. Even such committed labor leaders as Rose Schneiderman and Leonora O'Reilly began to lose heart and to conclude that women's last best hope in the hostile, patriarchal world in which they lived and worked was the state. Settlement workers, the General Federation of Women's Clubs, the Women's Trade Union League, and the National Consumers' League increasingly poured their energies into a campaign for legislation that would do for women and children what they could not do for themselves.

The problem that most disturbed women activists was child labor. Among the middle class, rising affluence and a declining birthrate had transformed attitudes toward children. Childhood ceased to be viewed as a useless period of life to be worked through as quickly as possible, and came to be sentimentalized as a special age, one over which mothers and teachers, schooled in the special needs of children, should rule. Children who labored in factories, in the fields, or in sweatshops could not receive this nurturing care.

In 1903 Mary Harris (Mother) Jones, a long-time labor organizer, focused the country's attention on the problem by going to Kensington, Pennsylvania, where thousands of textile workers, many of them children, were on strike. "Whatever your fight, don't be ladylike," Mother Jones was fond of saying, and in the decades around the turn of the century she probably participated in more labor strikes than any other labor leader in the country. She described the children in Kensington as "stooped little things, round shouldered and skinny, many not over ten years of age . . . some with their hands off, some with the thumb missing, some with their fingers off at the knuckle." She publicized their plight by marching them from Philadelphia to Oyster Bay, Long Island, President Theodore Roosevelt's summer home. The march (helped along by sympathetic trainmen who gave the marchers occasional free rides), together with pressure from settlement workers and women's clubs, led to the passage of stronger child-labor laws in Pennsylvania, New York, and Illinois that year and gave a boost to the child-labor movement around the country.

Middle-class reformers cheered, but their goals met stiff resistance from both parents and employers. Working-class parents who depended on the earnings of their children resented this state interference in family life; so, too, did manufacturers who relied on child labor. Even where child-labor laws existed, as they did in Massachusetts, agents could provide forged birth certificates that enabled children under fourteen to work at places like Lawrence. Despite years of campaigning, reformers never won adequate enforcement of state legislation and failed totally in their ultimate goal, an amendment to the Constitution that would bar child labor nationwide. Opposition, especially in the South where child labor was most prevalent, was too strong. When child labor finally began to diminish, the reasons had less to do with reformers' efforts than with the declining utility of children to industry (as it became more automated), the rising wages of their parents, and the spread throughout the country of compulsory school attendance laws.

Reformers enjoyed more success with other causes. To pro-

tect the nation's health they garnered support for the Pure Food
and Drug Act (1906), whose passage was widely credited to the
vigorous lobbying efforts of members of the General Federation
of Women's Clubs. To protect wives and children from drunken
husbands they campaigned for a constitutional amendment that
would prohibit the manufacture and sale of alcohol. And to
combat the fearsome rates of maternal and infant mortality that
plagued the country they lobbied for a national Children's Bureau that would collect data on child labor and dispense information on the proper care of infants.

The Children's Bureau was the brainchild of Lillian Wald and
Florence Kelley. Angered by a 1903 federal campaign to eradicate the boll weevil while the deaths of 300,000 babies a year
brought no public outcry, they proposed a federal agency devoted to the welfare of children. After nine years of lobbying,
reformers finally pushed the bill creating the Children's Bureau
through Congress in 1912, and President William Howard Taft
appointed Hull House resident Julia Lathrop its first head. Born
in Rockford, Illinois, and a graduate of Vassar, Lathrop was a
close friend of Jane Addams and had long experience in Illinois
social services. She was, in Wald's words, "irrespective of sex,
the best qualified person in the country . . . for the job."

Though limited by a pitifully small appropriation, Lathrop
maximized the bureau's impact by commissioning two pamphlets, *Prenatal Care* (1913) and *Infant Care* (1914), to be distributed free of charge to mothers throughout the country.
Between 1914 and 1921 the bureau gave away 1.5 million copies
of the *Infant Care* pamphlet alone. The pamphlets, in turn,
generated up to 125,000 letters a year to the bureau, indicating
that the pamphlets were widely shared and that they reached
not just middle-class mothers but poor ones as well. According
to bureau estimates, the pamphlets affected the care of roughly
half of all babies born between 1915 and 1930. Even immigrant
women who spoke no English often learned of the Children's
Bureau teaching through their daughters, educated in Little
Mothers' Leagues at school. "Don't give the baby herring.
Don't let the baby eat dirty things from the floor," young girls
admonished their mothers.

Much of the pamphlets' advice now seems harsh. *Infant Care*, for instance, proposed that mothers put a stop to an infant's crying without cause by ignoring its wails, so as to avoid producing a "household tyrant" who would make of its mother a "slave." But to mothers overwhelmed with cooking, cleaning, and laundry, such advice provided welcome protection from overwork.

The value of the Children's Bureau to poor women across the country, especially in isolated, rural areas, can be glimpsed in the thousands of letters they wrote thanking the bureau for the pamphlets and seeking further guidance in parenting. For women who had no adequate medical care, the Children's Bureau staff physicians patiently answered queries, referred them to doctors, and even sent gifts and money from their own pockets to help the destitute. "Words cannot express what I feel for you in my heart," responded one grateful mother.

A natural corollary to their efforts to abolish child labor and reduce infant mortality was the reformers' efforts to regulate women's hours, wages, and conditions of work. There seemed little use in protecting children if the women who bore and cared for them had no protection from overlong hours of work and subsistence wages. Male union members lacked enthusiasm for protective labor legislation, because they opposed state interference in labor-capital relations. In fact, most of the gains made by men in limiting hours and raising wages had come through union bargaining. In 1910 unionized workers in manufacturing, who were mostly male, worked an average of fifty hours per week, while nonunionized workers, a group that included most women, worked an average of sixty hours per week. The goal of protective labor legislation was to bring working conditions for women into line with those for unionized men.

Massachusetts led the way with an 1887 law limiting a woman's working day to ten hours, and during the 1890s other states followed. By 1914, twenty-seven states were regulating hours, and by the 1920s, fifteen states had minimum-wage laws. Across the country states also passed laws limiting the kinds of work women could perform—laws prevented women from working at night, carrying heavy weights, working in dangerous places such as mines, or in morally questionable places such as bars.

For a short time, it looked as though protective legislation of any kind would founder before a hostile Supreme Court. In the 1905 case *Lochner* v. *New York*, the Court struck down a ten-hour law for male bakers on the grounds that it violated the Fourteenth Amendment's guarantee against the deprivation of life, liberty, or property without due process of law. Due process meant that a law had to be reasonable, and the Court concluded that since baking was not a hazardous occupation there was no reason for the state to interfere with the right of employers and employees to sign whatever contract they wished.

But three years later *Muller* v. *Oregon* (1908) salvaged protective legislation, at least for women. *Muller* was a case concerning women laundry workers whose employer was arrested for forcing them to work overtime in violation of the state's ten-hour law for women workers. Florence Kelley marshaled the resources of the National Consumers' League to defend the law up to the Supreme Court. One of the league's members was Josephine Goldmark, whose brother-in-law was the lawyer and future Supreme Court justice Louis Brandeis. The league persuaded Brandeis to take on the case and league members spent months at the main branch of the New York Public Library compiling medical and sociological evidence on the particular dangers to women's health of long hours of labor. This work provided the foundation of what was to become known as the Brandeis Brief, one that relies on sources outside the law to build a legal argument. The brief persuaded the Court, which ruled that while it could see no social benefit sufficiently great to warrant interfering with the freedom of contract of male bakers, laundresses were another matter. The family life of the country required that the state take a special interest in protecting the health of female workers, who were either mothers or potential mothers, and who were less able than men to protect themselves.

Women reformers also fought to protect poorly paid working women by closing down the red-light districts. Many men participated in this effort, serving on vice commissions throughout the country, but they tended to take a different approach from women reformers. Men generally favored the regulation of prostitution, under which prostitutes were registered and regularly examined for venereal disease. Women, on the other hand, wanted to abolish prostitution altogether. Why should prostitutes be subjected to examination, reformer Maude Glasgow demanded in 1910,

> while the man who has voluntarily exposed himself to the contagion of a loathsome disease continued even after his infection by the prostitute to have business and social relations as before, with the result that innocent members of society are exposed to a dangerous and contagious disorder to which they have not exposed themselves and from which no effort is made to protect them?

Women reformers were convinced that abduction of young women was a key factor in the creation of prostitution, and between 1908 and 1914, reformers like Jane Addams published dozens of articles, pamphlets, and books that alleged young girls were being sold into virtual slavery. Filled with alarming case histories, these publications warned parents of sinister men who preyed on unsuspecting young women. These pimps would win their victims' confidence with declarations of love and the promise of employment, and then turn them over to brothels.

How widespread the so-called white slave trade was is impossible to establish in retrospect. There is no doubt that it existed, but it is also clear that writers, unable to believe that a woman would ever choose to be a prostitute, exaggerated its extent. In an effort to protect young women from such a fate, reformers pursued a number of strategies. They organized boardinghouses for single working women, "veritable virtue saving stations," according to Annie Marion MacLean. They demanded that cities create censorship boards for movies, bar liquor from dance halls, and assign policewomen (preferably trained in social work) to patrol all commercial amusements. At the state level they campaigned to raise the age of consent for marriage from fourteen to eighteen and to require a health certificate beforehand to ensure that men would be free of venereal disease. To thwart the white slave trade (a term that ignored the African-American and Asian-American women who were forced into prostitution), they lobbied at the federal level for the Mann Act (1910), which outlawed the transportation of women across state lines for the purpose of prostitution. Finally, reformers urged schools to teach courses in sex education to persuade young men that they should renounce the double standard and strive for the same standard of sexual restraint accepted by virtuous women.

The battles to abolish child labor, improve the nation's health, regulate women's working conditions, and eradicate prostitution all encountered stiff opposition. But these were just skirmishes in the larger engagement that Mary Beard described as women reformers' "war on poverty." The next step was a major battle.

The Advent of Social Insurance

It was one thing to regulate and educate; it was quite another to call on the state's resources to provide social insurance. By the early twentieth century social welfare policies enjoyed widespread acceptance in Europe. Germany had adopted national health insurance in 1883 and workmen's compensation in 1884. England adopted both in 1911, and even France, the country most like the U.S. in its reverence for individual freedom, provided state subsidies to voluntary organizations. European women workers were campaigning for paid maternity leaves and a few, like Sweden's Ellen Key, were beginning to agitate for state subsidies to allow mothers to raise children alone. But Americans resisted such an expansion of state power, even after supporters pointed out that Germany provided a whole range of services for less than what Americans paid privately for funeral benefits alone.

Private charities in America offered some of the fiercest opposition to state aid. Giving out money as a right, they argued, would destroy the recipient's will to work. Far better that charity remain in the hands of private organizations who, through careful casework, would ensure that money would go only to the worthy poor. Otto T. Barnard, the vice president of Charity Organization Society, argued that state subsidies to mothers would be the "entering wedge towards state socialism." Support for these pensions, he warned, breeds "candidates for alms . . . represses the desire for self-help, self-respect and independence and inflicts upon its beneficiaries what is termed in England the government stroke of paralysis." What was ultimately at stake, in Barnard's view, was not just self-respect, but, more importantly, American manhood. Support for pensions, he concluded melodramatically, "is not American; it is not virile."

Settlement leaders broke the deadlock against state assistance by focusing on the two policies for which they could marshal the most widespread support: mothers' aid and workmen's compensation. At the turn of the century, low life expectancy for working-class men and extended years of childbearing for their wives meant that one in seven white families and one in five black families were headed by widows. Most widows struggled to keep their children at home while they worked to support them, but those who could not earn enough routinely found themselves charged with neglect and their children institutionalized. Rose Schneiderman, who lost her father to a flu epidemic when she was ten years old, knew the pain of such separation firsthand. Though her widowed mother struggled to support Rose and her three siblings, periodic unemployment forced her to institutionalize first a son and then Rose. The experience turned the hapless daughter into an impassioned advocate of mothers' aid.

Illinois led the campaign to allow mothers to keep their children without having to work to support them. Eighteen states soon followed, but state pensions rarely paid enough to support a family, and few families qualified for even minimal assistance. Widows could usually count on some aid, but many reformers resisted the idea of granting funds to divorced women or women who had been deserted, fearing that a guarantee of assistance would encourage fathers to avoid their economic responsibilities. Moreover, even widows could be denied aid if there was any doubt about their moral fitness. Despite all these restrictions, however, mothers' pension legislation provided the first instance in which states took responsibility for ensuring a minimum income to a family in need.

The second victory for reformers was workmen's compensation. This was an easier battle because there were so many groups that wanted it: not only the women's clubs and social workers but also labor leaders and employers. Yet the popular resistance to social insurance in this country was so great that it took a major campaign to win even this modest level of protection. A key element of that campaign was Crystal Eastman's study of work accidents in the region around Pittsburgh in 1907–8. Eastman, the daughter of two Congregational ministers, grew up in upstate New York, graduated from Vassar College, took a master's degree in sociology at Columbia, and earned a law degree at New York University. Like so many other talented and highly educated women of her generation she gravitated toward social work, hoping to better the lot of America's poor. Her study of accidents in Pittsburgh became, in the words of Isaac Rubinow, "perhaps the strongest single force in attracting public opinion and arousing conscience concerning this one aspect of wage workers' rights in this country."

The conventional wisdom in Pittsburgh attributed 95 percent of accidents at work to employee carelessness, but Eastman found that only 21 percent of the accidents she studied over a year's time could be attributed to negligence. Even this number was open to question; long hours, relentless pressure to speed up, and fatigue made inattention inevitable. Eastman argued that workers were not responsible for most accidents. If she was right, then employers faced a potentially ruinous burden of litigation from employees who might seek recovery for their injuries. Far better, employers concluded, to accept a predictable system of compensation. Eastman helped write one of the first workmen's compensation laws in New York in 1910; other states quickly followed. These laws guaranteed too little money to compensate completely for most losses, but they were the start of social insurance that would protect families, especially women and children, against destitution.

The Struggle for Suffrage

The difficulty women reformers faced in winning legislative change brought home the importance of suffrage. In 1910 the fight for women's suffrage was more than sixty years old, a national campaign by the National American Woman Suffrage Association was twenty years old, and yet women could vote in only Wyoming, Idaho, Utah, and Colorado. Despite their increasingly active role in public life—as workers, professionals, clubwomen, settlement workers, and labor organizers—women (in common with black men in the South) were still classed with idiots and children when it came to the franchise.

Suffrage advocates frequently blamed the liquor interests for their difficulty in winning support, a not unnatural conclusion, since most people, including both suffragists and brewers, assumed that women would outlaw liquor if they had the vote. Yet the most fervent opposition to women's voting came from the South, where temperance forces were strongest. Most historians have therefore concluded that something larger than the brewers was at work.

Hard though it is to understand, given today's widespread apathy toward voting, early twentieth-century Americans harbored a deep-seated fear that women's suffrage would bring radical change to society. Women's suffrage challenged one of the fundamental assumptions of American politics: that the basic unit of political life was the family, with the father standing at its head representing and protecting his wife and children in the wider world. To grant suffrage to women would be to break up that fundamental unit. As a senator in 1866 explained, to give a woman the vote would be to put her "in an adversary position to man and convert all the now harmonious elements of society into a state of war, and make every home a hell on earth."

Given the country's strong tradition of individual rights, one might think that women's demand for suffrage would have succeeded more quickly in America than in Europe, where suffrage campaigns were also under way. But women's ideological advantage in the United States was offset by a crippling liability —the central importance of the family to maintaining social order. America had no aristocratic tradition of deference nor any dominating church. In America the family alone stood between the individual and chaos. To weaken the traditional hierarchy within the family, to place women on a political footing equal to that of men, risked undermining America's one bulwark against anarchy. Despite a tradition of individual liberty, therefore, many Americans looked on the demand for female suffrage as a radical assault on the social order.

The radical nature of suffrage had been clear from the start. When Elizabeth Cady Stanton organized the first women's rights meeting at Seneca Falls in 1848, the many goals that were at first identified as worthy of support did not include the vote. Women wanted property rights, the right to divorce abusive husbands, the right to an education equal to any man's, and the right to join any profession. But the idea of the vote seemed too extreme. "Thou will make us ridiculous," the elderly Lucretia Mott cautioned Stanton. And in the eyes of many men and women alike that is exactly how they looked. Men gradually agreed to extend property rights to women, because property in a wife's name could save a man from his creditors. They accepted coeducation, because universities needed students and society needed trained teachers. But the vote was something else. To give women the vote would mean recognizing them as individuals with their own rights and interests.

So radical did the suffrage demand appear that for decades few women thought it worth pursuing. Suffragists therefore labored under the considerable disadvantage of being generals with no army. The problem was made painfully clear in 1895 when Massachusetts (a hotbed of suffrage activity) conducted a referendum in which women were permitted to vote on the question of whether suffrage should be extended to females. The referendum was defeated, as had been expected, but the alarming fact was that far more men than women voted in favor of women's suffrage. In 1902 Susan B. Anthony ruefully observed, "In the indifference, the inertia, the apathy of women, lies the greatest obstacle to their enfranchisement."

Changes taking place outside the movement, however, gradually enabled suffragists to expand and legitimize their role. Women's increased employment, their educational attainments, their club work, and especially their reform activities transformed the suffrage movement from isolated, insistent women into part of a larger phenomenon—a movement of women to reform a world that most Americans, including most men, regarded as badly in need of change. By 1910 there existed an extensive interlocking directorate of women leaders in the reform and suffrage movements. Jane Addams and Florence Kelley were the two most important, holding between them offices in the General Federation of Women's Clubs, the Women's Trade Union League, the National Consumers' League, the Women's Peace Party, and the National American Woman Suffrage Association (NAWSA). This network of women gave suffrage leaders an audience they had lacked. The General Federation of Women's Clubs did not endorse suffrage until 1914, but throughout the preceding decade its local clubs listened to representatives of NAWSA explain the connection between the reform legislation the clubs supported and the need for more votes on behalf of those laws. Gradually, support for women's suffrage grew.

So, too, did opposition. Antisuffrage associations began to appear in the 1890s, principally in states like Massachusetts and New York where the suffrage movement was most active. Men belonged to these "anti" organizations, but women led them. Curiously, the "anti" leaders came from the same middle-class, educated background as did the suffragists. One of the most prominent antisuffragists was Annie Nathan Meyer, who had sought in the 1880s to open Columbia College to women and had helped found Barnard College. Her sister Maud was a leading suffragist.

The suffragists and their opponents agreed that men and women were fundamentally different, but they disagreed on the political implications of that view. To the antisuffragists, differences between the sexes destined women to the home and men to the world of business and politics. Suffragists, by contrast, insisted that differences between the sexes made women's suffrage all the more important. Men had done much to ruin the world through their competitive, aggressive, and unchecked individualism. If women had the vote, they could balance these unfortunate qualities with their own more cooperative, nurturing, and community-oriented characteristics. A few suffragists went so far as to claim that women were superior to men, but most accepted the more moderate position of Jane Addams. "We have not wrecked railroads, nor corrupted legislatures, nor done many unholy things that men have done," Addams observed; "but then we must remember that we have not had the chance." Nevertheless, Addams and most other suffragists believed that women and men had different temperaments and backgrounds and thus different social responsibilities. Only with the vote could women carry out those responsibilities in the modern, industrialized, urbanized world. Only with the vote would municipal housekeeping succeed, and would unsanitary housing, poisonous sewage, contaminated waste, adulterated foods, ill-ventilated factories, infant mortality, prostitution, crime, political corruption, and drunkenness be overcome.

Moreover, granting the vote to women would help overcome the class divisions that threatened to rend the American social fabric. Suffragists had not always talked this way. Indeed, throughout the late nineteenth century suffragists had argued the reverse, that votes for white, middle-class women would outweigh the votes of immigrant and black men. By 1910, however, the social reform movement had led suffrage leaders to emphasize the common ground on which immigrants and white native-born women stood, their common need for the vote. Harriot Stanton Blatch, daughter of Elizabeth Cady Stanton, played an important role in drawing working women into the suffrage movement. Having recently returned from England where she had been impressed by the militant tactics of Emmeline and Christabel Pankhurst's suffragettes, Blatch launched the Equality League of Self-Supporting Women in New York, participated in the garment workers' strike, and attracted twenty thousand women workers to her banner. By 1910 the organization had been renamed the Women's Political Union and had flouted convention by holding open-air meetings, inaugurating suffrage parades, sending working women to Albany to testify about working conditions, campaigning in election districts, and stationing women watchers at the polls.

The theme of social motherhood, so important in winning middle-class support, proved even more appealing to working-class, mostly immigrant women. "In our homes, as wives, mothers, and daughters," labor leader Leonora O'Reilly declared, "we need the ballot to do justice to our work as home-keepers. Children need pure milk and pure food, good schools and playgrounds, sanitary homes and safe streets." Working women also needed the vote to improve working conditions. "I hold that the humanizing of industry is woman's business," Rose Schneiderman told a suffrage rally; "she must wield the ballot for this purpose."

Some suffragists even believed that women's suffrage would help overcome racial divisions. In 1909 a group of white and black social reformers, including Mary Ovington and W.E.B. Du Bois, met at Henry Street Settlement to discuss the possibility of forming an organization that would fight for equal rights for blacks in America. The following year the National Association for the Advancement of Colored People—the NAACP—was founded. Members of the biracial organization believed that if anyone needed the vote in America it was the black woman. She would use it, black leader Nannie Helen Burroughs declared, "in defense of her virtue" against white men, to control prostitution, to win equal rights in the work force and in public accommodations, to combat lynching, and to work more effectively toward compulsory education in the South. Black women were active throughout the country on behalf of women's suffrage. Mary Church Terrell, a graduate of Oberlin, a teacher, a member of the Washington, D.C., board of education, and president of the National Association of Colored Women, addressed the 1898 convention of NAWSA on "The Progress of Colored Women," and lectured throughout the country on behalf of women's suffrage and the progress of black women. Ida Wells-Barnett, educated at Fisk University, a journalist and crusading leader of the antilynching movement, founded the first black women's suffrage organization in Chicago, and worked closely with Jane Addams.

For the most part, however, African Americans remained segregated from the white movement in their own clubs, and many white leaders viewed them as a threat to the suffrage campaign. To support black suffrage risked losing the white South. In 1903 NAWSA adopted a states' rights policy, which gave to each state organization the freedom to establish membership qualification in its branch and to make any arguments on behalf of suffrage it deemed fit. In practice this policy allowed Southerners to argue, as Mississippi's Belle Kearney did at the 1903 NAWSA convention, that "the enfranchisement of women would insure immediate and durable white supremacy honestly attained." Although settlement leaders argued consistently that blacks must have equal rights with whites, leaders of NAWSA asked blacks not to participate with whites in suffrage activities for fear of alienating white Southerners. Not surprisingly, many black women lost interest in the suffrage battle. "Personally," said Margaret Murray Washington, black clubwoman, educator, and wife of Booker T. Washington, "woman suffrage has never kept me awake at night." Race proved the one insurmountable obstacle in the suffrage campaign. Suffragists overcame regional differences; they overcame religious differences; they even overcame class differences; but, sad to say, except in rare instances, they could not overcome racial differences.

The Progressive Party

The magnitude of this failure was not, however, immediately apparent. Indeed, the suffrage movement had never seemed so successful as the country entered the century's second decade. Inspired by the example of militant tactics among suffragists in England, by the courage and vitality of striking women workers, by the legislative successes of social reformers, and by welcoming audiences around the country, suffrage leaders redoubled their organizing efforts. Parades, motorcades, open-air speeches, silent pickets, mass rallies—all gave evidence of new energy in the struggle. In quick succession came two important victories, Washington in 1910 and California in 1911, which showed what the new combination of flamboyant tactics and careful organizing could do.

The extent of women's success became apparent in the Presidential election of 1912. Settlement workers drew up a list of minimum standards of social welfare and submitted it to the Republican Party. The platform committee would have nothing to do with it, but Theodore Roosevelt seemed interested, and when he bolted the convention to found his own party he seemed more interested still. In facing the toughest race of his political life, Roosevelt needed whatever help he could muster. He visited Hull House and talked to Jane Addams about reform and women's suffrage, a cause to which he had not yet committed himself. According to Grace Abbott, who observed the meeting,

Addams explained why she thought women's suffrage a vital issue. "Well, that's that," Roosevelt responded. "I think you're right, Miss Addams, and if you're for it, I'm for it, and I'll support it." And thus the man known throughout the country for his celebration of female domesticity accepted not only women's demand for a place in the public sphere but also their blueprint for reforming it.

When the new Progressive Party convened in Chicago to nominate Roosevelt, it also adopted the reformers' list of demands. For the first time a major political party endorsed an eight-hour day in continuous, twenty-four-hour industries; a six-day week for all; the abolition of tenement manufacture; the improvement of housing conditions; the prohibition of child labor under sixteen; and the careful regulation of employment for women. It also called for a federal system of accident, old-age, and unemployment insurance. Most startling of all, the platform endorsed women's suffrage. "The Progressive Platform contains all the things I have been fighting for for more than a decade," Jane Addams announced.

She exaggerated. There were some things that the Progressive Party did not stand for. It did not stand for peace, as she did, but rather proposed the building of two battleships a year. "I confess that I found it very difficult to swallow those two battleships," she later remarked. She objected also to Roosevelt's decision not to seat black delegates from several Southern states. Few social reformers felt entirely comfortable with Roosevelt. His jingoism, not to mention his paternalistic condescension toward women, made him less than an ideal candidate. They were realists, however, and they welcomed their first chance to have a politician of unquestioned national influence champion their cause.

When the convention finally opened, the participants viewed it as the climax to years of struggle. When Jane Addams rose to second Roosevelt's nomination, the crowd cheered and applauded just as loudly as they did for Roosevelt himself. She wore a white dress, and she addressed the audience quietly and calmly. She emphasized the importance of the platform. "I rise to second the nomination stirred by the splendid platform adopted by this convention. . . . A great party has pledged itself to the protection of children, to the care of the aged, to the relief of overworked girls, to the safe guarding of burdened men. Committed to this human undertaking it is inevitable that such a party should appeal to women, should seek to draw upon the great reservoir of their moral energy so long undesired and unutilized in practical politics." There were other speeches that day, but the newspapers gave most of the attention to Addams, calling her "one of the ten greatest citizens of the republic." Her presence symbolized not only a triumphant moment for American women but more importantly the victory of the movement "for the aid of those who are now overwhelmed in the flood of economic error and social wrongs."

The Progressive Party Convention represented the high-water mark of women's political efforts for many years to come. In that moment women were able to capitalize on public concern over the destructive side of industrial growth to put together a coalition of reform groups that would support their new vision of state responsibility. In the end that coalition proved too weak to bring victory. The Progressives went down to defeat, as the three major parties split the vote, and the Socialists amassed an unprecedented 897,000 votes. Despite this loss, however, women had made clear that they were political actors to be taken seriously. In little more than a decade, they had played a pivotal role in laying the foundation of the modern welfare state. For a disenfranchised group theirs was no small victory.

3

Claiming the Rights of Men
1912–29

The First Feminists

In the years around 1912 the suffrage movement began to include a new breed of women. They called themselves feminists, and more than protective labor legislation or the right to vote they wanted emancipation of women from the conventions that circumscribed their lives. Women reformers had long emphasized women's duties; feminists stressed women's rights. Intent on liberating themselves from every kind of sex discrimination, they demanded the freedom that men took for granted. Concern for women's rights had never been absent from the suffrage movement, but as the campaign for the vote became enmeshed in the drive for social reform, suffrage leaders spoke less often of women's rights and more about society's need for the political power of women. Feminists sought to return to the tradition of rights talk.

Feminism found its first full expression in a Greenwich Village club called Heterodoxy, founded in 1912 by reformer Marie Jenny Howe. As one recruit later recalled, the group demanded only one thing of a member, "that she should not be orthodox in her opinions." Married, but childless, Howe had long been an organizer. A Unitarian minister until her wedding in 1904 at the age of thirty-three to reformer Frederic C. Howe, she devoted the first years of her married life to suffrage and the National Consumers' League. Heterodoxy, however, marked a new departure.

Its members included lawyer and social activist Crystal Eastman, publisher with her younger brother Max of the radical
magazine *The Masses*; journalist Ruth Hale, founder of the Lucy
Stone League, which championed women's right not to take
their husband's name upon marriage; Dr. Josephine Baker,
head of the country's first bureau of children's hygiene; teacher
Henrietta Rodman, defender of married women's right to work;
psychologist Leta Hollingworth, critic of G. Stanley Hall's theory of female mental inferiority; and anthropologist Elsie Clews
Parsons, advocate of trial marriage. In addition there were suffragist Doris Stevens; journalist Rheta Childe Dorr; black leader
and NAACP member Grace Nail Johnson; socialist trade-
unionist Rose Pastor Stokes; Wobbly leader Elizabeth Gurley
Flynn; author and literary patron Mabel Dodge; and, most senior and distinguished of all, writer, lecturer, and theorist Charlotte Perkins Gilman. Some were married, some single. Some
lived with men, others with women. They were all part of the
revolution gripping Greenwich Village in the years before World
War I, one that fostered rebellion against realism in art, against
formalism in philosophy, and against bourgeois respectability
in social values. No longer satisfied with winning political power,
they were beginning to reconsider womanhood itself and all of
the ways society constricted and limited women's lives.

The Village was a relatively isolated community before the
West Side subway connected it to the rest of Manhattan in 1917.
Low rents attracted artists, writers, and teachers who wanted
community without the moral restrictions that small-town
America typically imposed. Residents often spent their evenings
at Mabel Dodge's salon where they mixed with Wobbly leader
Big Bill Haywood, socialists Margaret and William Sanger, an-
archist Emma Goldman, political commentator Walter
Lippmann, and psychiatrist A. A. Brill. They discussed Sigmund
Freud's insistence on the centrality of sex in human experience,
argued over Havelock Ellis's still more startling view that sexual
restraint posed a danger to human well-being, analyzed the
Ashcan School of painting, and debated the IWW's idea of "one
big union."

On February 17, 1914, Heterodoxy furthered this intellectual ferment by calling the first feminist mass meeting at Cooper Union to consider the question "What Is Feminism?" Speaking to a packed auditorium where garment worker Clara Lemlich had called for a general strike five years earlier, Marie Jenny Howe sought to define this term, unheard of a half-dozen years before and now on everyone's lips. Feminism, she declared, was women's effort to break "into the human race," and to gain the whole range of activities that men enjoyed.

"We thought we discussed the whole field," Rheta Childe Dorr later recalled of Heterodoxy meetings from 1912 to 1917, "but we really discussed ourselves." They met every other Saturday for lunch, and from speakers and each other they learned about pacifism, birth control, the Russian Revolution, infant mortality, anarchism, women's education, black civil rights, and free love, and they reflected on how these changes affected them. They constituted a kind of consciousness-raising group long before the term was invented, and though they had come of age in a period of social activism, their concerns were increasingly inner-directed and individualistic. "We intend simply to be ourselves," Marie Howe declared, "not just our little female selves, but our whole big human selves." They stood for an important change taking place among American women as they entered the work force, the universities, the professions, and politics—a shift away from self-sacrifice and toward self-fulfillment. Even more decisively than Jane Addams, they were breaking with the "family claim." Not that the break was easy, or ever complete. As one college-educated contemporary complained, "Our families make us feel like murderers rather than joyous adventurers."

The changes that Heterodoxy's feminists sought were most obvious in two matters: their commitment to women's economic independence and their preoccupation with sexuality. In 1909, speaking before the WTUL with NAWSA president Anna Howard Shaw, Charlotte Perkins Gilman had urged that women claim the vote as a first step toward emancipation from the strictures of the home. Shaw, in contrast, urged that women had earned the vote through generations of domestic service, that they did not need to change themselves but merely needed political power to bring their nurturing talents to the public sphere. To the WTUL audience, Shaw won the debate hands down.

At Heterodoxy, in contrast, Gilman's call for economic independence won wide acceptance. Gilman's stance rested on a new concept of women's nature, one that stressed women's and men's essential similarity. Though she believed that women had been hurt by millennia of domestic confinement, Gilman insisted that better schooling and broader experience in the world would quickly erase the sex differences that evolution had created. Women scientists offered mounting evidence to support Gilman's critique of the traditional belief in innate female difference. Columbia psychologist Leta Hollingworth, in tests on college students, demonstrated that women did not, as had long been assumed, suffer mental decline during menstruation. Her colleague Helen Thompson Woolley, in tests on students at the University of Chicago, demonstrated that men and women differed much more among themselves on psychological tests than from one another. And anthropologist Elsie Clews Parsons, after reviewing the literature in her field, reported that much that was taken to be natural in female behavior did not exist among women in other cultures.

Given this evident variety in human aptitudes and behavior, Gilman believed that women should be free to choose their work without regard to sex and regardless of whether they married and became mothers. In fact, Gilman insisted that women would remain subordinates within the work force until work became a lifelong expectation for them. "Until 'mothers' earn their living," Gilman warned, " 'women' will not."

Making way for the wife and mother would require some fundamental changes, Gilman conceded. First, society would have to accept the idea of married career women, and second, marriage would have to be modernized through a combination of cooperative housekeeping and the relegation of such tasks as cooking, laundry, and child care to professionals.

Fellow club member Henrietta Rodman, a teacher in the New York City public schools, founded the Feminist Alliance to put Gilman's theories into practice. New York's schools denied employment to married women on the grounds that wives were too burdened by household duties to be effective teachers. Outraged by this policy, Rodman did not inform the board of education of her own marriage. She was not alone. Many women teachers kept their marriages secret, continuing to work under their maiden names until they became pregnant and could conceal their marriage no longer. Though Rodman never had children, her indignation at the injustice of the board's policy drove her to campaign not only for the end of discrimination against married women teachers but also for a maternity leave policy. New York City school officials dismissed Rodman for insubordination when she charged them with "mother-baiting," but in 1915 they granted her demands, permitting women to continue teaching after they married and even after they had become mothers.

Gilman's vision of economic independence for women united the members of Heterodoxy in a way that their second major concern—sexual emancipation—did not. They all agreed on the importance of eradicating the double standard, but older women like Gilman wanted to do so by insisting on male sexual restraint, while younger women called for female sexual freedom. The younger women looked for support to the writings and speeches of Emma Goldman, the fiery anarchist.

A Lithuanian Jew born in 1869, the strong-willed Goldman escaped an arranged marriage at the age of sixteen by emigrating to America. In New York she discovered anarchism and free love. One of her lovers, Alexander Berkman, spent fourteen years in jail for his role in the attempted assassination of steel tycoon Henry Clay Frick in 1892. Through her speeches and the editorship of her monthly *Mother Earth* (1906–17), Goldman called for revolution and excoriated the women's movement for the superficiality of its goals. Emancipation, she believed, required much more than the winning of legal rights. Like Gilman, Goldman deplored women's "parasitism" and called for their economic emancipation, but she also advocated women's sexual liberation. Gilman, revealing her Victorian upbringing, saw sex as a drain on intellectual achievement and a threat to personal autonomy. Goldman, in contrast, saw sexuality and intellect as mutually reinforcing. "The greatest shortcoming of the emancipation of the present day," Goldman

declared, "lies in its artificial stiffness and its narrow respecta-
bilities, which produce an emptiness in woman's soul that will
not let her drink from the fountain of life. . . . The demand for
equal rights in every vocation of life is just and fair; but, after
all, the most vital right is the right to love and be loved."

As the feminists debated, social change abetted the Goldman
view. By 1913 young, urban, middle-class women were bobbing
their hair, shortening their skirts, wearing makeup, smoking in
public, and spending afternoons at tearooms dancing the tango.
Vice inspector Belle Moskowitz, who began her career by trying
to protect immigrant girls from the corruption of the dance hall,
warned in 1915 that this "evil condition" was "working upward
into other strata of society."

Many of those at Heterodoxy who identified with this new
rebellious spirit in sexuality were struggling to emancipate themselves from a maternal destiny, but others saw sexuality and
maternity as compatible ideals. Inspired by Ellen Key's *Century
of the Child* (1910), they linked motherhood with erotic love
and called for programs that would permit women to enjoy both.
The Swedish-born Key argued that every woman should set
aside a decade for having three to four children, while being
supported by the state. Within Heterodoxy Rheta Childe Dorr
dismissed Key as a "reactionary," while Crystal Eastman applauded her vision. "If the feminist program goes to pieces on
the arrival of the first baby," Eastman declared, "it is false and
useless."

That feminists of Heterodoxy could espouse such divergent
ideas testifies to the breadth of their vision, as well as the potential for future conflict. All feminists believed that women
should band together to claim personal emancipation, but they
disagreed about what emancipation meant and how best to
achieve it. To some, sex was but an incident in a woman's life,
something best ignored. To others it was a central, defining
characteristic, one that social policy must never forget. In these
differences of emphasis lay the potential for much future strife,
but in the early teens the growing clamor for suffrage drowned
out the dissonance under the surface.

Winning the Vote

Despite a flurry of Western victories, suffragists were still losing more state campaigns than they were winning when Woodrow Wilson won the Presidency in 1912. Impatient with this glacial pace, a young Quaker militant, Alice Paul, and her friend Lucy Burns exhorted NAWSA to switch to a campaign for a federal amendment. Washington, D.C., presented a much more manageable target than state capitals, they observed, and with the 1912 Democratic sweep of both the executive and legislative branches the target was suddenly even more concentrated.

A 1905 graduate of Swarthmore College, Paul had spent several years as a social worker before attending the London School of Economics in 1908–9. Inspired by the exploits of the Pankhursts, she joined British suffragists as they marched through the streets, starved themselves in prison, and attacked the "party in power" for denying the vote to women. During one of her prison terms Paul met Burns, a redheaded Irish-Catholic graduate of Vassar who had pursued graduate work in Germany before coming to England and joining the suffragists' struggle. Paul returned to America in 1910 to complete a doctoral dissertation on the legal status of women in Pennsylvania, but the suffrage battle remained much on her mind. In 1912 she renewed her friendship with Burns, just back from London, and the two women dedicated themselves to transforming the American suffrage movement along English lines.

They began by persuading Jane Addams to intervene on their behalf with NAWSA leadership to put them in charge of the organization's congressional committee. From that position they recruited a group of like-minded women to form the Congressional Union (CU), an organization devoted exclusively to the fight for a federal amendment. Recruits ranged from the radical Crystal Eastman, who brought with her most of the members of Heterodoxy, to the wealthy Alva Belmont, who had been converted to militant action during a trip to England. Not all feminists became militant suffragists, but the overlap was substantial, and increasingly militants gave feminism its political meaning.

Leadership in the CU quickly passed to the charismatic Paul,

whom Heterodoxy member Doris Stevens called the Lenin of
suffragism. She was "cool, practical, rational," Stevens observed. "And if she has demanded the ultimate of her followers,
she has given it herself." Paul did not want a large, inactive
membership; she demanded committed workers, willing to ded-
icate themselves single-mindedly to winning a federal amendment by whatever means necessary. While NAWSA reached
two million members, Paul's followers never rose above fifty
thousand. They formed the "shock division" of suffragism, according to Inez Haynes Irwin, while NAWSA "formed the main
army."

Relations between NAWSA and the CU soon turned stormy.
NAWSA leaders believed in grass-roots organizing, patient education, and nonpartisan campaigning. Paul, in contrast, insisted on centralized control, provocative demonstrations, and
holding the party in power responsible for women's not having
the vote. These differences led to a permanent rupture in the
1916 Presidential campaign. Leaving NAWSA, Paul and her
followers joined forces with Western women voters to form the
National Woman's Party (NWP) and defeat the Democrats.

When the Democrats won yet again, Paul stepped up the
attack. NWP members picketed the White House, chained
themselves to the White House fence, and ceremoniously
burned the President's speeches. NAWSA leaders deplored
"those wild women at the gates," but when the picketers were
arrested and sentenced to prison, and especially after they embarked on a hunger strike to which officials responded with
forced feedings, the militants generated wide publicity and even
sympathy. All the women had done, as Alva Belmont told the
press, was to stand there "quietly, peacefully, lawfully, and
gloriously." Despite NAWSA objections to their rivals, the
group probably profited from the militants' tactics. Worried
about what the NWP might do next, Congress and the President
looked with increasing favor on NAWSA as the lesser of two
evils.

The popularity of the moderates owed as much to a timely
change in leadership as it did to the escalating tactics of the
militants. In 1915 Carrie Chapman Catt succeeded Anna Howard Shaw as president of NAWSA. Shaw, president from 1904

to 1915, had proven a poor administrator. Catt, by contrast, was widely recognized as a highly skilled leader. A college-educated teacher and journalist from Iowa, Catt had devoted most of her adult life to state suffrage campaigns. Twice widowed, she had enjoyed both the personal and financial support of her two husbands, the second of whom offered her a contract that gave her half the year to campaign for suffrage and left her a wealthy woman at his death in 1905.

Like other reform-minded women Catt believed that the vote would be a first step toward effecting a range of social reforms. But, grass-roots organizer that she was, she also recognized the wide variety of reasons that by the 1910s had come to unite women in the suffrage movement. In 1917 Catt announced that she did not know whether the vote was a right, a duty, or a privilege, but that "whatever it is, women want it."

Though distressed by what she regarded as the "stupendous stupidity" of Paul's tactics, Catt quickly accepted the dissident's view that victory lay with a federal campaign. In 1916 she persuaded NAWSA to shift its strategy to a dual-pronged approach: fighting for a constitutional amendment while continuing campaigns in the states where victory seemed most important. Everyone agreed that a major victory in an Eastern state would help the national cause enormously, and resources poured into New York as the most promising target. Mimicking the precinct-by-precinct organization of Tammany Hall politicians, suffrage workers redoubled their efforts in New York, and in 1917 they won.

Universal suffrage appeared within reach, when suddenly World War I threatened to tear the women's movement apart. Since the turn of the century international peace had become an increasingly important issue among women activists. In 1915, eighty-six delegates from all the major women's groups, including Catt, Gilman, Addams, and younger radicals like Eastman, attended the opening meeting of the Woman's Peace Party in Washington, chaired by Catt. After only two days of debate they settled on a pacifist platform, representing the views of "the mother half of humanity," who were no longer willing to see the fruits of their labor squandered by war.

But U.S. entry into World War I all but destroyed the women's peace movement. Jeanette Rankin, a Montana suffragist who had just been elected to Congress, voted against a declaration of war, and a small group of radicals, led by Crystal Eastman, continued to agitate for peace, as did Jane Addams, at tremendous cost both to Hull House and herself. The National Woman's Party simply refused to endorse U.S. entry into the war and continued its single-minded assault on the President and Congress. But NAWSA gave in to the rising tide of patriotism and abandoned its pacifist stance.

By Catt's calculation the war gave women the best chance they would ever have to win the vote, and she refused to risk losing popular support at that critical moment. Setting her belief in pacifism aside for the duration, she worked to turn the war to the suffragists' advantage. She began by exploiting Wilson's idealistic claim that the war was being fought for democracy. Democracy, she declared, begins at home. Following up with a heavy dose of realism, Catt warned that it was unwise to deprive women of the vote just when their war work was needed. And, indeed, the country was relying on the efforts both of middle-class clubwomen who were selling bonds, saving food, and organizing benefits for the troops as well as working-class women who were taking on men's jobs in factories. During the war NAWSA's membership doubled, reaching its peak of two million by 1919.

Catt's one-two punch, combined with the NWP's renewed picketing at the White House, finally beat down Wilson's resistance. On January 9, 1918, he called on House Democrats to support the federal amendment as "an act of right and justice," and the next day the House endorsed women's suffrage. Later that year Wilson told the more reluctant Senate that the amendment was "vital to the winning of the war." On June 4, 1919, the Senate finally agreed. A prohibition amendment was ratified that year as well, bringing to simultaneous fruition two of the principal reforms that middle-class women had fought for since the late nineteenth century. Fourteen months after the Senate suffrage vote, on August 16, 1920, the thirty-sixth state ratified the women's suffrage amendment, under which no state could deny the vote "on account of sex." Not that all women thereby gained the right to vote. Regulation of the franchise remained a state matter, and states could still deny or limit the possibility of voting for reasons other than sex.

Only the South held out in the ratification process. Fearful still that women's suffrage would jeopardize not only the subordination of women but also that of blacks, male legislators in most of the South declined to join the rest of the country in granting women recognition as political beings. It is ironic that NAWSA's sacrifice of black women, so costly to women's sense of common purpose, never brought the suffrage movement the expected payoff.

Irreconcilable Differences

For years suffragists and antisuffragists alike had predicted that if women won the vote, they would transform American politics. Evidence to support this view began to mount even before ratification of the Nineteenth Amendment in states, like Illinois and Massachusetts, that had extended women the vote on their own. Analyzing election returns in Illinois between 1913 and 1915, Edith Abbott discovered that women were substantially more likely than men to vote for reform candidates, while black leader Ida B. Wells-Barnett credited the votes of black women for the election in 1915 of Chicago's first black alderman. In 1916 women drawn to Woodrow Wilson as the peace candidate gave him critical support in states like California, where they had the vote. In 1918 Massachusetts female voters upset antisuffragist Senator John W. Weeks, and in New York that year women helped defeat at least four old antagonists in the legislature.

The League of Women Voters, successor to NAWSA, joined with the Women's Joint Congressional Committee (the umbrella organization for the country's principal women's groups) to educate the electorate, democratize politics, and press for reform legislation. Confronted with this feminine threat, politicians hurried to meet women's demands. In symbolic recognition that politics no longer belonged to men only, officials moved polling places from saloons and barbershops to schools. Democrats and Republicans both appointed women as equal members of their national committees and named women to government posts.

Congress established the Women's Bureau in the Department of Labor in 1920 to monitor women's working conditions; passed the Cable Act in 1922, giving women equal citizenship rights with men; and sent a child-labor amendment to the states for ratification in 1924.

The states were no less active. By 1925, twenty states had passed laws admitting women to jury duty, Michigan and Montana passed equal-pay laws, and Wisconsin passed an equal-rights act. Responding to women's demands for protective labor laws, all but four states limited working women's hours; eighteen states prescribed rest periods and meal hours; sixteen states prohibited night work in certain occupations; and thirteen had minimum-wage regulations. Even the South, long resistant to women's demands, joined in the spirit of reform. Georgia showed women lobbyists new respect, and in Virginia legislators granted reformers eighteen of their twenty-four requests, including a children's code and a vocational education law.

Much of this success merely extended reforms won earlier in the century, but, emboldened by their success, women began pushing in new directions. Determined to reduce the country's alarmingly high rates of maternal and infant mortality, they decided to press the federal government to do something it had never done before: spend federal funds on health care. In 1921 the Children's Bureau proposed the Sheppard-Towner Act to provide states with matching federal funds to help set up programs in which public-health nurses would instruct mothers on infant care and doctors would provide preventive health checkups. Even so decentralized and modest an intervention into private affairs, however, encountered stiff resistance. Opponents characterized the act as "German paternalism," and "official meddling between mother and baby which would mean the abolition of the family."

Undaunted, supporters mounted a determined campaign to win passage of the bill. Organizations ranging from the National Consumers' League to the Daughters of the American Revolution (DAR) worked together to secure endorsements from thirty-four governors and marshal expert testimony at congressional hearings. Dr. Josephine Baker, head of the New York Bureau of Child Hygiene and a member of Heterodoxy, testified to the power of intervention by revealing that infant mortality in New York had declined by half since she began battling the problem in 1908, while Florence Kelley asked ominously, "What answer can be given to the women in a myriad of organizations who are marveling and asking, 'Why does Congress wish women and children to die?' " A majority of Congress probably opposed the bill, and President Harding offered only tepid support, but fear of what twenty million organized women might do if spurned prompted Congress to pass the Sheppard-Towner Act in 1921 and to inaugurate, however cautiously, the modern welfare state.

Despite women's triumphs, the tempo of reform began to slow by the mid-twenties. The Supreme Court struck down minimum-wage laws in *Adkins* v. *Children's Hospital* (1923) on the grounds that such legislation violated the Fourteenth Amendment's guarantee against unreasonable infringement of freedom of contract. The child-labor amendment won ratification in only six states between 1924 and 1930. And the campaign to win women the right to serve on juries ground to a halt in the face of a new wave of opposition. For several years the threat of a "woman's vote" had pushed laws of special interest to women through Congress and state legislatures, but by mid-decade it was clear that women were voting not as a separate block but like the men in their families. Moreover, like all new voters, they were voting in smaller numbers than those with longer experience at the polls. Not everyone was surprised. Seasoned suffrage leaders like Anna Howard Shaw had anticipated that once the vote was won underlying divisions of ethnicity, class, race, and religion would reassert themselves among women. "I am sorry for you young women who have to carry on the work in the next ten years," Shaw told Emily Blair, when suffrage seemed assured; "[S]uffrage was a symbol, and now you have lost your symbol. There is nothing for the women to rally round." But the problem was deeper than the loss of a symbol, deeper even than the multiple differences that had always divided women. Larger political and generational forces were pulling the women's movement apart.

Most importantly, the spirit of reform on which women had depended so long to advance their causes was dying. The war eroded that spirit even as it brought progressivism to full power. By unleashing a fierce insistence on 100 percent Americanism and, with the Bolshevik Revolution in Russia, 100 percent antiradicalism, the war wrecked the progressive/left-wing coalition of the prewar years, turning friend against friend. Rose Pastor Stokes and Rheta Childe Dorr, both active on behalf of working women and social reform generally in the 1900s, both members of Heterodoxy and the NWP in the 1910s, took very different paths after the war. Stokes joined the Communist Party, while Dorr became a conservative Republican.

Some of the damage was repaired after the war, as a large number of women's organizations, divided over American entry into the hostilities, reunited under the general leadership of the National Council for Prevention of War (NCPW) to campaign for disarmament, an end to conscription, and an investigation of the munitions industry. This unity proved short-lived, however, as Warren Harding's Secretary of War, John W. Weeks, whom Massachusetts women voters had removed from the Senate in 1918 because of his antisuffrage views, took the offensive against them. Worried over the growing popularity of the women's peace movement and his difficulty in winning defense appropriations from an economy-minded Congress, Weeks sent army officers around the country to denounce disarmament, arms control, and the peace movement in general.

Especially effective was General Amos Fries, head of the Chemical Warfare Service, who contended that the purpose of the NCPW was to establish Communism in America. This charge so alarmed members of two NCPW affiliates—the Parent Teachers Association and the General Federation of Women's Clubs—that they promptly withdrew from the parent organization. Warming to the fight, Fries produced a "spider's web" chart, which described the interconnectedness of American women's organizations and alleged that these groups intended to disarm the nation and promote a Bolshevik takeover. The list included every major women's organization from the Women's Trade Union League to the American Home Economics Association, along with twenty-nine of the country's most prominent women leaders, including Carrie Chapman Catt, Jane Addams, Julia Lathrop, and Florence Kelley.

Seen through the "spider's web," legislation like the Sheppard-Towner Act took on a sinister cast. By 1923 the DAR
withdrew its support of the health bill, while the American
Medical Association mounted a powerful campaign against it,
denouncing the bill as an "imported socialist scheme" that competed unfairly with private doctors. Though the Medical Wom-
en's National Association, which had long played a central role
in the development of public-health programs, dissented from
the AMA position, arguing that private physicians had never
given preventive medicine adequate attention, it was not strong
enough to prevent the bill's defeat in 1929.

The political backlash against the "spider's web" greatly
weakened the women's movement. But women were further
hampered by growing divisions among themselves. The first
decade of the twentieth century had witnessed a widespread
consensus on the unifying needs of womanhood: the need to
gain political power to make women's separate voices heard, to
create policies of special concern to women, and to impose on
men the same standard of morality to which most women sub-
scribed. During the second decade, however, as a younger generation began arguing that women should claim sexual freedom
rather than impose sexual restraint on men, as American entry
into World War I drove a wedge between women once united
by pacifism and a progressive view of politics, and as the winning
of the vote posed the question "What next?" women came to
differ over what womanhood meant and what their goals should
be.

The differences in goals became apparent as early as the NWP
convention called in 1921 to consider where feminism should
go after the vote. With the exception of NAWSA every major
women's organization sent delegates. Florence Kelley, speaking
for the National Consumers' League, recommended pressing
for more protective labor legislation. Crystal Eastman advocated a broader program, including state-funded "motherhood
endowments" (to pay mothers for raising their children), birth
control, and equal rights. Black women wanted the NWP to
direct its attention to black women's continuing inability to vote
in the South, despite passage of the Nineteenth Amendment.
Others hoped that women would focus their energies on peace.

But Alice Paul rejected all of these alternatives and argued that the focus should be on a "purely feminist program," directed at removing all laws that continued to restrict women's freedom.

Ever since writing her thesis on the legal status of women in Pennsylvania, Paul had been concerned about the extent to which women remained bound by law. With suffrage won, she set researchers to work identifying women's continuing legal disabilities. Their legal survey revealed that many states across the country still denied women the right to equal pay for equal work, to serve on juries, to work as public officials, and to be employed at certain jobs or under certain conditions. Wives suffered the added burdens of not being able to hold their own earnings without their husbands' consent, make contracts, choose their domicile, or exercise equal guardianship rights. To overturn these laws piecemeal would require enormous, and, in Paul's mind, unnecessary effort. Having succeeded once with a federal amendment, Paul urged that women resort to the amendment process once again to secure for women complete equality with men.

Reformers like Florence Kelley and Women's Bureau chief Mary Anderson recoiled in horror at this suggestion. Abolishing legal distinctions between the sexes, they warned, would risk invalidating the protective labor laws which women, including many members of the NWP, had fought to secure. "So long as men cannot be mothers," Kelley declared, "so long legislation adequate for them can never be adequate for wage-earning women; and the cry Equality, Equality, where nature has created inequality, is as stupid and as deadly as the cry of Peace, Peace, where there is no Peace."

Initially sympathetic to the reformers' protest, Paul advised her lieutenants in March 1921 to be "very certain that none of the legislation which you introduce in any way disturbs any protective legislation that may have been passed in your state for the welfare of women. . . ." But as the debate developed, the line between protection and discrimination often proved difficult to draw. Maximum-hours laws, defended by reformers as protecting women's health, could limit their opportunities. In Wisconsin, for instance, where an equal-rights act included a guarantee that women would not be denied "the special protection and privileges they now enjoy for the general welfare," the state's attorney general ruled in 1923 that women could be excluded from employment as legislative employees because "legislative service necessitates work during very long and often unseasonable hours. . . ." Laws prohibiting night work, defended by some reformers as necessary to protect women's safety and morals, also barred women from lucrative jobs. According to Harriot Stanton Blatch, "In many highly paid trades women have been pushed into the lower grades of work, limited in earning capacity, if not shut out of the trade entirely by these so-called protective laws." The people being protected, in Blatch's view, were not women workers but the men with whom they might otherwise compete.

Gradually members of the NWP came to the conclusion that protective labor laws for women were incompatible with equal rights. If labor legislation was needed, and many in the NWP still believed that it was, it should be extended to men, not limited to women. Unlikely though such an achievement seemed in the increasingly conservative political climate of the 1920s, the NWP settled on an all-or-nothing strategy. In 1923 it introduced an Equal Rights Amendment—the ERA—into Congress, which read: "Men and women shall have equal rights throughout the United States and every place subject to its jurisdiction." With one simple amendment, the NWP sought to end forever all distinctions between men and women in laws affecting family law, possession of property, political rights, and employment opportunity.

Virtually every women's organization in the country opposed the NWP's new amendment, beginning with the League of Women Voters and followed by the WTUL and the National Consumers' League. Within the government, members of both the Children's Bureau and the Women's Bureau opposed the ERA. Protective labor laws helped far more women than they hurt, the reformers argued, because women worked overwhelmingly in female occupations, for longer hours and at lower pay than men. In the great majority of cases protective laws merely brought women workers a little closer to the standard already reached by most men. In abolishing those laws the NWP would not be placing women on an equal footing with men but rather would be permitting employers to go back to exploiting women as they had in the past. Before hours were limited, scoffed Pauline Newman of the WTUL, women "were 'free' and 'equal' to work long hours for starvation wages, or free to leave the job and starve!" In the view of most reformers the ERA was not an egalitarian measure but an elitist one, at odds with the needs of the average woman worker. As Mary Anderson of the Women's Bureau declared, "Women who are wage earners, with one job in the factory and another in the home, have little time and energy left to carry on the fight to better their economic status. They need the help of other women and they need labor laws." Even some members of the NWP harbored doubts about the course that Paul had set. As Mary Beard wrote a fellow NWP friend, the party was running the risk of "forsaking humanism in the quest for feminism."

Disagreements over the ERA stemmed in part from personal differences dating back to the teens. Carrie Chapman Catt had long regarded Alice Paul as a loose cannon. But more than old animosities fanned the flames of conflict. Opposing positions on the ERA derived from fundamentally different worldviews. The world of ERA supporters stressed individualism and competition, while working-class women and their supporters saw the world in communal terms. The former stressed the ways in which women were like men and shared their aspirations, while the latter emphasized women's vulnerability and the double burden of work and family under which many women lived. To members of the NWP the working mother was a modern heroine, without whom women would forever be consigned to social, political, and economic dependency; to reformers she was a calamity, to be avoided by a "family wage" for fathers and "mothers' aid" for widowed mothers. Because supporters of the ERA believed that women and men were essentially the same, they believed that equality of treatment would lead to equality of outcome. Because opponents believed that women were weaker and more heavily burdened, they believed that equality of treatment would simply ensure continuing inequality of conditions. These differences reached even into the language that the two sides used. While supporters of the ERA tended to speak in the abstract language of "equality" and "rights," reformers couched their case in the concrete language of maternity. According to friends, Jane Addams could only explain Alice Paul's "barren position" in fighting for the ERA as a function of her "ignorance of society and life." Never was the centrality of maternalism to women's lives more clearly expressed; never was the chasm dividing reformer from ERA supporter more starkly revealed.

Who was right? There was evidence on both sides. Unions suffered repeated reverses in the 1920s, leaving women less protected than ever before. Most women worked in low-paying jobs and did not compete directly with men. Protective labor legislation sheltered them from exploitation without subjecting them to job competition from men willing to work longer hours. And yet the expanding economy of the 1920s was creating new job opportunities that could be placed beyond a woman's reach by the passage of protective labor laws. Business expansion created a growing need for clerks, stenographers, typists, switchboard operators, and salesclerks, while the leisure industry created jobs in theaters, bowling alleys, and amusement parks. Women made rapid gains in these fields and in banking and real-estate sales, and newspapers trumpeted female firsts throughout the decade: the first kettle drummer in 1922, the first deep-sea diver in 1924, and, most dramatic of all, Amelia Earhart, former teacher and settlement worker, member of the NWP, and in 1927 the first woman to cross the Atlantic by plane, flying in a crew of three.

When Florence Kelley first sought to protect department-store workers at the turn of the century, most were working as salesclerks. By the 1920s women made up half of all buyers, who thought of themselves not as industrial workers but as businesswomen. As new opportunities developed, protective labor laws did place limits on the jobs women could take, and threatened to introduce sexual division where none yet existed. Night laws kept women from working in bowling alleys. Maximum-hours laws kept women from higher-level white-collar jobs that required extended hours. Despite the beleaguered position of the NWP during the 1920s, opposed on all sides by women's clubs and labor groups, time was on its side. The ERA enjoyed scant support, but it would not die.

The Battle over Birth Control

The struggle over the Equal Rights Amendment not only divided feminists, it also narrowed their vision. By 1923 only a handful of those who had first gathered around the luncheon tables at Heterodoxy remained committed to the broad agenda of those early years. Crystal Eastman was one of the few. Though she joined the National Woman's Party and called for equal rights, she continued to campaign for "motherhood endowments," sexual freedom, and birth control. Most feminists, however, concentrated their efforts on either the ERA or protective labor legislation, and abjured calling attention to other, still more controversial demands. The campaign to legalize birth control, in particular, looked like a bad bet to most. At best it detracted from what feminists regarded as more central concerns. At worst it threatened to sabotage their efforts by seeming to sanction immorality. Those who believed that economic independence and heterosexual freedom depended on a woman's ability to control her fertility had to make their own way. In this effort, no one did more than Margaret Sanger.

Born in 1879 in Corning, New York, Sanger was the sixth of eleven children born to Anne and Michael Higgins. Her mother was a housewife, her father the owner and operator of a stone monument shop. Anne Higgins maintained the Catholic faith of her Irish ancestors, but Michael was an outspoken atheist and advocate of left-wing political ideas. Though Margaret loved her father, who supported women's suffrage, she blamed him for her mother's chronic ill health and the family's financial insecurity. While Michael lived past eighty, Anne Higgins died at forty-nine of tuberculosis, and the drudgery, in Margaret's view, of raising eleven children on the income provided by a man who was usually too busy arguing great social issues to attend to business. The contrast between her parents' fates was one source of Margaret Sanger's ambition to win reproductive autonomy for women.

In her autobiography, Sanger remembers envying the pretty, well-to-do mothers who lived in the nice houses on the hill in Corning and wore white dresses as they played with their children. One of those children was Katharine Houghton, a daughter of the Corning Glass family. Katharine would later attend Bryn Mawr, marry Hartford, Connecticut, physician Norval Thomas Hepburn, give birth to four children (including future film star Katharine Hepburn), become a militant suffragist, join the NWP, and become a close ally of Margaret Sanger. As a child, however, she was just one of the distant figures whose afternoon play impressed upon Margaret the lesson that being healthy and having the leisure to play with one's children was connected in a critical way to not having too many of them.

After her mother's death, Margaret studied to be a nurse, but before she could earn her degree, she was swept off her feet by William Sanger, a dashing young architect, whom she married in 1902. The couple settled down in the suburbs of New York City, and Margaret bore three children, but after a decade they grew restless. William came to dislike architecture, while Margaret found life as a suburban matron stultifying. Seeking to recapture the excitement of their first married years they moved to a Manhattan apartment in 1910 and entered into the radical, bohemian life of Greenwich Village. William struggled, unsuccessfully, in a new career as a painter, but Margaret flourished in the stimulating environment of the city. She became an organizer, first for the Socialists and then for the Wobblies, while working as a visiting nurse/midwife for Lillian Wald's Henry Street Settlement. In addition, she began to have extramarital affairs. These experiences, together with the memory of her mother's hard life, reinforced each other and led to her career as an advocate of birth control.

Contact with the radicals and bohemians of Mabel Dodge's Greenwich Village salon, most particularly Emma Goldman, proved especially important in shaping Sanger's career. Goldman had been smuggling contraceptive devices into the United States from France since at least 1900, and in speeches around the country had been recommending their use. Women, Goldman declared, wanted "fewer and better children, begotten and reared in love and through free choice, not by compulsion, as marriage imposes." Contraception, the fiery anarchist declared, was not only a woman's right but an anticapitalist tool. "Children glut the labor market, tend to lower wages, and are a menace to the welfare of the working class."

Sanger found Goldman's work inspiring and adopted it as her own, bringing to it a single-minded urgency that surpassed even Goldman's zeal. She found support, for a time, from radicals, and, in turn, worked with them in the great garment and textile strikes. When workers struck at Lawrence in 1912 the Socialists sent her to the mills to bring the children to New York to stay with foster families until the strike was over. In part a publicity effort, in part an effort to get the children badly needed food and medical care, the rescue effort brought widespread attention.

Though committed to radical causes, Sanger increasingly emphasized the inadequacy of economic revolution for women who had no control over their bodies. In 1914 she decided to follow the Wobbly method of "direct action" by openly defying the Comstock law prohibiting the circulation of contraceptive information and devices through the mails, in a new journal she called *Woman Rebel*. Exhorting working-class women "to think for themselves and build up a fighting character," Sanger advocated birth control on the grounds that "women cannot be on an equal footing with men until they have full and complete control over their reproductive function." Though Sanger never published any contraceptive information, she soon found herself indicted for violating the Comstock law. If she was going to be indicted, Sanger decided, she would give the government something really to complain about, a document that went beyond advocacy to open description. In a brief pamphlet entitled *Family Limitation*, she gave clear advice about contraceptive technique. Asking IWW colleagues to distribute the 100,000 copies she had printed, she fled the country to avoid jail.

Traveling to England in 1914, she met and had an affair with Havelock Ellis. Author of the six-volume *Studies in the Psychology of Sex* (1907–10), Ellis was the reigning authority on human sexuality. Breaking with Victorian tradition, he argued that women were even more sexual than men. Ellis advocated trial marriage before couples made a lasting commitment, approved of masturbation as a form of relaxation, accepted homosexuality (which he called inversion) as natural, and recommended contraception. For several months Ellis supervised

Sanger's research on sexuality and contraception at the British Museum. He then urged her to visit Holland, where she observed a birth control clinic run by midwives.

When Sanger returned to the United States in 1915, having decided to work exclusively for birth control, she had become a celebrity, a fact that may have played a part in the government's decision to drop its charges against her. She took advantage of her newfound freedom to set off on a cross-country speaking tour, making 119 stops in an effort to raise money and support for her cause.

Sanger's experience in Holland convinced her that the best way to help women was through a system of women-run clinics, and in 1917 she opened the first, a storefront clinic in the Brownsville section of Brooklyn, where she distributed birth control information to the poor Jewish and Italian women of the neighborhood. During the ten days the clinic was open before the police closed it down, 464 women visited. Arrested and this time sent to prison, Sanger became a martyr in the eyes of radicals.

But the acceptance by radicals proved fleeting. Some, especially among the men, viewed contraception as a low priority compared to the working-class struggle. Those who did support birth control, like Emma Goldman, were often among those rounded up during World War I and either jailed or deported. Besieged and distracted, Sanger's radical allies turned away from birth control, as the most easily expendable plank in the radical program. When Sanger wrote in the mid-twenties to Rose Pastor Stokes for help in organizing a birth control conference in New York, Stokes responded that the goals they had once shared could only be achieved "by working for the abolition of capitalism and for the establishment of Soviet governments."

A few feminist supporters remained. Elsie Clews Parsons, Doris Stevens, Crystal Eastman, and Katharine Houghton Hepburn all viewed birth control as a need that united all women and an issue that could weigh against the centrifugal forces being exerted in the 1920s by protective labor legislation and the ERA. In the appreciative words of Crystal Eastman, birth control is an elementary essential in all aspects of feminism. Whether we are the special followers of Alice Paul . . . or Ellen Key . . . we must all be followers of Margaret Sanger. Feminists are not nuns. That should be established. We want to love and be loved, and most of us want children, one or two at least. But we want our children to be deliberately, eagerly called into being, when we are at our best, not crowded upon us in times of poverty and weakness.

Alice Hamilton also proved a friend, endorsing birth control as a cure for poverty. As she wrote in the *Birth Control Review* in 1925, the poor should have "the knowledge and power which [has] long been in possession of those who need it least."

But most leading feminists remained suspicious or ambivalent. When Sanger appealed to Carrie Chapman Catt in 1920 to support the cause, Catt equivocated.

Please be assured that I am no opponent even though I do not stand by your side. . . . Your reform is too narrow to appeal to me and too sordid. When the advocacy of contraception is combined with as strong a propaganda for continence (not to prevent conception but in the interest of common decency), it will find me a more willing sponsor. . . . There will come some gain even from the program you advocate—and some increase in immorality through safety. The gains will slightly overtop the losses however, so I am no enemy of you and yours.

Charlotte Perkins Gilman would later endorse birth control, but in the 1920s she was a far more formidable critic than Catt. Gilman voiced her objections in Sanger's own journal, the *Birth Control Review*. Birth control, she contended, would not improve marriage but transform it into "unromantic, dutiful submission to male indulgence." For in making sex less hazardous it permitted men's sexual aim to gain precedence over women's. "When men talk of sex, they mean only intercourse," Gilman explained. "For women it means the whole process of reproduction, love, and mating." To Gilman and Catt birth control threatened to bolster male tyranny by forcing women to assume a male-defined sexual role.

Unable to build either a radical or feminist consensus on the centrality of birth control to women's emancipation, Sanger looked increasingly to wealthy women, like Katharine Houghton Hepburn and Elsie Clews Parsons, who agreed with her that the most important goal for women was controlling their fertility, who were willing to say so publicly, and who were able to support the campaign financially. Such support allowed Sanger in 1921 to found the American Birth Control League, the national lobbying organization which in 1942 became Planned Parenthood.

In 1921 Margaret Sanger divorced William Sanger, and two years later she completed her transformation from left-wing labor agitator to the single-minded leader of the well-heeled in pursuit of birth control for women by marrying millionaire J. Noah Slee, the manufacturer of 3-In-One oil. For Slee it was a marriage of passion, for Sanger one of convenience. She insisted that Slee respect her independence, which he did, allowing her to travel extensively, in America and abroad, and to continue affairs with other men, including Havelock Ellis and H. G. Wells. Sanger also depended heavily on Slee's fortune, which was the single most important source of funds for the birth control movement from the 1920s on.

The aim of the American Birth Control League was to make birth control respectable in this country, which, in the absence of grass-root support, meant winning the endorsement of influential opinion makers—especially doctors, but also academics, eugenists, and other experts. Eugenists were a group of scientists and pseudoscientists who supported birth control as a way of limiting births among the "unfit." For decades eugenists had been calling for the well-to-do and the well educated to avoid race suicide by having more children, but these entreaties had clearly done no good. Now the eugenists changed their tune, urging instead that contraceptives be made available to the poor to keep their numbers down.

With the eugenists on her side, Sanger sought next to secure the support of doctors. At her trial in 1917 for having violated an 1873 law prohibiting the dissemination of contraceptives by opening the Brownsville clinic, she argued in her own defense that the law should be struck down as unconstitutional because it forced women to risk pregnancy against their will. The judge ruled against her, but he said something in his opinion that was to prove of enormous importance. The law was reasonable, he ruled, because it allowed doctors to prescribe condoms for "the cure and prevention of disease." When the law was written legislators no doubt intended to protect men from disease-bearing prostitutes, but the judge broadened the disease clause to include women. His dictum meant that doctors could prescribe contraception for any woman whose health would be impaired by pregnancy.

Sanger interpreted the judge's opinion as a mandate for doctor-staffed birth control clinics, and in 1923, just as Paul was about to submit the ERA to Congress and Sheppard-Towner began coming under fire from conservatives, she opened the Clinical Research Bureau on lower Fifth Avenue in New York City, the first doctor-staffed birth control clinic in the United States. Under the medical direction of first Dr. Dorothy Bocker, and later Dr. Hannah Stone, the clinic dispensed contraceptive information, fitted diaphragms, and kept clinical records for thousands of women.

Most of the women who came to the Sanger clinic were poor, and Sanger looked to the network of health clinics sponsored by the Sheppard-Towner Act as a model of what she might accomplish. If Sheppard-Towner could provide money for clinics in which nurses could teach mothers how to care for themselves and their babies, it could also provide contraceptive services in those very same clinics. Embattled with the American Medical Association (AMA), however, Julia Lathrop and Grace Abbott were not about to endanger their program further by associating it with birth control. Fifty-five clinics existed in twenty-three cities in fifteen states by 1930, but Sanger could never reach as many women as she might have—especially in rural areas—had she enjoyed the use of Sheppard-Towner facilities.

Not only did Sanger fail to win the support of the Children's Bureau, she confronted the almost unanimous opposition of the medical community. The AMA harbored a long-standing aversion to anything that smacked of lay medicine, sensationalism, or quackery. Two factors, however, moved doctors to begin talking about contraception. The first was a growing belief among them that sexual continence was not really good for people. The second was the fear that if they did not act on contraception, Margaret Sanger would take what little control they had over it away from them.

No one did more to turn the medical profession around than Dr. Robert Latou Dickinson, one of the foremost obstetricians and gynecologists of his day. From 1923 to 1926 he supervised a study of contraceptive practices among New York women in the hope of demonstrating to doubting colleagues the safety and effectiveness of contraception. What little was then known suggested that douching did not work very well and that the relatively new diaphragm could be harmful, causing nasty infections if left in place too long. In three years, however, Dickinson was able to collect information on only 124 patients, while Sanger's New York City clinic was able to study 1,655 women in 1925 alone. Dickinson concluded that he must join with Sanger to further his work, but his colleagues would have nothing to do with the Sanger clinic, which, because of the political machinations of the Catholic Church, had been denied a license by the state. The two sides remained deadlocked until 1929, when New York City police inadvertently came to the birth controllers' aid.

Disturbed by the growing popularity of the clinic, which by the end of the decade was treating five thousand new patients each year, the New York City Police Department dispatched an undercover woman police officer in late March 1929 to pose as a client. After a medical history and pelvic examination, Policewoman Anne McNamara was fitted with a diaphragm. Two weeks later eight police officers returned to the clinic, drove out patients, arrested staff members, and confiscated medical records. The young prosecutor who handled the case proved no match for Sanger, who turned pretrial hearings into a referendum on doctors' professional autonomy. Dickinson and other distinguished leaders of the New York medical community testified that Officer McNamara had exhibited medical indications for birth control under the legal standards of the time and, after two such hearings, charges were dismissed. What Sanger and Dickinson had not been able to accomplish with years of exhortations, the police accomplished almost overnight with their violation of the confidentiality of the doctor-patient relationship. After 1929 the doctors were on Sanger's side, ready to study the effectiveness and safety of contraception, although the AMA would not finally endorse contraception publicly until 1937.

The continuing reluctance of doctors to give their unqualified support was due in large part to the persistent legal cloud under which birth control advocates operated. Throughout the twenties it remained illegal to send birth control information through the mails or to import birth control devices. Since most diaphragms were manufactured abroad these laws had a serious chilling effect on the movement. The law, clearly, had not caught up with the new morality, and would not begin to do so until 1936, when a federal district court in New York City ruled in *U.S.* vs. *One Package of Japanese Pessaries* that the federal government could not interfere with the importation of diaphragms for legitimate medical use.

Despite continuing legal difficulties, by the end of the 1920s Sanger had greatly advanced the cause of birth control. She succeeded far more, however, with middle-class women than with those less well off. One research project in 1925 suggested that, among young married women aged twenty-five to twenty-nine with one child, about 80 percent of middle-class women but only 36 percent of poorer women used contraception. In Muncie, Indiana, contraception was universal among the middle class, but only half of the working-class families practiced it. As one Muncie working-class wife reported, "I just keep away from my husband. He don't care—only at times. He's discouraged because he's out of work. . . . I certainly believe in birth control! But I don't know anything about it." Lack of contraception was especially evident in the South. Among those who used it, blacks relied more on douching, whites on withdrawal and condoms. For many women, especially among the poor, abortion remained the birth control method of last resort. A study of ten thousand mostly working-class clients at Sanger's clinic revealed that half the women had undergone abortions, averaging two to three each.

Sanger deserves principal credit for the success of the birth control movement, but that success did not come without certain costs. In medicalizing birth control Sanger relinquished what she had initially seen as a woman's right to control her body to the discretion of doctors, which tended to keep birth control a privilege of the privileged. Sanger might also be faulted for pushing the diaphragm as hard as she did, particularly after her clinical staff began to discover that it was not working that well among poor women, who frequently did not have either the bathroom facilities or the support of their spouses that made diaphragm use more effective among middle-class women. But Sanger had compelling reasons for advocating the diaphragm despite its limitations. First, properly used, it was the most effective form of birth control available before the 1960s. And second, unlike the condom, it was a woman's contraceptive. Sanger's overriding concern was to put into women's hands a means of self-protection that would make them independent of men. Although Sanger relied on eugenists and doctors when it suited her needs, she always insisted on keeping her clinics under women's control, and she was guided, from beginning to end, by one overriding, profoundly feminist ambition—that of setting free all women, rich and poor, from Victorian inhibition and unwanted childbearing.

Turning Inward

By the end of the 1920s feminism as an organized movement was in retreat. General Fries's infamous "spider's web," the battle over the Equal Rights Amendment, and the struggle over birth control each took a toll. Apart from members of the NWP, few women still called themselves feminists, especially if they were young. In 1927 Dorothy Dunbar Bromley wrote, " 'Feminism' has become a term of opprobrium to the modern young woman." Young women had contempt for those "who antagonize men with their constant clamor about maiden names, equal rights, woman's place in the world, and many another cause." Among women growing up in the 1920s, according to psychologist Phyllis Blanchard, feminism meant being lonely and unmarried.

And yet, even as feminism as a political movement splintered, a privatized form gathered strength. A younger generation, taking for granted the gains of their elders, tried to work out the consequences of those changes in their personal lives. As the feminist idea that there was unity in gender began to erode, women turned inward to focus on their own private concerns. One young woman expressed the view this way: "We're not out to benefit society. . . . We're out for Mary's job and Luella's art, and Barbara's independence and the rest of our individual careers and desires."

The preoccupation with sexual freedom and economic independence that took hold in Greenwich Village in the years before World War I spread like wildfire in the years after the war, reaching into small towns throughout the country by the mid-twenties. As radios, movies, and cars flooded the market, they transformed the culture of the young, undermining the values of restraint and self-denial that had governed their parents' generation. Even youths supported entirely by their parents felt a greater independence. By 1930 over half of all American girls of high-school age were in high school, and 10 percent of college-age women attended college. Spending more time with those their own age than any prior generation, young women found their behavior shaped more by their peers than by their parents.

Young women whose mothers had entertained suitors on their back porches, within parental earshot, were now "dating" far from home, lured by a growing array of commercial entertainments and abetted by the automobile. There was 1 car for every 4.5 persons in America by 1930, and though it was hardly a "house of prostitution on wheels," as labeled by a juvenile judge in Muncie, Indiana, it nevertheless offered escape from adult supervision.

Many couples used their new freedom for sexual exploration. Helen and Robert Lynd found that in Muncie one-third of the girls and one-half of the boys had attended petting parties. Another study of college youth revealed that 92 percent of coeds petted. Most young women viewed petting as an end in itself, but for roughly a third, it eventually led to sexual intercourse, more than double the rate for women just a decade older. Despite this sudden jump, to "go all the way" remained a strong taboo for young women in American society, and few did so except with a fiancé.

The heterosexual exuberance of the 1920s carried with it negative consequences for female friendship. Suddenly, close ties between women seemed a little old-fashioned, if not actually unnatural. Many women who had long thought of their relationships with other women as valuable began to think of their feelings as abnormal and perverted. In responding to Katharine Bement Davis's survey of sexual practices in about 1920, one woman reported, "In my city some business women are hesitating to take apartments together for fear of the interpretation that may be put upon it."

However women chose to arrange their private lives, they were spending less time at home than ever before. Many engaged in volunteer work. The League of Women Voters, the Parent Teachers Association, the American Home Economics Association, and the Young Women's Christian Association were just a few of the organizations whose membership rolls ballooned in the 1920s. Disagreements over which goals to pursue after winning the vote did much to weaken women's sense of gender solidarity but failed to dampen women's enthusiasm for joining groups of various kinds; indeed, the period between the two world wars marked the zenith of women's volunteer work.

For a still small but growing number of wives, leaving home meant going to work. Work-force figures for women overall rose only modestly in the early twentieth century, from 21 percent in 1900 to 25 percent in 1930, but among married women they doubled, rising from 6 to 12 percent. By 1930, single women comprised only a little more than half of the female work force (down from two-thirds in 1900), while the rest were either married (30 percent), widowed, divorced, or separated (17.5 percent).

This shift can be traced to a variety of factors. A decline in immigration following the outbreak of war in Europe in 1914 reduced the number of boarders on whom many married women's budgets had long relied, and the Immigration Act of 1924, which imposed strict quotas, brought additional reductions. At the same time, industrial changes and regulatory laws removed the last of the garment industry from home production. Moreover, compulsory school attendance laws and child-labor laws, along with the growing importance of education, led to a further decline in household income as families struggled to keep children in school longer. Many mothers went to work just to replace the income lost through these various changes.

Sometimes the reason for a married woman's working was simply a desire in an increasingly monied economy to be actually paid for her labor. As a married Southern mill worker put it, "Why should not a married woman work [for pay], if a single one does?" For others work was a way to deal with the escalating conception of need brought by the flood of consumer goods. "Who is to decide [what real need is]?" inquired a woman trade unionist from Seattle. "Suppose my husband's wages are enough to keep the family from starving, but if we want to get the children's teeth fixed, and have the right doctor, and give them a good education, we need more money than he is making." In Muncie, Indiana, a cleaning woman married to a pipe fitter combined a desire to better her family's well-being with an appreciation of the independence that money brought to justify taking a job. "I have felt better since I worked than ever before in my life. . . . We have an electric washing machine, electric iron, and vacuum sweeper. I don't have to ask my husband any more because I buy these things with my own money."

These rising aspirations affected more privileged women, too, leading to a new emphasis on college and careers. Female college graduates tripled, while women who earned doctorates almost quadrupled during the 1920s. In the same period, the number of women professionals rose by 50 percent, while the female work force increased by only 25 percent. Three out of four women professionals worked in fields traditionally dominated by women (libraries, social work, teaching), but the remainder were finding new opportunities as journalists, editors, lawyers, doctors, professors, scientists, civil servants, and businesswomen.

Many of these well-educated women, like their less privileged peers, were continuing to work after marriage. In 1910 12 percent of all professional women were married. By 1930 the figure had more than doubled. In some professions the figures rose even higher. One-third of all women physicians and lawyers were married by the 1930s.

Margaret Mead, a Barnard College graduate of the mid-twenties, was an exemplar of this younger generation of feminists. Her mother, a graduate student at the University of Chicago before her marriage, had been active in the suffrage and reform movements of the progressive period, while catering to the needs of her husband, a professor, and raising five children. Margaret Mead looked back on her mother's life, questioned whether her sacrifices had been worth making, and decided that she was not going to make the same mistakes. She was not going to put off her dissertation until her children were grown. She was going to be an anthropologist and be married, too. When she was ready, she would have children. In 1923, just out of college, she married. In 1928 she published her first book, *Coming of Age in Samoa*. By the time she bore her only daughter, in 1939, she had achieved international fame for her studies in cultural anthropology.

Few women, married or not, enjoyed Mead's personal success. But she stood for something important—an emerging view that women should seek economic opportunity, even if married. A survey of women college students in the twenties shows that 38 percent wanted to combine career and marriage. Among Radcliffe graduates questioned in 1928 75 percent thought that marriage and career could be combined. As Dorothy Dunbar Bromley wrote in 1927, younger women knew that "there is hardly a man who will never take advantage of his wife's economic dependence upon him or who will never assume that it gives him special prerogatives." Although Bromley advised that women sacrifice work for marriage if the two could not be reconciled, she clearly held up the combination of the two as ideal.

Despite these changes in attitude, the proportion of married women at work remained extraordinarily low by today's standards—9 percent in 1920, rising to only 12 percent by 1930. The only significant exception to this pattern was the black married woman. In 1920 25.5 percent of black married women in Detroit and 46.4 percent in New York worked for wages. Pushed north by the invasion of the cotton-destroying boll weevil, growing numbers of black women took jobs in domestic service once held by single immigrants. These domestic positions, which accounted for three-quarters of the jobs held by black women in the 1920s, improved the standard of living of blacks living in the North, but they failed to lift any significant number out of poverty. As one black woman, newly arrived in Pittsburgh in 1917, remarked, "They give you big money for what you do but they charge you big things for what you get."

Those women who either wanted or needed to work often found combining marriage and work impossible because of limited opportunities. Poor, uneducated women found themselves confined to unskilled work, with no prospect of advancement, while more privileged women faced persistent prejudice against women workers, not to mention working wives. Even in teaching, which claimed the great majority of women professionals, barriers remained, especially at the college level. In higher education women comprised over one-quarter of all college faculties in the 1920s, but they were overwhelmingly unmarried and tended to cluster in the lower ranks, in "women's" fields (like home economics), and at women's colleges.

Men in most schools believed that women on the faculty would automatically lower the prestige of the institution. In 1919 Harvard reluctantly appointed fifty-year-old Alice Hamilton to its first position in industrial medicine (with the understanding that she would never march in commencement or attend football games) because her pioneering work in that field made her the only reasonable candidate. Sixteen years later she retired without a single promotion.

Rules against employing wives added to the difficulties women faced. In the public school system, more than 60 percent of the boards of education in 1,532 cities polled by the National Education Association in the mid-twenties continued to discriminate against married women in new hiring. In 50 percent of all school systems women had to resign upon marriage. In many colleges antinepotism rules complicated employment prospects for academic women married to academic men. Only rarely would an institution hire both a husband and a wife, a fact that prompted one disappointed scholar to cry, "Can it be in the divine order of things that one Ph.D. should wash dishes a whole lifetime for another Ph.D. just because one is a woman and the other a man?" Even at women's colleges, men found greater favor than women. At Barnard, Dean Virginia Gildersleeve, hoping to maintain a sex balance in her faculty, hired men for the higher ranks and at higher salaries, secure in the knowledge that there were plenty of well-qualified women eager to accept whatever positions she offered them.

Some of the problems women faced were subtler, as in the self-conscious "masculinizing" that many fields underwent as women entered them in significant numbers. Medicine is only one example of a discipline once regarded as an art that turned into a research discipline by the 1920s. Sinclair Lewis marked the change in his novel *Arrowsmith*, whose protagonist was a doctor, modeled on Katharine Houghton Hepburn's husband, Tom. Published in 1924, the same year that women physicians in Kansas reported to the Medical Women's National Association on the success of a public-health campaign they had named "Fitter Families for Future Firesides," the novel chronicles the career of Dr. Martin Arrowsmith. Beginning his career as a clinician, Dr. Arrowsmith grows disillusioned with the medical practice of his day, especially with the public-health enthusiasts whose "Better Babies Week," "Tougher Teeth Week," and similar efforts reveal a greater dedication to softheaded reform than to advancing the frontiers of science. At the end of the novel Arrowsmith leaves clinical medicine altogether to become a pure scientist, heroic and honorable, but inevitably alone, doomed to withdraw from his community and even his family to pursue his vision. There was little room in this vision for the women doctors who had carved out a special place for themselves during the Progressive Era in public-health and preventive medicine. Although by the 1920s the percentage of women medical students had risen once again to the 5 percent rate that women had claimed in 1890, before the wholesale closing of women's medical colleges and the shift in medicine to coeducation, the percentage rose no higher until the 1950s.

Women also faced discouraging prospects in government. Though aided by a 1919 ruling that opened all civil service tests to women and the formal recognition as early as 1923 that there should be equal pay for equal work, other policies undercut

these gains. Preference in hiring for veterans enabled government agencies to hire male veterans before hiring better-
qualified female applicants; the right of individual agencies to
specify whether they preferred men or women for specific jobs
helped women at the Children's Bureau and Women's Bureau
but hurt them elsewhere. Moreover, the equal-pay ideal was
gutted by a system of reclassification that downgraded work that
was being done by women so that it could be paid on a lower
scale.

If women found barriers in academics and government, industry proved even more difficult to break into. Apart from
businesses closely identified with female consumers—clothing,
food, and home products—women found options limited.
Women often deplored the artificial limitations placed on them,
but with organized feminism in retreat, it was difficult to lodge
an effective protest. The cost of the privatizing of feminism was
that women bore their defeats individually, believing that if only
they had been better qualified they might have been hired or
promoted.

In addition to the obstacles that faced women in the workplace, domestic responsibilities remained too burdensome for
all but the most ambitious, or the most desperate, to work
outside the home. For poor, uneducated women the difficulty
of combining work and domestic responsibilities remained enormous. A third of all dwellings had no electricity in 1930; medical
services, especially in rural areas, remained limited; and fertility
rates continued to be high. Middle-class white wives enjoyed
greater job opportunities and increased technological assistance, but these advantages rarely outweighed another important change: the rising standards of child care and home
maintenance that attended middle-class status in the 1920s.
Higher wages meant that families were able to buy more clothes,
and with washing machines housewives washed them more
often. By the 1920s middle-class families (and those who aspired
to middle-class status) were changing sheets once a week and
changing underwear every day.

Nowhere did the demand on women's time increase more
dramatically than with child care. Children had long been the
principal responsibility of mothers. But at the turn of the cen-

tury, that responsibility had been adequately met if a child could be kept fed, clean, and dry. By the 1920s, as part of the effort to combat infant mortality, mothers were scrupulously watching their children's diets, weighing them often and seeking better medical care. As the children grew older, mothers could not relax. They had to attend child-study meetings, become involved in the Parent Teachers Association, read books and magazines about child rearing, supervise their children on playgrounds, and transport them to lessons and social events. Some experts, like behaviorist John B. Watson, warned mothers not to indulge their children or smother them with attention, but even he recommended that mothers be ever vigilant in the shaping of their child's habits. Mothering became more scientific and efficient, and yet it took more time than ever.

Women who tried both to work and meet these new standards were often driven to exhaustion. In 1919 Freda Kirchwey, an editor at *The Nation* in lower Manhattan, walked across the Brooklyn Bridge each noon to her home in Brooklyn Heights to nurse her infant son, Michael, rather than allow him to be bottle-fed. "I did it for nine months. It wasn't easy and I don't say this admiringly—I think I'd have gotten a lot more satisfaction out of having a baby if I'd taken some time off. It was very hard." Despite her efforts to meet the considerable demands of both work and mothering, Kirchwey never fully succeeded. In later years Michael accused her of having placed her career ahead of her family, and complained bitterly of the "regime of alternate acceptance and rejection" to which he believed he had been subjected.

No one spoke more sensitively about the problems that faced women trying to combine work with motherhood than Crystal Eastman. Married and the mother of two, Eastman lived in England during most of the twenties, working as a writer. How to reconcile economic independence with motherhood was, for her, the central dilemma for feminists in the 1920s. "Women who are creative," she wrote, or "who have administrative gifts, or business ability, and who are ambitious to achieve and fulfill themselves in these lines, if they also have the normal desire to be mothers, must make up their minds to be a sort of supermen, I think."

Believing that children needed a mother's care when they were young, Eastman advocated maternity allowances that would enable women to be economically independent while mothering their young, but she also believed that men should take a larger responsibility at home than they typically did. She urged feminists to raise their daughters to be independent and their sons to do housework. Putting her program into practice, however, proved difficult. She and her husband found modern marriage so stressful that they did better living apart. In "Marriage under Two Roofs" (1923), she advocated this kind of arrangement as the best solution for the modern, emancipated mother, and then was surprised when her children developed the view that fathers were visitors while mothers were people who worked all day and did housework in the evening and on weekends.

Few women believed that their independence could be won by reforming men. Ethel Puffer Howe, a psychologist trained in philosophy at Harvard, established the Institute for Coordination of Women's Interests at Smith College in the 1920s. Following in the tradition of Gilman, she hoped to resolve the "intolerable choice between career and home" by developing cooperative nurseries, kitchens, laundries, and shopping arrangements. The institute lasted only six years. More typical of the ways in which educated women were responding to the rising standards of housekeeping in the 1920s was the decision of the General Federation of Women's Clubs in the mid-twenties to abandon its support of social reform in favor of a campaign on behalf of home economics and the broader use of electrical appliances in the home.

Visionaries like Eastman and Howe imagined a world in which women and men would work side by side, each encouraging the other to develop his or her capacities to the fullest. In practice men often felt ambivalent about their female partners' vision. For all their admiration of equality, many men did not like living with a "new woman." Frederic C. Howe, husband of Heterodoxy's founder Marie Jenny Howe, confessed his own difficulty with the idea of gender equality in 1925: "I hated privilege in the world of economics; I chose it in my own home." Not all husbands of "new women" were so honest.

In 1928, journalist Dorothy Thompson, daughter of the minister's wife who had died of an attempted abortion in Hamburg Village, New York, in 1901, married novelist Sinclair Lewis. Thompson felt attracted, she said, by "the pull of his genius and my faith in his almost agonized protestations, at times, that he *needed* me." This pull and the birth of a child made it increasingly difficult for Thompson to sustain her career. "My brain has gone phut," she wrote a friend in 1930. After three years of marriage, in which Lewis became steadily more involved in writing and drinking, she returned to her profession and won wide acclaim for her reporting on Germany and Hitler's rise to power. While her career gained momentum, Lewis's declined. In 1937 he left her, proclaiming that her work had ruined their marriage. "American women are like that," he would remark in later years. "Killers of talent."

Having a working wife, especially a successful one, challenged Lewis's manhood, which meant, most fundamentally, his ability to fulfill his traditional responsibility to support his family. Men did not want to compete with women. Nor did women find it easy to compete with men, given the power that men had to set the rules by which women must do so, and their own reluctance to abandon domestic roles that they valued highly. Those who advocated that women combine careers with marriage tended to underrate both the significance of society's negative judgment of working wives and the importance of women's domestic presence both to themselves and their husbands.

By 1929 assaults on feminism, together with growing internal tensions, had all but destroyed the sense of a strong, unified woman's world that had flourished in the first two decades of the century. Those who believed that access to the world of men would prove a worthy substitute, however, often faced bitter disappointment. Until women and men could achieve greater mutual understanding with respect to sex, until both could accept the legitimacy of women's working, until they could share the burdens of domesticity or find some other way to lighten that labor, claiming the same rights as men could not guarantee freedom for women.

4

Crisis Years
1929–45

Backlash

The stock market crash in 1929 dealt a stunning blow to, among many other things, the cause of women's rights. Few people had any interest in the careers of the "new woman" at a time when male breadwinners were losing their jobs at an unprecedented rate. By the winter of 1932–33, as the country reached the depths of the Depression, a thousand homes were being foreclosed each day, local governments could no longer meet relief payments, thirty-eight states had closed their banks, factories across the country stood idle, breadlines stretched for blocks outside Red Cross and Salvation Army kitchens, city hospitals reported sharp increases in death by starvation, and thousands of homeless families lived in makeshift shacks constructed of flattened tin cans, scraps of wood, and other debris. Unemployment stood at 25 percent, while pay cuts affected much of the rest of the population, producing an overall decline in wages and salaries of 55 percent. The deflation that accompanied the economic collapse helped consumers a little by reducing prices 25 percent, but wage earners across the country were still 30 percent worse off than they had been before the crash. As families struggled to maintain their former lives in the face of reduced income, women's long-term movement from Victorian dependency to greater self-assertion came to a halt.

In fact, the economic downturn unleashed a vicious backlash against working women. Efforts to understand the causes of the

Depression led many to blame women, especially married women, for having taken men's jobs. In 1932 Congress passed Section 213 of the Federal Economy Act, which prohibited more than one family member from working in the federal civil service. Despite the gender neutrality of the legislation's wording, everyone understood that it was aimed at wives. Women's groups set aside their differences and campaigned to repeal Section 213, but they did not succeed until 1937, by which time sixteen hundred federal women workers had been forced to resign.

The battle continued at the state and local level. In half the states, bills were proposed to prohibit the hiring of married women in *any* job. Women activists defeated these measures, but their task was not easy. Public-opinion polls revealed widespread popular opposition to the working wife. In 1936, when the Gallup Poll asked whether wives should work if their husbands had jobs, a resounding 82 percent of all respondents (including 75 percent of all women) responded no. Many men held to this view even in the face of their own unemployment. One jobless working-class husband declared that "the women's place is in the home. I would rather starve than let my wife work." Another insisted, "I would rather turn on the gas and put an end to the whole family than let my wife support me." To allow a wife to work would mean that a man had relinquished his last hold on patriarchal authority, his very claim to manhood. Most women accepted this prejudice against the working wife, not only out of concern for men's psychological vulnerability but because most women were either housewives, and therefore dependent on their husbands' earnings, or they were single, widowed, deserted or divorced working women for whom the married woman worker represented unwelcome competition. Although the proportion of married women in the work force had climbed steadily throughout the 1920s, they remained a small minority of the female population as a whole. Working wives themselves often regarded their claim to a job as more tenuous than that of a man. Automotive worker Mrs. Helen Gage said she "would not give my job up to another woman, but I will give my job up to a man, as a man has more responsibilities than a woman."

Even in professions like teaching, where women's place had long seemed secure, the Depression brought a backlash, which produced a drop in women's share of the teaching force from 81 percent in 1930 to 76 percent in 1940. By the 1930–31 school year, even before schools felt the full impact of the economic crisis, only 23.4 percent of all cities hired married women, compared to 39 percent three years earlier. In Ames, Iowa, three women who had worked as teachers had to take other jobs after they married. One became a factory operative, another a domestic, and the third a house-to-house canvasser. The same preference for hiring men was evident in other fields. Women librarians, who had occupied 91 percent of the jobs in that field in 1930, held only 85 percent of them by the decade's end. Women social workers fell from 80 percent to 66 percent. Other women lost jobs in business, such as bookkeeping and insurance, as men moved down into previously female occupations.

Employers varied in their willingness to hire married women. A 1939 study by the National Industrial Conference Board found that policies barring married women were especially common in large offices, banks, insurance companies, and utilities. Department stores, on the other hand, generally welcomed married women. The part-time nature of much saleswork suited both the women and their employers, and so, despite hostility from customers and labor organizations, only 11 percent of large retail businesses discriminated, compared to 84 percent of all insurance companies. In the clothing, textile, canning, candy, and meat-packing industries, where conditions were traditionally seasonal and exploitative, concern over marital status was virtually unknown. In sum, the lower the wages, the less the prejudice against working wives. At bottom what mattered was not a woman's marital status but her willingness to work for a wage no man would accept.

Women's slide down the occupational ladder during the 1930s had a predictable effect on their wages. While the general shift of women workers from agriculture and domestic service into factory work and then increasingly into white-collar work had raised female earnings from 47 percent of male earnings in 1900 to roughly 56 percent in 1930, the reverses women suffered in the 1930s slowed further improvement.

Despite these setbacks, women's occupational distribution offered a measure of protection. The Depression had a devastating impact on heavy industry, where male workers predominated, but the service and clerical sector, which employed large numbers of women, actually expanded in the 1930s. Even though men moved down into the elite women's occupations, the lower clerical and service fields expanded more than enough to make up the loss. As a consequence, women's overall participation in the labor force increased during the Depression to a higher level than ever before. During the 1930s women entered the labor force at twice the rate of men. The number of women workers rose 25 percent, and, despite popular prejudice against the working wife, the proportion of married women who worked rose as well. In 1930, only 29 percent of women wage earners were married, but in 1940, 35 percent were. The increase came principally from women in their twenties, who married and succeeded in keeping their marriage a secret until they became pregnant.

Nonwhite women could only rarely claim the limited protection of gender, except within their own groups. Factory positions were beginning to open up to them, but the pay never kept pace, even with white women's low wages. In Texas during the thirties, the weekly wage of white factory women was $7.45, while Chicanas took home $5.40 and black women only $3.75. Most businesses barred minority women from the clerical and sales positions that white women were coming to dominate. In a Women's Bureau study conducted in 1938, Hollywood film studios, which employed large numbers of women clerical workers, proved a little more liberal than most businesses in the country. Even within this group, however, Metro-Goldwyn-Mayer was one of the rare employers to respond that it did not discriminate on the basis of either "race or color." Paramount suggested a guarded liberality in stating it "might employ orientals if qualified." But the office manager at Universal Pictures refused to go even that far. Though he declared that his firm did not "consciously discriminate on the basis of race," he appears to have meant that the firm did not intentionally discriminate against Jews, because he went on to say that "of course" they "wouldn't hire colored." With views such as these, even among relatively liberal employers, it is not surprising that roughly 70 percent of all Asian women workers and over 90 percent of all blacks and Latinas continued to labor in agriculture or in some form of domestic service when less than 40 percent of white women workers were employed in these least-remunerative occupations.

Even in agriculture and domestic work, employment was uncertain. As the Depression deepened, the boll weevil continued its deadly march eastward across the South, and the great drought of the thirties dried up land in the Middle West. Unable to pay their debts farmers lost their property to banks. Field hands forced off the land into migrant labor lived hand to mouth as they followed the harvest, exploited and cheated wherever they went. The competition for scarce migrant jobs became so fierce that many Mexican families who had come to the U.S. in the 1920s in response to the growing demand for agricultural laborers found themselves deported in the 1930s. At the same time, downwardly mobile white women, searching for any work they could get, pushed women of color out of domestic work. In 1930 42 percent of all black women worked; by 1940 only 37.8 percent did so, as their jobs, in the words of black educator Nannie Burroughs, went "to machines, to white people," or "out of style." In many large cities, black women's only hope of employment was the "slave market," a name given to street corners where groups of black women gathered, waiting for white women to drive up and offer them a day's work. Investigators estimated that New York City alone had two hundred such markets, where black women vied for jobs paying only $1.87 a day.

Within this generally gloomy picture were some bright spots, dividends of an earlier feminist movement that persisted into the Depression years. These, however, proved qualified successes. Hollywood offered the surest route to fame and fortune for talented women, as long as they were white and beautiful. With tickets selling at ten to twenty-five cents apiece, movie theaters attracted sixty to ninety million viewers (50 to 75 percent of the population) every week. In the 1930s Mae West, Katharine Hepburn, Marlene Dietrich, Bette Davis, Rosalind Russell, and Greta Garbo all presented images of towering female strength, but the conventional ending for most movies remained that of a woman's renouncing her independence for the fulfillment of marriage and family life. Babe Didrikson, the most outstanding female athlete of her generation, won national titles in basketball, track, and golf, but despite her success she found it difficult to support herself as a professional athlete. In the world of music, black women triumphed: Marian Anderson in opera; Ella Fitzgerald in jazz; Billie Holiday and Bessie Smith in the blues. But prejudice hounded them all, despite their extraordinary talent. Bessie Smith lost her life near Clarksdale, Mississippi, in 1937 because the county hospital to which she was taken following an auto accident would not accept a black person, no matter how famous.

By the end of the decade anxiety about the "forgotten man" had overwhelmed concern for the "new woman." Those who argued on behalf of women workers no longer dared to assert women's *right* to work. Supporters settled instead for defending their need to work. A study conducted by the National Federation of Business and Professional Women at the end of the thirties concluded that women "worked only because their families needed the money they earned. They preferred not to work outside the home." A columnist added, "Ninety percent of these women would rather be at home sewing on buttons." Hoping to take advantage of the protective benefits of occupational segregation, women vocational experts avoided the advice that feminists had always given to break down barriers. Counselors urged instead that women enter fields where they would minimize competition with men. This strategy, which protected women in the short run, ensured women's inferior economic status for decades to come.

Making Do

Faced by falling income, many women fell back on housekeeping skills in order to make do with less. They returned to canning and baking, turned their backyards into vegetable gardens, made over old clothes, deferred medical care, moved to smaller quarters with lower rent, heated only one room, and cut off the electricity and telephone. To bring in extra cash, many also returned to home industry. Women took in boarders, laundry, and sewing, and even set up small businesses. Sociologists Robert and Helen Lynd found "little signs in yards" in Muncie, Indiana, announcing "the presence of household beauty parlors and cleaning and pressing businesses." Some women set up grocery stores, while others established small bakeries, restaurants, and dressmaking shops.

For poor farm women, the great majority of whom had no electricity, running water, or access to doctors, making do proved even more challenging. When Margaret Hagood visited white tenant farmers in the South, she found women living much as their grandmothers had, cooking on a wood stove, preparing meals from scratch, canning up to five hundred quarts of produce out of their own gardens each year. "Since the canning season coincides with the time for summer field work [in which all family members are needed], much of [the canning] is done at night or before breakfast," she wrote. Washing was done by hand over a fire in the yard; sewing, on the family's one appliance, a foot-powered sewing machine.

Economic pressure brought not only a redoubling of women's money-making efforts but also a return to the extended family arrangements that had been common earlier in the century. In his memoir *Growing Up*, journalist Russell Baker recalls his half-Irish, half-Cuban aunt in Bellevue, New Jersey, who cared for her husband, two infant daughters, two unemployed brothers-in-law, widowed sister-in-law, niece, and nephew (young Russell) in four rooms. Social worker Elizabeth Wood discovered eleven people living in three dark rooms in Chicago, while Hagood found up to twelve people living in three-room shacks in the rural South.

Such hardship discouraged many young people from marrying, and resulted in a plummeting marriage rate, which did not start to rise again until 1934. "Do you realize how many people in my generation are not married?" school principal Elsa Ponselle asked Studs Terkel, when he was writing his oral history of the Depression. "There were young men around when we were young. But they were supporting mothers." When the young man she was dating lost his job, the result was devastating. "It hit him like a ton of bricks," she remembered. "And he just disappeared."

As the marriage rate fell, so, too, did the birthrate. More than 25 percent of American women born in the first decade of the twentieth century (those who were between twenty and thirty at the beginning of the Depression) never bore children, a higher rate of childlessness than in any other decade, before or since. Those who did bear children struggled to have fewer of them. A Gallup poll revealed that a solid majority of the public, 63 percent, had come to favor the teaching and practice of birth control. One unemployed father reported, "Before the depression I never gave a thought to birth control. . . . Had we been able to foresee the depression, we would have felt differently about it."

By mid-decade manufacturers were turning out 1.5 million condoms a day. Drugstores, groceries, dance-hall bathrooms, gas stations, even the Sears Roebuck catalog, offered the rubber prophylactics for sale. Despite their wide availability, however, condoms represented only 10 percent of the contraceptive market. The rest of this $350-million-a-year industry was dominated by over six hundred products sold as "feminine hygiene." In this ocean of jellies, suppositories, and douches, diaphragms constituted a modest 1 percent of the market and remained a predominantly white, middle-class device, despite Margaret Sanger's best efforts.

When contraception failed, growing numbers of women turned to abortion. State laws permitted abortion only to save the life of the mother, but since a number of common illnesses, including tuberculosis and diabetes, could be lethal to a pregnant woman, many doctors performed abortions openly under this legal loophole. Others did so quietly, even without medical reasons, if the mother was a longtime patient. Hundreds of women sought abortions at the Sanger clinic in New York, where physicians, wary of jeopardizing the birth control movement but not wishing to turn needy women away, referred the "overdues" to private practitioners. Women who could not turn to a sympathetic family physician often sought out one of the abortion clinics, which proliferated in the 1930s. In Chicago one clinic paid off the police to avoid prosecution and performed two thousand abortions a year for an average fee of $50 (two and one-half times the average woman's weekly salary in that city). Women who could not afford so high a fee turned to midwives who worked without a fee. Or they turned to back-alley abortionists, in whose filthy rooms women risked their health and not infrequently their lives.

The strain of economic hardship further limited the birthrate by sapping interest in sex. Even as Ethel Merman was belting out Cole Porter's 1934 hit song "Anything Goes," fear of pregnancy, anxiety over unpaid bills, and resentment over their husbands' failure to provide turned many women against intercourse, as sociologist Eli Ginzburg discovered in his study of unemployed families. One wife "supposed it was [her husband's] right to have sexual relations," so long as he was "working and supporting her. . . . Now she avoids it. She has limited sexual relations to once a week and even tried to get out of this." For men, despair over losing their position as breadwinners often had a similar outcome. As one wife of an unemployed man put it, "They're not men anymore, if you know what I mean."

When a man's despair reached this point he sometimes just disappeared. Pressed financially, growing numbers of husbands abandoned their wives and children, not bothering to seek a divorce because of the cost. In 1930 12.7 percent of all households had female heads. By 1940 15 percent did. The Depression created a special strain on the ties that bound black women and men together. A Pittsburgh mother of six children applied for relief in 1931, after her husband, a steelworker, was laid off from a job he had held for several years. Shortly after the company told him "he needn't trouble looking for a job as long as there are so many white men out of work," he left and never returned. In 1930 about 30 percent of all black households were female-headed (more than twice the rate for whites). In the North the figure was higher.

Though the Depression led to the collapse of some families, its principal effect was to reinforce the tendencies present before the stock market crash. Families who had enjoyed good relations tended to be drawn more closely together by adversity, and to cling more strongly to traditional roles. Repeatedly, investigators came to the same conclusion. If a wife had to work for her family to survive, she did. But she typically regarded her work as a temporary expedient, until her husband got a break. So little did the Depression affect traditional gender roles that, as Mirra Komarovsky discovered, even the strain of unemployment rarely altered them. Indeed, unemployed men often did less housework than they had before losing their jobs, despite having more time to help their wives. Those who had lost the principal source of their dignity as men would not risk further degradation by performing the work of a woman. Although women in the Depression often did better psychologically than men, because their traditional roles took on added meaning, they did not gain greater power as a result. Indeed, women in most families found it more difficult than ever to assert their rights.

Friends in High Places

Even as economic collapse threatened the quest of many women for greater autonomy, the feeling of crisis created new opportunities. The Depression of the 1930s made criticism of the American industrial system acceptable once again, and women reformers who had long worked on behalf of social welfare finally found a broad audience for their ideas. Just as important, the election of 1932 catapulted Eleanor Roosevelt into the White House. For the next twelve years hardly a day passed without her reminding President Franklin Delano Roosevelt of the pressing need for social justice.

The niece of Theodore Roosevelt, Eleanor worked at a settlement house in New York City and in the National Consumers' League before marrying in 1905. Between 1906 and 1916 she bore five children and settled into the role of a dutiful, upper-class wife of a promising reform Democrat. While the struggle for women's suffrage flourished around her, she dismissed politics as "a sinister affair," best left to the men of the family, and busied herself with domestic duties. Her views began to change, however, when in 1917 she discovered that her husband was in love with her social secretary, Lucy Mercer. Devastated, she sought to bury her unhappiness in the social welfare work that had brought her satisfaction before her marriage. Then, in 1921, she faced a second trauma. A year after rising to the top of the Democratic Party and running unsuccessfully for Vice President, Franklin was stricken by polio. These two experiences transformed the Roosevelts' relationship from a traditional marriage into a political partnership. Joining the League of Women Voters, the Women's Trade Union League, and the women's division of the Democratic Party, Eleanor established her independence and at the same time became indispensable to her husband. She monitored the New York State legislature; observed legislative pressure politics; and learned to defend her point of view, even if she caused "disagreement and unpleasant feelings." For the first time she made friends with women from outside her social class, and with them she learned about trade unionism and worked to pass maximum-hours and minimum-wage laws for women. In addition, she kept up her work in the National Consumers' League and promoted U.S. entry into the World Court.

By 1928, when F.D.R. became governor of New York, Eleanor Roosevelt was not only an old hand at politics, she had also made her mark as an important women's advocate. Four years later, when F.D.R. reached the Presidency, she was ready to play a national role. Franklin Roosevelt would probably not have reached the White House without Eleanor's assistance. He certainly would not have achieved his reputation as a defender of the downtrodden without her influence. Because of her clear stand on social issues, blacks, women, and young leftists usually came to Eleanor rather than Franklin with their requests. If she supported what they wanted, she would get them a hearing with the President. Most close Presidential advisers regarded Eleanor as a dangerous idealist and thought it their duty, as one put it, "to get the pants off of Eleanor and onto Franklin." But the worsening economic crisis allowed Eleanor to play a critical role in transforming her husband into a more active reformer than either he or his male advisers initially thought wise.

Eleanor Roosevelt's Victorian upbringing made her see the Depression as a moral failure—the result of a national preoccupation with material gain. Believing that women were more sensitive to moral issues than men, she urged that women assume responsibility for rebuilding the country's "moral fiber." She was quick to add, however, that morality alone would not bring the country out of the Depression. The only way to ensure prosperity for all, Eleanor Roosevelt argued, was to make changes in the country's economic structure that would prevent future depressions. "One part of the country or group of countrymen cannot prosper while the others go downhill," she told a group of women in 1933. "We must reorganize our economic structure so it may be possible for those willing to work to receive adequate compensation."

As First Lady, Eleanor Roosevelt relied heavily on the assistance of a wide network of women professionals and reformers whom she had come to know during the 1920s. Many of them came from Republican backgrounds, as one would expect of the predominantly upper-middle-class circles from which they came. The Republicans' increasing hostility to reform, however, pushed a growing number into the Democratic Party. They were mostly well-off and well educated. About a third never married, but many of them, in the tradition of the "Boston marriage," formed lifelong partnerships with other women. About one-half were daughters, sisters, or wives of politicians. Mostly in their fifties, they conveyed a sense of dignity and seriousness that younger women found difficult to equal. Working in the male world of politics, they were wont to claim, in Eleanor Roosevelt's words, that "it is the person and not the sex which counts." But few supported the Equal Rights Amendment, and they thought the National Woman's Party wrong for dismissing the need for protective labor legislation for women. "When all is said and done," Eleanor Roosevelt observed in *It's Up to the Women* (1933), "women *are* different from men. They are equal in many ways, but they cannot refuse to acknowledge their differences. Not to acknowledge them weakens their case. Their physical functions in life are different and perhaps in the same way the contributions which they are to bring to the spiritual side of life are different."

One of Eleanor Roosevelt's first acts as First Lady was to call a White House Conference on the Emergency Needs of Women, in November 1933. Gathering together the government ap-

pointees and social reformers who made up her broader circle
of women friends, she told the conference, "Either a certain
number of jobs must be found for a certain number of women
or . . . a certain amount of money must be allocated for giving
women work." Within the month Ellen Woodward, head of
women's projects at the Federal Emergency Relief Association
(FERA) and the Civil Works Administration, found work for
100,000 women in jobs ranging from sewing to nursery-school
teaching. But despite Woodward and Eleanor Roosevelt's best
efforts, women never comprised more than 19 percent of those
employed on work relief, most of them in sewing rooms, despite
the fact that they constituted 37 percent of the unemployed.

Hoping to expand women's representation in the New Deal,
Eleanor turned to her closest political associate, Molly W. Dewson, head of the Democratic Party women's division. A former
social worker, parole officer, dairy farmer, and suffragist, Dewson became Florence Kelley's chief assistant in the National
Consumers' League in the 1920s. Heading up the league's drive
for state minimum-wage laws for women and children, Dewson's
initials were said to stand for Minimum Wage Dewson. By the
end of the decade, however, a series of setbacks in the courts
persuaded her that the best way to expend her energies was
through strengthening women's activities within the Democratic
Party. By the time Franklin Roosevelt reached the White
House, she had proven so valuable an organizer that she became
director of the women's division of the Democratic Party.

In Dewson's view, the "men's organizations did not know
what to do about the foot-loose voters—the 20 percent that
decide elections." She worked to make Democratic women that
20 percent. Her first step was to replace the party's deadly,
twelve-page political brochures with Rainbow Fliers, one-page
outlines of Democratic policies. By the 1936 election they accounted for 80 percent of all campaign literature. Schooled in
the grass-roots campaigning of the suffragists, Dewson next
turned to the problem of organizing women voters. In small
towns throughout the country, she taught women to educate
themselves on Democratic policies, and then to go door to door,
speaking to friends and leaving Rainbow Fliers that husbands
might read when they returned from work. At the Democratic

Convention of 1936 there were 219 women delegates, compared to 60 at the Republican convention. Moreover, Dewson pushed through a rule on the platform committee that every member (all of whom were men) had to have an alternate of the opposite sex. Because male members missed so many meetings, women alternates played a crucial role on the committee.

Dewson's success impressed F.D.R. early on and put her in a good position to recommend political appointments. She quickly made it clear that she intended to use that power to appoint women to political office, even though patronage was an aspect of the old political system she hoped eventually to overturn. Her initials were now said to stand for More Women Dewson. Dewson placed more than one hundred women in New Deal positions, including Ellen Woodward at FERA, Emily Blair at the National Recovery Administration, Clara Beyer in the Bureau of Labor Standards, and Florence Allen as a judge in the U.S. Court of Appeals.

Dewson's most important appointment was Frances Perkins, a former Hull House resident with a B.A. from Mt. Holyoke and an M.A. in sociology and economics from Columbia University. Married to economist Paul Wilson and the mother of one daughter, she kept her own name and pursued a career in social reform. While still a young woman she worked as a legislative lobbyist for the National Consumers' League and investigated the Triangle Shirtwaist fire. In her subsequent career she held a series of professional positions in which she worked to improve workers' health, safety, and working conditions. In 1928 F.D.R. appointed her New York State's industrial commissioner, and in 1932 Dewson and Eleanor Roosevelt persuaded the President to make her Secretary of Labor, the first cabinet office ever held by a woman. Perkins found it difficult to accept the position, notwithstanding the honor. Her husband, who had shown signs for more than a decade of mental illness, was by 1933 in a sanitarium in New York. She worried about the effect on him of her coming under intense public scrutiny. Moreover, she did not want to disrupt her sixteen-year-old daughter's life. Knowing that Perkins was hesitant, Dewson applied pressure. "After all, you owe it to the women." And moving from exhortation to intimidation: "Don't be such a baby, Frances. You do the right thing. I'll murder you if you don't." In the end, Perkins agreed to go to Washington, with the understanding that she would return home to Manhattan on weekends.

Frances Perkins's position as head of the Labor Department proved difficult from the start. Labor leaders opposed her because she did not have a union background. The department resented her because she criticized the focus of their efforts throughout the 1920s, which was to hunt down and deport aliens who might be radicals or who might be undercutting wages for native-born Americans. Even Perkins's female colleagues in the department criticized her. Mary Anderson, chief of the Labor Department's Women's Bureau, complained that Perkins "leaned over backwards" not to favor women and "did not want to be thought of as a woman too closely identified with women's problems." Perkins, for her part, believed that her effectiveness as Secretary of Labor depended on her not appearing to be engaged in special pleading, even for a cause she believed in.

Building a Welfare State

Despite disagreements about the proper use of their power, women in the Roosevelt Administration did more to improve the lives of American women than had officials in any prior administration. Their first priority was the cradle-to-grave system of social insurance that women reformers had been advocating since the turn of the century. As head of the Committee on Economic Security, Perkins supervised the drafting of the necessary legislation, a job that got bogged down almost immediately in political conflict. After months of heated debate, the committee reluctantly decided against a system of health insurance because the American Medical Association so strongly opposed it, but it agreed on the following: provisions for old-age insurance, unemployment insurance, and care of the disabled. Moreover, it included a provision for Aid to Dependent Children essentially as written by the Children's Bureau. Grace Abbott and her successor as chief of the Children's Bureau, Katherine Lenroot, used this opportunity to revive the health programs they had lost when conservative congressmen revoked the Sheppard-Towner Act in 1929. They provided for a cooperative program with state health departments to care for mothers and children, established a rural maternal nursing and educational program, medical care for crippled children (hoping that this would open the way for generalized federal health insurance), and services for homeless, dependent, and neglected children. Finally, they proposed an aid program that would meet the essential financial needs of young children living in their own homes whose fathers were dead, had deserted them, or were mentally or physically incapacitated. For Abbott this last provision, in particular, was a triumph. She had long regretted that so many states limited "mothers' aid" to widows. Now a much broader group of families would be eligible.

Congressional hearings on the Social Security Act provoked a chorus of outrage. Cries of "socialism" echoed through the halls, while businessmen warned of the imminent demise of thrift, initiative, and the American way of life. A New Jersey senator protested that the bill "would take all the romance out of life. We might as well take a child from the nursery, give him a nurse, and protect him from every experience that life affords." By the time Congress was done revising the bill, however, all but a few Republicans voted for it.

The Social Security Act was a major achievement. It put the government on record as assuming a modicum of responsibility for the aged, the disabled, and the poor. But there were glaring defects, especially as modified by Congress. Under pressure from Southern Democrats, the Social Security Act excluded agricultural and domestic workers (that is, most blacks). The payroll taxes used to pay for old-age benefits were regressive, burdening those least able to pay by taxing all workers at the same rate. And the states retained so much control over administration of the act's provisions that tremendous inequity existed from one state to another, leaving the great majority of eligible families in the South uncovered. Moreover, while other Western nations were developing a blend of social policies, including family allowances, health services, housing allowances, and assistance that benefited poor and nonpoor alike, Congress drew a sharp distinction between welfare programs, like Aid to Dependent Children (ADC), which were paid for out of general tax revenues, and social insurance, like old-age pensions, to which workers contributed from their own wages. This distinction tended to stigmatize women and children who received welfare as less worthy than the elderly who received social security benefits. To make matters worse, ADC benefits could be withdrawn if a mother could not satisfy a morals test. In other words, any woman who set a bad example for her children (by drinking, not keeping her home clean, or "entertaining" men) could be denied benefits. The bill compounded difficulties for mothers by providing allowances for children only. Mothers themselves received nothing.

Despite frantic lobbying efforts by Margaret Sanger and others, the revival of a national system of maternal and child health services paid no attention to birth control. Sanger estimated that the country needed three thousand contraceptive clinics, about ten times the number of existing private and public clinics combined. A few federal agencies began funding birth control surreptitiously, including the Farm Security Administration, which paid public-health nurses to bring contraceptive information to poor farm women and women in migrant labor camps. Political realities, however, stood in the way of broader action. Most important was the Democratic coalition's dependence on Catholic support, which F.D.R. would do nothing to jeopardize. In the 1920s Eleanor Roosevelt had served on the board of Sanger's American Birth Control League, but when in 1932 F.D.R. became a Presidential contender she stopped discussing birth control publicly.

The biggest government initiative came, ironically, in the South, where state governments began to worry about the black birthrate. In 1937 North Carolina became the first state to offer birth control through its public-health program. It was followed by South Carolina, Virginia, Georgia, Mississippi, Alabama, and Florida, all states in which there were few Catholics and many blacks. In the end the support for birth control came from fear of the rising cost of relief.

Though flawed, the Social Security Act was for Frances Perkins a major triumph. She was far less enthusiastic about another legislative measure working its way through Congress in 1935. The National Labor Relations Act, a bill to provide for the federal supervision of union elections, was the brainchild of New York senator Robert Wagner. Labor leaders were solidly behind it, but they secured neither Roosevelt's nor Perkins's support until the bill passed the Senate. F.D.R. thought it politically unwise for him to be seen as overly supportive of labor. Perkins had different reservations. In her view labor leaders simply could not be counted on to help most workers. The AFL had always adopted an elitist stance toward the unskilled, especially women and minorities, and Perkins thought that workers had more to gain from a government that protected them through protective labor laws. Eleanor Roosevelt and Mary Anderson, director of the Women's Bureau, agreed. As Anderson wrote to Eleanor Roosevelt: "I suppose it is too much to expect these men will ever put us on a par with them. It will be the next generation, maybe even the next, before that will happen."

But progress was being made in the unionization of women as a new generation of labor leaders, typified by the head of the United Mine Workers, John L. Lewis, fought in the tradition of the Wobblies to unionize whole industries. Under the leadership of the newly constituted Congress of Industrial Organizations (CIO), women won significant gains in the automotive industry, where they constituted about 7 percent of all workers, and the electrical industry, where they made up 25 percent. In the garment and textile industries, where women predominated, a new militancy on the part of the AFL won the biggest gains of all. The International Ladies Garment Workers Union, part of the AFL, had peaked at 105,000 members in 1920, only to suffer a sharp decline in the 1920s, falling to 40,000 members by 1933. Then, in 1934, a membership drive in New York brought racial integration and a dramatic rise in membership to 200,000. Women pressers became the best paid women in Harlem, at $45 to $50 dollars for a thirty-five-hour week. Moreover, strikes throughout the South, though ultimately unsuccessful, gave many white women workers in that region their first experience in taking forceful action on their own behalf. Even where women did not form a large portion of a unionized work force, women family members benefited whenever their husbands won wage increases through successful strikes, as they did in 1937 when the Women's Emergency Brigade (made up mostly of wives) played a supportive role in the General Motors sit-down strike conducted by the United Automobile Workers in Flint, Michigan.

The Communist Party played a particularly important role in championing the cause of women workers. Though the party was never a major political force (it polled only 120,000 votes in the Presidential election of 1932), it made significant contributions to industrial unionizing during the thirties, controlling about a third of the CIO by the end of the decade, and it took women's contributions seriously. As the major radical organization of the day, it offered an important vehicle for change for many reform-minded women, including many black women. Women comprised a third of the party's members, had their own publications, and contributed a column to the *Daily Worker*. In addition to labor organizing, women worked alongside men to defend the poor, the homeless, and the victims of racial attacks. Communist men distinguished themselves by their commitment to social equality; nevertheless, many harbored fairly traditional ideas about women's roles. When Esther Allen tired of the constant, impromptu entertaining that accompanied party organizing, she yelled at her husband, "Who the hell does all the goddamn work? While you sit on your ass making the revolution, I'm out there in the kitchen like a slavey. What we need is a revolution in this house." But he ignored her, and life continued on as before.

While their practice did not always live up to their egalitarian rhetoric, Communists provided important inspiration for women seeking a wider role not only within the labor movement but among intellectuals as well. As writer Mary McCarthy later recalled, "For me, the Communist Party was *the* party, and even though I did not join it, I prided myself on knowing that it was the pinnacle." While the United States was collapsing, the Soviet experiment seemed exciting and promising. By 1937, word of the Moscow trials and Stalin's tyranny began undermining support among intellectuals, but membership in the party continued to grow, peaking at over 100,000 in 1944.

While political controversy divided the Left, Frances Perkins continued to believe that federal legislation offered the surest protection for workers in general and women in particular. In

1938 she proposed to Congress a Fair Labor Standards bill, which would outlaw child labor in interstate commerce and set a minimum wage of twenty-five cents per hour for a forty-four-hour week, rising in two years to forty cents per hour for a forty-hour week. The bill would cover twelve million workers, about one-quarter of the work force, who were earning less than the minimum wage.

Despite wide support in Congress, two groups opposed the bill: Southerners, who feared losing their inexpensive work force, and organized labor, which feared the minimum wage would become the maximum wage. As with the Social Security Act, Congress gutted much of the bill presented to it by exempting agricultural and domestic workers and those in seasonal industries. The law helped women in Southern textile and Northern shoe factories, but not in canneries, where workers worked too few weeks each year; nor did it cover clerks in retail stores or those in any business not engaged in interstate commerce. The law exempted so many workers that one representative jokingly suggested the following amendment: "Within 90 days after appointment of the Administrator, it would read 'She shall report to Congress whether anyone is subject to this bill.' "

Many thought that with passage of the Fair Labor Standards Act (FLSA), the bitter division between ERA supporters and protective-labor-legislation advocates would end. And, in fact, many social reformers, among them Alice Hamilton, dropped their opposition to the ERA. But the Women's Bureau, Eleanor Roosevelt, and others continued to argue that state laws remained necessary as long as federal laws exempted so many groups.

Confronting Racism

The power of white Southern Democrats to whittle away New Deal social welfare legislation brought debates over race to the forefront of American politics for the first time since Reconstruction. Before the decade was over these debates had become entangled with two other issues: first, the proper role of the federal government in protecting individual rights, and, second, the relationship of gender and race in American society. Discussion of these matters was to have important consequences for all women in the years that followed.

For several decades the NAACP and a small group of intellectuals and social reformers had been trying to combat the racist beliefs that prevailed in much of white America. During the 1930s, three women anthropologists, two white and one black, turned this mounting critique into a broader analysis of the deficiencies of American culture. One was Ruth Benedict, who in 1934 published *Patterns of Culture*, the most popular work of anthropology ever written. In a chapter entitled "The Pueblos of New Mexico," she not only presented one of the first positive depictions of Native Americans to the nation, she also used the depiction to convey a sharp critique of competitive individualism in the dominant culture. Isolated on a reservation, the Zuni tribe, for example, lived in a matrilineal culture that scorned individual power and violence and granted women far greater authority in family life than women could claim in white middle-class society. There was nothing inevitable about the highly materialistic, competitive individualism celebrated in Western white culture, according to Benedict. Indeed, such a culture entailed serious dangers, as the United States had discovered with the collapse of its economy. "[T]he dominant traits of our civilization need special scrutiny," she advised. "We need to realize that they are compulsive, not in proportion as they are basic and essential in human behavior, but rather in the degree to which they are local and overgrown in our own culture."

The following year Benedict's protégée, Margaret Mead, published *Sex and Temperament* (1935), a study of gender roles in three widely differing South Pacific cultures. Poking fun at the lingering power of the Victorian sexual code in American life, Mead argued that there was nothing natural, much less superior, about Western mores. Gender roles, she maintained, were the product of particular cultural conventions, not stages on an evolutionary scale culminating in the American ideal of feminine selflessness and masculine competitiveness. The peoples she studied patterned their behavior in widely varying ways, following none of the expectations of Western culture. Indeed, the men who, in her view, seemed the most contented (the mountain Arapesh of New Guinea) lived in a culture where both men and women lived according to a code of behavior that in America would be characterized as feminine, because of its emphasis on cooperation and nurturance.

Two years later Zora Neale Hurston, daughter of Lucy and John Hurston of Eatonville, Florida, underscored this mounting critique of the competitive individualism championed in white, male America in her novel *Their Eyes Were Watching God.* Several years after the death of her mother in 1910, Zora Neale Hurston left home, driven away by conflict with her stepmother. She supported herself as a maid, studied at Howard University in Washington, D.C., and in 1925 made her way north to be part of the Harlem Renaissance. Accepted on scholarship to Barnard College, she studied anthropology with Franz Boas, who sent her back to her birthplace in Florida to record the folktales of rural blacks before they could be obliterated by the surrounding white culture. *Their Eyes Were Watching God* grew out of this project, and for the first time showed white America a black rural culture, where happiness came not from an imitation of white society, which led men to measure themselves solely in terms of material success and women to marry for security rather than love, but from the ability to remain true to one's own heart, to work cooperatively with others, and to treat all people as equals. The critique of American culture offered by authors like Benedict, Mead, and Hurston contributed to a growing respect for cultural differences in America. But despite the work of these writers, few showed a genuine willingness to give minorities a full voice in American politics, and still fewer listened to women anthropologists' brief for female-centered cultures.

When New Dealers pushed the Indian Reorganization Act through Congress in 1934, for example, they failed to consult either male or female Native Americans. Though the so-called Indian New Deal professed a respect for tribal traditions, it imposed white concepts of political participation and civil rights through newly written tribal constitutions that had mixed consequences for women. In tribes that had traditionally barred women from political participation, women gained new power, but in tribes like the Zunis, the new constitutions often under-

mined women's economic and political status. According to one
new constitution, for instance, "Every member . . . who is the
head of a family that does not own any land . . . shall be entitled
to receive an assignment of new land." Because the New Deal
assumed that heads of families were male, excess land invariably
went to men, not women.

The New Deal's record with respect to black women was
slightly better, due to the political influence of black leader Mary
McLeod Bethune. One of seventeen children of black sharecroppers, Bethune attended a Presbyterian school for black
girls, became a teacher, and founded her own college, Bethune-
Cookman College, a Florida vocational school. Briefly married
to a man who did not share her missionary spirit, she raised
their one daughter alone while continuing to build her school
and to campaign for black civil rights. In 1927 she met Eleanor
Roosevelt, and in the years that followed educated her about
the need to include African-Americans in her vision of a more
equitable social order. By 1934, Roosevelt was saying, in a
speech to a conference on black education, "We must learn to
work together, all of us, regardless of race or creed or color.
. . . We go ahead together or we go down together."

Appointed through Eleanor Roosevelt's influence to head
Negro affairs at the National Youth Administration, Bethune
occupied a place apart in the New Deal women's network. But
she played a critical role in bringing the problems of blacks to
the Administration. "We have been eating the feet and head
of the chicken long enough," she said. "The time has come
when we want some white meat."

Bethune had an impact because she was not alone. For over
three decades middle-class black women had been engaged in
civil rights organizing. In the Young Women's Christian Association (YWCA), for instance, black women, who had been
accepted into segregated groups since the 1890s, worked steadily
to achieve control of their own branches and to direct the attention of the national association toward black needs. In
Brooklyn during the Depression, black YWCA leader Anna
Arnold Hedgeman led protests against major department stores
until she won young black women positions as clerks. In Harlem,
black women and men picketed white-owned stores, shouting

"Don't shop where you can't work" until store owners finally relented and began hiring blacks.

While some black women focused on winning economic rights, others carried on Ida Wells-Barnett's campaign against lynching, which had increased dramatically at the beginning of the Depression. Throughout the 1920s black women had been telling the white churchwomen of the South that these lawless executions would be stopped only when white women rose against it. Finally, in 1930, they inspired one white woman to take a stand. Jessie Daniel Ames, a suffragist from Texas and longtime member of the women's committee of the Commission on Interracial Cooperation, formed the Association of Southern Women for the Prevention of Lynching (ASWPL). On the face of it, lynching would not appear to be a woman's issue. Those who were lynched were virtually all men. But as black women had long argued, and as Ames slowly persuaded the white women of the South, lynching was not only a woman's issue but more specifically a white woman's issue, because it was so often done in the name of white female purity.

The antilynching campaign prompted white women for the first time to challenge the Southern code of chivalry that purported to protect them from black rapists. Pointing out that only 29 percent of those lynched had even been accused of rape, Ames called the bluff of the white Southern patriarchy. Lynching was done for many reasons, not simply to protect female virtue as white men often alleged. She ridiculed what she called "the crown of chivalry which has been pressed like a crown of thorns on our heads." As the white Southern writer Lillian Smith later described the white women's crusade, "They said calmly that they were not afraid of being raped. . . . Not only that, they continued, but they would do everything in their power to keep any Negro from being lynched and furthermore, they squeaked bravely, they had plenty of power."

No issue divided Franklin and Eleanor Roosevelt more than the antilynching movement. Eleanor believed that a federal bill against lynching should have the President's endorsement, but Franklin, fearful of losing Southern Democratic support for New Deal legislation, refused to endorse the bill as "must" legislation, and it failed to pass.

Though bitterly disappointed by their failure to achieve racial justice during the Depression, Eleanor Roosevelt and Mary McLeod Bethune, together with intellectuals like Ruth Benedict, Margaret Mead, and Zora Neale Hurston, represented an important new departure both in women's history and American politics. Six decades after the end of Reconstruction, and fifteen years after winning the Nineteenth Amendment, they demonstrated the possibility, at least, of transcending both racial and gender divisions to secure equal rights for all.

The Wages of War

World War II accomplished what no amount of political organizing could gain in the 1930s. It ended the Depression, and in doing so created such a critical labor shortage that women who had been barred for a decade from high-paying jobs suddenly found themselves in demand. During the war the number of employed women rose from twelve to eighteen million, and the very government officials, employers, and union leaders who had once opposed hiring women now celebrated the virtues of "womanpower."

In the most dramatic break with tradition, the army enlisted women into the military services. In March 1942 Congresswoman Edith Nourse Rogers of Massachusetts pushed a bill through Congress creating the Women's Auxiliary Army Corps, which, within a year, became the Women's Army Corps, whose volunteers were known as Wacs. Soon each of the other branches of the armed forces had their own female units. In the navy, women became Waves, in the Coast Guard, SPARs. Most women served as clerical workers or nurses, but a few who had trained as pilots before the war joined the Women's Airforce Service Pilots, test-flew new fighters to demonstrate how easy they were to maneuver, and made 75 percent of all airplane deliveries throughout the U.S. and Canada. By 1944 female nurses and doctors had won full officer status in recognition of their command positions over male corpsmen and patients. By the end of the war, hundreds of thousands of women had donned uniforms in the armed services and were earning equal pay with men holding the same rank.

In civilian life women's employment grew in every occupational field except domestic service. Women took jobs as taxicab drivers, bus drivers, railroad workers, lumberjacks, security guards, welders, and riveters. The biggest jump was in factory work, which claimed 2.5 million new workers, and especially defense work, where women's work-force participation grew by 460 percent. In defense plants women worked on tanks, airplane frames, engines, propellers, parachutes, ships, gas masks, life rafts, ammunition, artillery, and electrical equipment.

Though employers had long objected that women lacked the skills and strength to work in most industrial jobs, they found that, under the pressure of a critical labor shortage and with government contracts that covered all costs and guaranteed a profit, they could retool machines and simplify tasks so that women could quickly learn to perform 80 percent of all jobs with only brief training.

White-collar work claimed the largest share of new workers after manufacturing. Many women, including most women with a high-school degree or more, preferred clerical work to factory work, although the wages were not as high. The hours were shorter, the work less strenuous, the conditions better, and the status higher. Two million women took clerical jobs during the war, half in the government. By 1945 the clerical work force had doubled and become securely identified as women's work. Banks hired women to be tellers, while food stores experimented with women clerks.

Women made smaller gains in the professions, because of the extensive training required for most careers, but the war opened opportunities in medicine, when Harvard Medical School finally admitted women in 1944 and many hospitals began taking women interns for the first time. As male musicians left, the Chicago and Boston symphonies, among others, accepted their first women musicians. Giant corporations began hiring women chemists. Women lawyers were suddenly in demand, especially in government, and in Washington the number of women journalists tripled. While discrimination persisted, the demand outstripped the supply of women in virtually every field.

The war brought women a significant boost in earnings. The median income for all women, adjusting for inflation, rose 38

percent during the war, as employers competed for scarce workers. But the biggest boost came to women who took advantage
of the labor shortage by moving into better-paying jobs. During
the war, seven million women left their jobs and homes to
migrate to Mobile, Baltimore, Detroit, San Francisco, Los Angeles, and Seattle, where defense industries were booming. In
Mobile, Alabama, a domestic servant's wage rose from $9 to
$12 a week; a waitress could make $14, a salesclerk $21, and a
shipbuilder $37. Good jobs brought women a chance to pay off
debts left over from the Depression, to save for a house, or to
send children to college. Many poor women were able to provide
adequate food for their families for the first time in their lives.
The nutrition of the poorest third of the population came close
to equaling that of the richest third by the end of the war.

For many women, expanded opportunities offered greater
freedom than they had ever known. Margarita Salazar, the sheltered daughter of Mexican parents, entered a new world when
she went to work at a Lockheed subassembly plant in Los Angeles. For the first time in her life she mixed with Anglos. She
even dated servicemen. "We all blended in," she recalled,
"men, women, Mexican, Italian."

Wartime mobilization led not only to greater intergroup contact but to a marked loosening of sexual mores. Many teenage
girls, in a display of romantic patriotism, had sex with soldiers
who were about to ship out. "Victory girls," as they were called,
differed from traditional camp followers. They would not have
sex with civilians and would not accept money. But the consequence of their sexual enthusiasm was the same: skyrocketing
VD rates. At the same time marital infidelity soared, as young
wives, separated by war from their husbands, had affairs with
other men. For lesbians the wartime loosening of sexual mores
led to something of a "coming out" experience. In the women's
branches of the armed forces and in the female-dominated sectors of war industries, in particular, same-sex relationships
flourished.

The government helped create these economic and social opportunities. Secretary of War Henry Stimson issued a pamphlet
entitled "You're Going to Employ Women." The War Manpower Commission repeatedly urged employers to adopt a uni-

form wage scale for men and women, and the National War Labor Board ruled in 1942 that the manufacturing company Brown and Sharp could not pay women 20 percent less than it paid men for the same work. The Women's Bureau insisted that factories provide rest rooms, adequate toilets, cafeterias, good lighting, and comfortable chairs. And in school districts across the country the ban on married women teachers disappeared.

Not all women could take full advantage of these opportunities. Black women were able to recoup the losses of the Depression years by regaining domestic service positions and even winning jobs in laundries, cafeterias, and other commercial services as white women abandoned them for better-paying jobs. But jobs in war offices, stores, and factories proved much harder to gain, even with the creation in 1941 of the federal Fair Employment Practices Commission. The government hired its first black clerical workers since the time Woodrow Wilson had imposed Jim Crow on Washington in 1912, but usually confined them to segregated offices and promoted them six times less often than whites with similar efficiency ratings. In Detroit, Sears Roebuck lowered barriers enough to hire black women in the wrapping and stock departments, but would not hire them in sales, where they would meet the public.

By 1943 Mary McLeod Bethune, working through the National Youth Administration, won a promise from defense plants to hire black women, but success came more quickly in some regions than in others. Once Los Angeles factory owners accepted blacks, they vigorously opposed racism, firing any white worker who refused to work with blacks. Elsewhere, however, prejudice proved more intractable. It took black women who had completed vocational training courses two years of continuous protest to win jobs in Detroit. When victory came, it was poisoned by hate strikes led by white women who objected to sharing bathrooms and showers with black women. In Baltimore similar strikes shut down five plants. When mediation failed and citywide riots threatened, black and government leaders capitulated and installed new segregated locker and rest rooms. Even where blacks won the right to work in war plants they faced discrimination. They were hired for the dirtiest, hardest, most dangerous jobs. In Baltimore a black woman at the

Edgewood Arsenal spent her days lifting fifty-five-pound boxes of TNT for only $18 a week, while white women earned twice that wage working on the assembly line.

One group of women could not claim even these modest gains. Within weeks of the Japanese attack on Pearl Harbor, F.D.R. granted the War Department authority to remove all Japanese-American aliens and citizens to concentration camps for the duration of the war. Forced to work in the camps, women could earn, at most, only $4.75 a week. Monica Sone, a nisei (second-generation Japanese-American citizen), spent the war in a leaky chicken coop in a camp in Minidoka, Idaho. Only toward the end of the war was she offered the opportunity to continue with her schooling and to work outside the camp. This offer allowed her to break free of the restrictions her family had long imposed on her and hastened her Americanization, but it did so at a terrible price. She never fully overcame the guilt she felt in abandoning her parents and their culture.

Despite some limitations on women's opportunities and basic human rights, the war years represented a major shift. By 1943, according to *Fortune* magazine, there were "practically no unmarried women left to draw on." The increase of the work force after that point came overwhelmingly from the ranks of unemployed housewives. For the first time in U.S. history married women outnumbered single women in the labor force, and women over thirty-five, once considered unemployable, outnumbered their younger sisters.

The greatly expanded role of women in the work force, however, points more to the extent of the wartime crisis than to any fundamental redirection in employment patterns. The shift from young, single women workers to older, married women was part of a long-term trend. Throughout the early decades of the century, as women bore fewer children, kept those children in school longer, and strove to raise their families' standard of living, they looked for opportunities in the work force. As the economy gradually shifted from blue-collar to white-collar and service work, women found opportunities, even during the Depression, when public opposition to their doing so was especially high. The war accelerated this trend; it did not produce it.

In some ways the war reinforced traditional roles rather than impose new ones. For instance, the war heightened men's image as warriors and protectors of defenseless women, while diminishing their supply through the draft. By 1944 there were two women for every man in the twenty to twenty-four age group, and many young women began rushing to the altar out of fear that they might otherwise not marry at all. As these new wives rapidly became mothers, employers' primary source of cheap labor sharply diminished.

Adding to employers' recruitment woes, most husbands remained strongly opposed to their wives' working. To a 1943 Gallup poll that inquired "Would you be willing for your wife to take a full-time job running a machine in a war plant?" only 30 percent of men said yes. Twenty percent of the housewives who took war jobs did so over their husbands' objections and generally in spite of their continuing resistance. At the height of the war only 26 percent of all wives worked, and of those the great majority had no children under fourteen. Even black men, long accustomed to wives' working, objected to their taking defense-industry jobs. "The women are working on that defense and they's making lots of money, just quitting their husbands," complained one man.

If simple prejudice was not enough to ensure the perpetuation of traditional roles, the burdens of wartime housekeeping heightened the difficulty of taking on new responsibilities. Despite increasing prosperity, the rationing of food, clothing, and gasoline, as well as the termination of all household appliance production, forced housewives to continue making do as they had during the Depression. Women who also worked often faced six-day work weeks after the War Manpower Commission suspended maximum-hours laws in 1943 (over the vocal protests of women reformers). By the time most women left the day shift, stores and banks were already closed. Women who worked at night could shop during the day, but standing in long lines after eight to ten hours of work and trying to cope with rationing and depleted supplies on store shelves proved exhausting.

Under this double burden of domestic and work responsibilities, women sometimes had to quit or stay home simply to buy food for their families, catch up on the laundry, or care for their children during summer vacation. Government surveys found that women workers changed jobs twice as often and stayed home twice as much as men. For every two women workers hired in war production factories in June 1943, one quit. According to Bernard Baruch, who had run the War Industries Board in World War I, female absenteeism and turnover in one factory alone caused the loss of forty planes a month.

In 1943 Congress responded by designating funds under the Lanham Act for child-care centers. A number of companies built their own facilities, the most famous of which was that built by the Kaiser Corporation for its shipyard workers in Oregon. It provided round-the-clock care for children over eighteen months and hot dinners that workers could pick up when they called for their children. For the most part, however, child-care services remained woefully inadequate.

This inadequacy stemmed in part from ambivalence both among the public and within the government over the proper role for wives and mothers during wartime. Facing a critical labor shortage, the all-male War Manpower Commission strongly supported the expansion of child-care centers. The Children's Bureau, however, opposed the expansion out of fear that children would be warehoused in hastily constructed, poorly staffed centers. Group care for children under two, Children's Bureau officials warned, would result in "slower mental development, social ineptness, weakened initiative and damage to the child's capacity . . . to form satisfactory relationships."

By the end of the war the country was providing child care for only one in ten of those who needed it. And yet, those centers remained only partially filled, for few working mothers actually used day-care centers. They recoiled at the "relief" image that day care had long ago taken on, the inconvenient locations, the inadequate hours, the high weekly charges, and the risks involved should their children become sick. Most mothers made other arrangements, usually by leaving their children in the care of relatives or neighbors. Given the lack of either government or private consensus on the child-care issue, and the fact that the United States did not suffer an all-out attack, this country never approached the success of Britain, which, though a much smaller country, provided child care for three times as many children.

Women who overcame the problem of limited services to work in war industries found an additional problem: the hostility of male coworkers. Men resented the women whose arrival signaled the loss of their special status as craft workers. Employers simplified jobs that had belonged to men and relabeled them female jobs. Moreover, they forced older men, who with seniority had moved into less strenuous jobs, to return to heavier work so that women could be used in the physically less taxing positions. Catcalls, hisses, and whistles greeted the first women to walk onto the floor of war production plants. "I never walked a longer road in my life than that to the tool room," one woman aircraft worker later recalled of her first day on the job.

The Congress of Industrial Organizations, committed since the 1930s to welcoming all workers, provided the primary vehicle through which women fought these hostile reactions, but there was a great variety of response among unions, and even progressive unions did not always control their locals. The United Electrical Workers (UE), in which Communists played an important role, helped women most, accepting Ruth Young on its executive board and making women fully a third of all its organizers. The United Auto Workers (UAW) was not as open to women as the UE, but it too made gains, creating a Women's Bureau to deal with women's concerns.

Under even the best of circumstances, however, women admitted into unions could pursue their own interests only insofar as those interests coincided with those of men. Male unionists' overriding fear was that employers would quickly see the advantage of employing women and paying them less, and that men's future job security would be in doubt. This concern prompted male union officials to side with women on the equal-pay issue. Their theory was that women were inherently less productive than men, and that if employers had to pay them equal wages, managers would always prefer men. To guard further against the possibility of women's taking men's jobs, union leaders demanded that women be placed on separate seniority lists, with the implicit understanding that they would be eliminated when the men returned from war. As far as most male workers were concerned, women were a regrettable necessity who would have to be endured "for the duration." To ensure that women would not stay past the end of the war, union contracts granted seniority equal to the time spent in military service both to veterans previously employed by a unionized company and to those newly hired after discharge from the military.

Most women working in defense plants accepted the view that their jobs were temporary, and that veterans had a prior claim to high-paying jobs. According to the WTUL, "Women do not expect or want to hold jobs at the expense of returning soldiers." As the last hired, women could expect to be the first fired. Indeed, when war production ended, women quit at twice the rate they were discharged. Many young, single women left to marry returning GIs, while many married women with children to care for returned home. In Los Angeles 64 percent of all former homemakers wanted to leave their defense jobs.

Even women war workers who wished to continue working, which 75 percent hoped to do, did not always want to stay in the same job. In Detroit 15 percent of women in manufacturing who wanted to continue working planned to look for other jobs; in Seattle 23 percent planned to do so. In addition to believing that defense-plant jobs were men's by right, many women found defense jobs too strenuous, tedious, or exhausting. Some found the hours too long. Still others complained that the working conditions were too hot, dirty, or noisy.

To many women, however, especially those who had been in the work force before the war, the war-industry layoffs came as a crushing blow. Having achieved jobs that paid well, they wanted to hold on to what they had gained. Margie Lacoff, a war widow who was working as an electrician's helper in a navy yard at the end of the war, declared, "I like my work so much that they'll have to fire me before I leave." Some women who wanted to hold on to their jobs succeeded in doing so. A Women's Bureau survey of women in aircraft, shipbuilding, and electrical equipment in the fall of 1946 found that 45 percent of women workers had been able to keep their wartime jobs. Nine out of ten of those who remained, nevertheless, experienced a decrease in pay, from roughly $50 a week to $37 a week. Male workers' fear that employers would take advantage of the war to shift work from men to women who were paid less was, in fact, partly realized. Even in the auto industry, where women suffered a cutback from being 25 percent of the work force to only 9.5 percent in 1946, twice as many women remained at the end of the war as had worked there before.

There were limits to how much shifting employers felt they could get away with. In banks and grocery stores, where there were no unions, women moved permanently into positions as tellers and grocery clerks. In heavy industry, however, where unions were strong, employers were reluctant to perpetuate wartime changes. Fearful of strikes by male workers if too many women were kept on, mindful of the strong public support for granting job preference to veterans, and believing that men were more versatile workers because of their greater relative strength and lower turnover, managers reclassified most jobs, adding skilled or heavy-lifting components to formerly female jobs, so that by 1946 they were seeking men for 80 to 90 percent of their jobs.

The impact of the war experience, then, was mixed. For a small number of women the war provided an opportunity for upward mobility, which they were able to hold on to after the war. But for most the crisis nature of the conflict ensured that traditional values would be reasserted once the fighting was over. Eleanor Roosevelt, who had fought so hard for women throughout her life, revealed how completely the pressures of economic collapse followed by military conflict had scuttled the early twentieth-century feminist ideal of female autonomy and self-determination when, in 1944, she wrote that "The circumstances that surround women as a rule force most of them into certain channels. . . . The best [a woman] can do is to use the opportunities that come to her in life to the best advantage, according to her abilities. This is a little less true today than it was in the past, but nevertheless it still holds true, since women, or the greatest number of women, must subordinate themselves to the life of the family."

By the end of the war a Gallup poll revealed how little the war had changed things. Only 16 percent of all men and 20 percent of all women agreed that a married woman should work if her husband could support her. Moreover, the women's organizations that had once fought on behalf of women's concerns, including the Women's Trade Union League, the National Consumers' League, and the League of Women Voters, were all but dead. As far as government support for women was concerned, the period 1929–45 proved, on the whole, disappointing.

During the first four decades of the twentieth century, women reformers had placed enormous faith in the potential of the state to redress the balance of power in American society between men and women. The New Deal had gone far to fulfill that faith. But the war set in play forces that quickly undercut support for centralized state power. As war industries proved more productive than expected, policymakers came to believe that private business and local governments would function best if largely left free of government interference.

For the most part women leaders did not disagree. Many would have liked stronger social welfare policies and a more vigorous enforcement of equal-pay regulations, but they were not sanguine about the chances of the federal government following their lead. Even if women reformers could have claimed greater power, battles such as that over child care during the war were making it increasingly apparent that the interests of women and children were not always the same and that women did not speak with one voice.

Predictably, conflict over the Equal Rights Amendment reinforced this lesson. The National Woman's Party, hoping to win the level of support for the ERA that World War I had generated for suffrage, campaigned hard in Congress and won significant support, especially after the General Federation of Woman's Clubs and the National Education Association voted endorsement. But opposition from women workers and their supporters in the Department of Labor remained steadfast. Although the Supreme Court had upheld the Fair Labor Standards Act in 1941, and although growing numbers of women workers had gained union protection during the war, the vast majority labored in jobs not covered by either the FLSA or union contracts. For them state labor laws remained important. The Senate voted in favor of the ERA in 1946, but the vote fell one vote short of the two-thirds majority needed to send the amendment to the House. With the war over, the campaign lost impetus.

As for the significance of the war in drawing women into the work force, it seems clear that the war gave millions of women a much broader appreciation of their capacities. Even those who ultimately left the work force may well have passed the resulting boost in confidence to their daughters. On the other hand, the fact that married women became the majority of all women workers during the war is not attributable to the war alone. Rather, the shift in the female work force from young, single women to older, married women was part of a long-term transformation, reaching back to the turn of the century. In short, the war did not dramatically change women's lives. Indeed, its principal effect was to produce a sense of crisis, which, following as it did on the economic devastation of the Depression, made traditional family life, with all of its demands on women, seem more desirable than ever before.

5

Cold War Fears
1945–61

Promised Lands

In 1943 Betty Goldstein, a summa cum laude graduate of Smith College and a first-year graduate student at Berkeley, won a fellowship to complete her Ph.D. in psychology. Jubilant over the honor, she announced the news to her boyfriend. He gave a cool response. "You can take that fellowship," he told her, "but you know I'll never get one like it. You know what it will do to us." Fearful of becoming "the old maid college teacher," she turned down the grant, burying within her the disappointment that would erupt two decades later as her book *The Feminine Mystique*.

Sadly, the romance did not last, despite her sacrifice. She moved to New York, took an apartment in Greenwich Village with several college friends, and went to work for a small labor news service. Immersed in left-wing labor activity, she enjoyed her new life until, with the end of the war, her roommates began leaving one by one to marry and move to the suburbs. Beset by a "pathological fear of being alone," she married Carl Friedan, just returned from running an army show in Europe, and in 1949 bore her first child. Taking a leave from her job to concentrate on breast-feeding, she read Dr. Spock, bought *The Joy of Cooking*, and toyed with the idea of not returning to work after her year's maternity leave was up. In the end she went back, only to find herself fired when she became pregnant a second time. To her surprise losing her job came as something of a relief. It forced her to accomplish her secret wish: to leave New York City for the suburbs and a full-time career as a mother. She found a charming old Victorian house in Rockland County, New York, which Carl bought with a GI loan. "It was a wonderful house," Betty would remember. Situated on a knoll with a view of the Hudson, it had a front porch that was even longer and wider than the one where she had played as a child.

Betty had grown up in Peoria, Illinois, the eldest of Harry and Miriam Goldstein's three children. Her father, a Jewish immigrant, had built a business that started as a street corner button stand into Peoria's finest jewelry store. Her mother, the daughter of a physician, had worked as a society reporter on the Peoria newspaper until she married. Together they raised Betty and their two younger children in comfort, until the Depression struck. Years later Betty would recall the hard times that followed, as the family finances deteriorated and her mother lashed out at her father in "impotent rage." Having weathered a Depression childhood and a wartime youth, Betty Goldstein Friedan vowed that her own life would be different. "I was determined to be 'fulfilled as a woman' as my mother was not."

As Betty Friedan searched for a home in suburban New York, another young mother was moving to Chicago to share a cramped kitchenette apartment with her aunt. Ruby Lee Daniels, the illegitimate daughter of Mississippi sharecroppers, was part of a flood of poor black migrants from the South, pushed by the mechanical cotton picker and pulled by the unskilled jobs of the booming cities of the North after World War II. As second- and third-generation immigrants left the area of Chicago around Hull House, migrant blacks took their place. Daniels made almost four times as much doing janitorial work at Montgomery Ward as she had working as a waitress in Clarksdale, Mississippi. To her, as to thousands of other rural blacks, Chicago was the Promised Land.

Daniels came from a part of the South with the worst poverty, most violence, poorest schools, and highest rate of illegitimacy in the country. She had a better education than most, having finished the eighth grade at a school endowed by Sears Roebuck magnate Julius Rosenwald. But like so many other women of her background, she had known poverty all her life. Married young and quickly separated, she had borne two children, but never found a man she could count on for long. Her real family was made up of female friends and relatives, who took her in when she was homeless, passed on word of potential employment, and helped her raise her children. When she left Mississippi after World War II, she gave one of her sons as "a gift child" to a childless friend, and took the other with her, planning to move in with her Aunt Ceatrice, who was renting a kitchenette apartment in Chicago. There she hoped to make a new life—to find a good job, a reliable man, and a home of her own.

The hope for a better life, which Friedan and Daniels shared, rested largely on the remarkable economic growth of the postwar years. During the war, savings reached a historic high as people banked 25 percent of their disposable income—triple the proportion saved during decades before or since. These pent-up savings, combined with a yen for consumer goods long denied, and a continued high level of military spending spurred by Cold War tensions, staved off the depression that so many feared would follow World War II. Between 1935 and 1950 income rose 50 percent. For the first time since the Depression significant numbers of poor families began to climb out of poverty. In 1940, at least 33 percent of all Americans lived in poverty; by 1950 that figure had fallen to 27 percent; by 1960 to 21 percent; and by 1990 to 13 percent.

Poverty typically falls with greatest force on the aged and the young. Social security benefits were beginning to help the elderly, especially as legislators pegged benefits to the workers' best-paid years, rather than their lifetime earnings. Government benefits to veterans aided the young. And the economic growth of the postwar years created opportunities in urban areas that pulled people of all ages out of the poorest, rural sectors of the country and into the booming cities.

Of all the material aspirations encouraged by this new prosperity, home ownership stood at the top of most women's lists. The home was a woman's domain, where she worked as well as where she lived. Pressed to choose, most men put scarce resources into the down payment on a car; most women put spare resources into their home. Ruby Lee Daniels had a chance at owning her own home only once in her life. In 1961 she made a $200 down payment on a house on Chicago's West Side. Soon thereafter, her common-law husband, Luther Haynes, bought a car. Not able to keep up the payments on both, Luther Haynes insisted on keeping the car.

Despite such differences in priorities, owning a home was a nearly universal dream in postwar America for both men and women. As late as 1940 half of all young adults twenty to twenty-four years old lived with their parents. In 1945 98 percent of American cities reported housing shortages. By 1947, 6 million families (out of 35 million nationwide) were doubling up with families or friends, and another 500,000 were occupying temporary quarters. People were living in trolley cars, abandoned silos, and Quonset huts left over from World War II. One couple even set up housekeeping in a department-store window as a way of advertising their homelessness. Home ownership in America had held steady at about 45 percent from 1890 to 1945. In the fifteen years following the war, however, it shot up to 62 percent.

No one did more to capitalize on this dream of home ownership than William and Alfred Levitt, who became the Henry Fords of home building by applying methods of mass production to housing. In the late forties William Levitt embarked on the biggest private housing project in American history. Buying up four thousand acres of potato fields in Hempstead, Long Island, about twenty-five miles east of New York City, he started work on 17,500 homes in what was to be known as Levittown. To minimize costs, he broke down construction into twenty-six steps. Teams of workers executed specific tasks: bulldozing the land, paving the roads, pouring foundations, planting trees, joining the walls and roof, installing the plumbing and electricity, and painting. Every house was identical: one story high, covering twenty-five by thirty-two feet, with a living room, kitchen, two bedrooms, and a bathroom. The price: $7,990.

On March 7, 1949, William Levitt opened his sales office. Waiting outside was a long line of prospective buyers, many of whom had been there for five days, braving the raw, wet, cold winds in the hope of securing a new home before they were all sold. One of the women on the line of buyers was pregnant and had gone into labor. The developer's assistant had rushed her to the hospital so she wouldn't have her baby in the street. Returning to set up a canteen of hot coffee and soup to warm those who stood on line, he greeted a team of news photographers sent out from New York City to take pictures. On the day the sales office finally opened, William Levitt sold 1,375 identical houses in three and a half hours. Underselling his nearest competitors by $1,500 per house, Levitt still made $1,000 profit on each home. Those Cape Cod houses became the single most powerful symbol of the dream of upward mobility and home ownership for American families. With a thirty-year mortgage, no down payment, and tax deductions for homeowners, it was cheaper to buy a house in Levittown, where mortgage costs ran $56 per month, than to rent an apartment in New York City, where apartment rentals averaged $93 per month.

Levittown offered a suburban retreat at an affordable price. The roads in the new community curved to accentuate the country setting. No industry spoiled the bucolic atmosphere. And each new Cape Cod house constituted a self-contained, private world, with a green lawn, a television set built into the living-room wall, and a Bendix washing machine built into the kitchen's laundry alcove. Although Levittown houses were small, a husband could convert the attic and then build an addition easily, since the houses covered only 15 percent of the lots. William Levitt liked to think of his homes, and their possibilities for do-it-yourself expansion, as the country's principal bulwark against leftist subversion: "No man who owns his house and lot can be a Communist," asserted Levitt in 1948. "He has too much to do."

The critical importance of the suburban home as a weapon in the Cold War emerged with special clarity a decade later, when Vice President Richard Nixon engaged Soviet premier Nikita Khrushchev in impassioned dialogue at the opening of the 1959 American National Exhibition in Moscow. In what came to be known as the "kitchen debate," the two men argued over the relative merits of American and Soviet household appliances. To Nixon, American superiority in the Cold War rested not on weapons but on the secure and abundant family life of the modern suburban home. America's washing machines, refrigerators, and television sets would stave off class warfare and thwart the appeal of Communism.

Suburbs had been around since the late nineteenth century. When migrants from home and abroad began crowding into urban centers, more prosperous inhabitants pushed out to the urban periphery. Unlike Europe, where the scarcity of land had long encouraged civic conservation, America enjoyed abundant countryside. That abundance encouraged in New World citizens a pattern of picking up and moving elsewhere rather than restoring and improving what was at hand. The American suburb grew steadily in the early decades of the twentieth century, slowed to a standstill during the Depression, and then exploded after the war. Demand for housing on the part of young families living in cramped apartments or squashed in with relatives fueled that explosion, but Congress lit the match.

Congress's most important initiative was the Serviceman's Readjustment Act of 1944 (the GI Bill of Rights). This bill provided veterans with unemployment compensation, medical benefits, loans to start new businesses, and subsidies to continue their education or acquire new skills. Passage of the GI Bill gave the young a sudden boost. Among other things, it funneled over six million students, nearly half of the veteran population, into the nation's colleges, universities, and training programs. By 1947 GIs constituted half the college enrollments. But since 98 percent of veterans were men, the GI Bill helped men much more than it did women, giving them an enormous competitive advantage in the marketplace and significantly reinforcing the traditional American belief in the male breadwinner.

The government also established the Veterans Administration, which, among other things, set up a program to help the fifteen million sailors and soldiers who fought in World War II purchase homes. The program insured long-term mortgages at very low rates. Down payments of less than 10 percent were routine, and no down payments were common. Half of those who purchased new homes in 1949–50 were GIs in their mid-thirties with young children. Many came from middle-class backgrounds, but a significant number had working-class origins. In the suburban development of Milpitas, California, most of the male residents were autoworkers, while in a Levittown built in New Jersey roughly half the men held clerical, sales, or blue-collar jobs.

The government also authorized the Federal Housing Authority, established during the Depression, to provide home builders with "production advances," without which the Levitts, among others, could not have undertaken huge projects in advance of any sales. These benefits led to others. Homeowners could deduct the interest on their mortgages and their property taxes from their income taxes, giving them a marked advantage over those who remained, by choice or poverty, in rental housing.

Finally, the government's decision to greatly expand its financing of highways made suburban living possible by giving rapid access to distant bedroom communities. In the 1950s 85 percent of new homes were built in the suburbs, and by 1960 as many Americans lived in the suburbs as in central cities. Overall, the rate of home ownership was double that of Germany, Switzerland, France, Great Britain, and Norway.

The federal government contributed to this pattern of democratization in home ownership, but only by helping the housing industry and veterans. It did nothing for female workers, who lost their wartime jobs to returning male veterans and found that there were no postwar plans designed to help them find new jobs, new homes, or mortgages with easy terms. Nor, with the end of the Lanham Act, could women with children to support easily find day care.

The government took no action on behalf of women workers, because no organized movement forced it to do so. This absence of pressure stemmed in part from America's distinctive wartime experience. America suffered 400,000 dead in World War II, a large number, but one dwarfed by the 25 million deaths suffered by the rest of the world. The devastation of war in Europe, especially, forced on these countries problems that the United States did not face—chief among them, how to help women become mothers and workers at the same time so that repopulation and rebuilding could go forward together. Because America did not need to rebuild or repopulate, support in this

country for social welfare policies to assist women both as mothers and workers never developed.

Compounding the obstacles created by gender was the factor
of race. William Levitt frankly acknowledged that Levittown
barred black buyers. He explained to a reporter that this was
"not a matter of prejudice, but one of business. As a Jew I have
no room in my mind or heart for racial prejudice. But, by various
means, I have come to know that if we sell one house to a Negro
family, then 90 to 95 percent of our white customers will not
buy into the community."

In 1948 the Supreme Court declared racially restrictive cov-
enants in housing unconstitutional, but this decision did little
but increase white panic over the prospect of blacks moving
into their neighborhoods. In practice, blacks who wanted to buy
a house in a white neighborhood had to arrange the purchase
individually with a sympathetic white seller. Tina and Joseph
Hill, a black couple in Los Angeles, bought a house on a predominantly white street in the late forties. Joseph, a serviceman
during the war, drew on his GI benefits; Tina, a production
worker at North American Aircraft, contributed her wartime
savings. Their purchase did nothing, however, to shield them
from the wrath of their new neighbors. Only when it became
clear that Joseph had a shotgun and knew how to use it did the
cross burnings and other forms of harassment stop.

Compounding those problems suffered because of race and
gender, the Federal Housing Authority did not approve mortgage funds for integrated communities or mortgages for female-
headed families. While the government funneled production
advances into suburban builders' businesses and offered mortgages for new suburban homes, the homes and apartments in
older, presumably less creditworthy urban areas slowly decayed.
And while highways spread their tentacles across the landscape,
public transportation, on which women more than men relied,
declined. The federal government added to this inequity through
its public-housing policies. Bowing to conservative forces, which
were pressing for a return to local economic controls in the
postwar years, federal officials left to localities the determination
of need and site selection for housing projects. Since few towns

outside large cities would admit to a need for public housing, most projects were built in existing slums. Rather than constructing public housing at low density on the less costly land outside the central cities, as was the practice, for instance, in Great Britain, the federal government further concentrated the poor in the central cities and reinforced the image of the suburbs as a refuge from the social pathologies of the disadvantaged.

For a moment, in the late 1940s, it looked as though the story in Chicago might be different—that poor blacks might be able to become part of the prospering white neighborhoods spreading out from Chicago's urban center. Black housing manager Robert Taylor and white reformer Elizabeth Wood decided to buck the tide of public-housing practice around the country. Taking advantage of the Federal Housing Act of 1949, they resolved to build small-scale public housing projects on vacant land in white neighborhoods. But their plan never made it through the Chicago City Council. And their efforts to move carefully screened black families into white neighborhoods provoked ugly race riots. Federal housing money, in the end, went to the building of high-rise buildings in black areas. The only vestige of the integrationist dreams of reformers were the names given to the new projects—Robert Taylor, Elizabeth Wood, W.E.B. Du Bois, Ida Wells-Barnett, and Jane Addams. For Ruby Lee Daniels and many other women like her, the Promised Land turned into a sad continuation of the poverty and fear they had known in rural Mississippi.

In sum, though the growth of American suburbs extended the privileges of middle-class life to a broader segment of American society than ever before, only white families with male heads could take full advantage of government-subsidized prosperity. For most blacks the way out of the inner city was effectively blocked, either by racism, or, in the case of many black women like Ruby Lee Daniels, by poverty and the stigma attached to not having a husband. In a period that celebrated traditional family life, 25.3 percent of all black wives were either separated, divorced, or widowed, compared to 10 percent of all white women who had ever been married. These handicaps led to significant demographic shifts in the postwar years. In Chicago, for instance, crowding among blacks increased, as up to twenty-two hundred black migrants a week flowed into the city. While white families settled into new houses, black families faced rodents "big enough to ride on," by one black woman's account, in the crowded apartments of the inner city.

The Apotheosis of Motherhood

After fifteen years of privation and war, the lure of traditional domesticity proved powerful wherever a woman lived. Marriage and birthrates, which had begun to rise in the early years of the war, soared after 1945. By 1950 the average marriage age for women had fallen to twenty, and more women were marrying between fifteen and nineteen than in any other age group. According to one study, most Americans thought that single people were "either sick or immoral, too selfish or too neurotic." Never in the past century had marriage been so popular. A baby boom quickly followed this wave of early marriages. During the 1950s a million more children were born each year than during the 1930s. Even college-educated women joined the trend, with a birthrate only slightly lower than the average.

To the despair of women professors, two out of three women who entered college dropped out before graduating. Most of those who did so either wanted to marry or feared that too much education would ruin their marital prospects. Economically, their fears made sense. The road to upward mobility for women after World War II lay in the direction of marriage to well-educated men (most of whom opposed working wives), not in the direction of careers. A 1952 advertisement for Gimbel's department store summed up the anticollege sentiment. "What's college?" the ad asked. "That's where girls who are above cooking and sewing go to meet a man so they can spend their lives cooking and sewing." Following the widespread view that a woman's place was in the home, a declining proportion of women college students prepared for careers in law or medicine or pursued other graduate degrees. Only black women college students deviated from this pattern. Greatly outnumbering black male college students, and therefore less likely to marry a highly educated man than their white counterparts, nine out of ten black women college students completed their degrees.

Family life had always been important to American women, but it came to serve as the focus of their hopes and aspirations to an unusual degree in the postwar years. To those who had grown up in the poverty of the Depression only to confront the trauma of World War II, the importance of security, both in monetary and emotional terms, took on an almost religious significance. The Cold War did nothing to diminish that feeling. "Security" was a big part of the family's attraction, Betty Friedan later remembered. " 'Security,' as in 'risks,' was in the headlines, as in atomic secrets, Communist espionage, the House Un-American Activities Committee, loyalty oaths, and the beginning of blacklists for writers." Commenting on the trend toward young marriages, another observer commented, "Youngsters want to grasp what little security they can in a world gone frighteningly insecure. The youngsters feel they will cultivate the one security that's possible—their own gardens, their own . . . home and families."

A woman's most important role within the postwar family was that of mother. By the 1940s most women, other than poor black women in the rural South, began this part of their lives in a hospital, a far safer but less supportive environment than the one their mothers had experienced in their homes. Actress Julie Andrews, who delivered a baby in a New York hospital in the 1950s, later recalled her anguish as she lost control of her own labor. "I begged, but they wouldn't let my husband go with me into the delivery room," she remembered. "They were wheeling me into bright white light, lifting me onto another table, strapping my legs down in long white leggins, clamping my feet and hands in stirrups. For the first time in my whole labor I felt helpless and afraid. And then the doctor tried to clamp an ether mask on my face. I was terrified, then angry. They were going to make me miss the climax. . . . I fought so that when they took the mask off I was still conscious."

Despite such experiences, childbirth ranked as the "most satisfying moment" in the lives of almost half the married women in a 1961 Gallup survey, and two-thirds rated motherhood the "chief joy of womanhood." The centrality of motherhood for postwar women held for all groups. When Lee Rainwater interviewed working-class mothers in the late 1950s, she found that motherhood was the central focus of their lives. "The working class woman," Rainwater explained, "tends to feel that she has only her body, her energy and her good conscience to offer as evidence of her worth—having children is the most dramatic and absorbing accomplishment she can offer to the world that she has done well." Studies of poor black mothers reported similar findings. Robert Bell found that among black mothers living in Philadelphia, over two-thirds volunteered that they would rather be a mother than a wife.

More surprising was the centrality of motherhood in the lives of well-off and well-educated women, those who had led the long decline in birthrates in the decades before World War II. Elaine May, in her study of middle-class women from the 1950s, found no less maternal involvement among her subjects than Rainwater found among hers. And the reasons for this involvement were largely the same. "[W]omen whose aspirations for personal achievement had little chance of realization in the wider world put their energies into full-time motherhood," May observed. "But motherhood could only be full time as long as there were young children at home." The best way to extend their career, therefore, was to increase "the number of small children." From 1930 to 1945 much of the satisfaction of motherhood had been sacrificed, first to economic exigency and then to war. Postwar women made up for lost time. By 1957 more third and fourth children were being born to women of all classes than at any other time in the twentieth century.

Especially in a child's early years good mothering was a full-time job. Despite marked improvements in sanitation and medical treatment since the turn of the century, childhood diseases remained an absorbing concern. Antibiotics were not widely used until the middle of the 1950s. Until then scarlet fever, ear infections, pneumonia, rheumatic heart disease, and meningitis could either kill swiftly or turn into a long-term, debilitating illness, requiring careful nursing attention. Polio remained a scourge, crippling tens of thousands of children each year, until the development of the Salk vaccine in 1954 and the Sabin vaccine in 1960. Because of the risk that even a minor ailment could turn into a life-threatening disease, mothers watched carefully for even the slightest symptoms of these diseases, such as a sore throat, headache, stomach cramps, lethargy, high fever, or stiffness of the neck and back.

In moments of medical crisis women traditionally had turned to their female relatives for advice and assistance, but one of the consequences of the increasing geographic mobility of American families, especially with the spread of the suburbs, was a breakdown of kinship ties. This trend, though evident across the country, was most obvious among middle-class families. Expert advice in the form of magazine articles and child-rearing manuals, geared specifically to middle-class mothers, proliferated in the postwar years to fill the void. Working-class women continued to rely on traditional child-rearing practices: "I don't go by the book, I go by the way my parents raised me," reported one autoworker's wife. Middle-class women, on the other hand, were more likely to have cut ties with both kin and inherited wisdom and were turning with increasing frequency to expert opinion—most importantly that of Dr. Benjamin Spock.

The first edition of Spock's *Baby and Child Care*, published in 1944, represented a major new departure in child-care advice. The feminists of the Children's Bureau and the research psychologists of the 1920s and 1930s had all insisted that children be held to rigorous schedules, fed only every four hours, and toilet-trained early. Spock, assuming the greater freedom that improved standards of living among middle-class families made possible, took a more relaxed approach. He urged mothers to follow their own common sense, not to worry excessively about schedules, not to impose toilet training upon the unwilling, but to offer gentle guidance and encouragement. In offering his counsel, Spock took pains to instill confidence in young mothers. "You know more than you think you do," Spock reassured his readers. As the best-educated mothers the country had ever produced, they were uniquely qualified to build a better tomorrow, he assured them. Stressing the importance of close mother-child bonds, he speculated that creative people owed their talents to "the inspiration they received from a particularly

strong relationship with a mother who had especially high aspirations for her children."

Along with the confidence-building, however, came some
stern warnings. Above all, mothers must avoid two dangerous
tendencies: rejection and overprotection. In a chapter entitled
"Special Problems," Spock discussed the working mother, who,
he warned, was guilty of the first sin. By working she left behind
a child who might feel abandoned and who therefore might
become a juvenile delinquent. Mothers who wanted to leave
young children for paid work should seek psychological counseling. It was best to leave home only for a trip to the beauty
parlor, to see a movie, to buy a new hat or dress, or visit a good
friend. The good mother was the one who was always there for
her children. *But*, while mothers should always be available,
they should guard against being overprotective. Such suffocating
attention could lead to "Momism," a condition identified during
World War II as a psychological defect suffered by soldiers
whose mothers had so sheltered their sons that they could not
function in wartime. The ideal mother was ever present but
never controlling. Most experts thought that this precarious
balance could be achieved, but only if women were married to
strong men who assumed their rightful economic and sexual
dominance in the home so that women could channel their
sexual energy into marriage rather than toward their sons.

In the spirit of "togetherness," Spock urged fathers to participate in the care of their infants, but warned them against
going too far. "Of course, I don't mean that the father has to
give just as many bottles, or change just as many diapers as the
mother. But it's fine for him to do these things occasionally.
He might make the formula on Sunday." Other experts, more
insistent about the dangers of confusing children about proper
gender roles, spoke more directly. "Live your gender," urged
one advice writer, because children need "manly men and womanly women" as proper role models.

Cold War tensions reinforced the heavily gendered themes
of the experts. Some claimed that the family must stay strong
for the battle against Communism. FBI chief J. Edgar Hoover
praised homemakers and mothers in 1956 for the unique role

they played in fighting "the twin enemies of freedom—crime
and communism." Sexuality must be contained, discipline en-
forced. The links between the most private sexual reveries and
the most public foreign-policy debates were illustrated constantly in the popular press. A sexy woman was widely described
as a "bombshell." A skimpy bathing suit became a "bikini,"
named for the South Pacific islands where the U.S. tested its
nuclear warheads. Homosexuals were harassed and driven from
government jobs because their sexual orientation was deemed
a sign that they could not submit to the discipline expected of
all patriots. Lesbians who frequented the gay bars of Buffalo,
New York, reported greater pressure from their peers to conform to rigid butch/femme roles. Even Margaret Sanger and
the birth control movement fit in with this new mania for national security. Pointing to the dangers of overpopulation in the
Third World, which would lead to poverty, hunger, and Communism, Sanger adopted the slogan "National security through
birth control." Alfred Kinsey, whose studies revealed the extent
of the sexual revolution that had taken place in this country,
was accused of aiding world Communism. But the best illustra-
tion of paranoia were the bomb shelters that a few especially
fearful Americans began building in their backyards in the late
1950s. In these steel- and concrete-encased structures, built to
protect their inhabitants against nuclear annihilation, families
could enjoy real togetherness.

Postwar family life remained home-oriented, even when not
lived underground. Working-class women, especially, focused
attention on their families, joining clubs only rarely. But even
middle-class women played a less active role in community affairs and politics than their mothers or grandmothers had.
Middle-class women often served as volunteers and joined the
PTA, but they were no longer as visible on the national level
as they had been during the Progressive Era and the New Deal.
Among the few active women, Democratic congresswoman Helen Gahagan Douglas fought valiantly against the Red-baiting
tactics of young Richard Nixon in her unsuccessful bid to win
a California Senate seat in 1950. Maine Republican Margaret
Chase Smith, who entered the Senate in 1948, exercised important influence in turning her colleagues against Senator Joe

McCarthy's crusade against alleged Communists in government. Women also remained active as volunteers in political campaigns and in the movement against nuclear armament. But the old fervor was gone.

In 1950 the Women's Trade Union League disbanded, even though women made up only 14 percent of all unionized workers, and many left-wing unions with large female memberships—such as the cannery union—disbanded under the pressure of Red-scare attacks. Three years later the Democratic Party, to the dismay of Frances Perkins and others, abolished its women's division in an economy move. At the same time Alice Leopold, chief of the Women's Bureau, became Assistant to the Secretary of Labor for Women's Affairs, a shift that reflected the bureau's declining political influence. And by 1960, the League of Women Voters had shrunk to half the size it had been in the 1920s.

According to many of the psychiatrists, sociologists, and other family experts of the day, women's limited participation in public life was altogether natural. After four decades of feminist-inspired writings that emphasized the social roots of gender roles, the postwar years marked a return to the naturalistic and stridently antifeminist thinking of the late nineteenth century. The same forces that drove so many women to embrace family life inspired a new traditionalism among experts on female nature.

In psychiatry, where an influx of European psychoanalysts fleeing Hitler gave naturalistic views an added boost, the Freudian belief that woman's anatomy was her destiny gained ascendency. In 1945 Helene Deutsch wrote that the normal, feminine woman accepted her distinctive sexuality and lived through her husband and children. Women who through some unfortunate turn in their psychic development did not follow this pattern developed a "masculinity complex," in which the "cold, unproductive thinking" of manhood overwhelmed the "warm, intuitive knowledge" of womanhood. Ferdinand Lundberg and Marynia Farnham made the case for natural femininity even more starkly in their 1947 best-seller, *Modern Woman: The Lost Sex*. Tracing feminism to the neurotic impulses of women who had been abused by their fathers in childhood and were seeking revenge by claiming a share of masculine power, Lundberg and Farnham urged that women seek not to imitate men but to accept their femininity through subordination to their husbands and the joyful acceptance of motherhood. Higher education and careers, they warned, would lead to the "masculinization of women with enormously dangerous consequences to the home, the children dependent on it, and the ability of the woman, as well as her husband, to obtain sexual gratification."

These traditionalist views were not confined to psychoanalysts. Talcott Parsons, the dean of American sociologists, declared that differentiation and specialization within family life were an essential part of the development of complex, industrial societies. Echoing social Darwinists of the nineteenth century like Herbert Spencer, Parsons argued that by providing emotional support at home, women freed men to play "instrumental" roles in the economic world beyond, making possible increased productivity and abundance for all. A woman who failed to play her proper role threatened not only the happiness of her family, but the economic well-being of the Western world.

Even the women's colleges, long staunch advocates of rigorous liberal-arts education, became part of this traditionalist trend. Colleges should not treat women as "men in disguise," the president of Mills urged in 1950, echoing the popular psychoanalytic wisdom of the day. They should instead provide a "distinctively feminine curriculum," constructed around a course on the family, that would not cut women off from their domestic destinies.

The ideal of motherhood proved so powerful in the postwar years that it affected even the writings of those who challenged the new traditionalism most energetically. In *Women and the Modern World* (1952) sociologist Mirra Komarovsky attacked demands for a more feminine curriculum as "neo-anti-feminist," and condemned the placid housewife as someone who "risks a self-abased subjection to tyranny and a deterioration of personality." She conceded, however, that feminism had erred "in its disparagement of the homemaker." In her own work, Komarovsky strove to understand motherhood's attraction while examining the ways in which it conflicted with women's increasing education and their experience at work. Of the scholars who most influenced her in seeking this middle course, Komarovsky singled out Margaret Mead.

Mead, who bore her only child in 1939, with Dr. Benjamin Spock in attendance, found that maternity shifted her perspective on anthropology. In her earlier books, *Coming of Age in Samoa* (1928) and *Sex and Temperament* (1935), she had portrayed motherhood as an incident in the life cycle, a positive experience but not significant for the culture at large. The power of the eugenists in the 1920s and the rise of Hitler in the 1930s had made her especially sensitive to the evil uses to which biological determinism could be put, and in her writings she strove to minimize any suggestion of its importance in human life. By the time she wrote *Male and Female* in 1949, however, Mead had begun to discuss the ways in which biology might work dialectically with environmental forces to shape culture. Maternity became the central feature of this dialectic, the one great problem that all cultures must confront in organizing gender roles. How, she asked, do societies deal with universal experiences, like pregnancy and childbirth?

While Mead emphasized the need to take maternity into account in explaining the different ways that culture patterns gender roles, she scorned biological determinism, which in the hands of those like Lundberg and Farnham was used to legitimize female passivity. Mead had long been interested in psychoanalysis, but she believed that Lundberg and Farnham had erred badly in their uncritical acceptance of Freud's belief that "penis envy" lay at the root of the female personality structure. Drawing on the work of dissident psychoanalysts Karen Horney and Clara Thompson, Mead argued that women suffered not so much from "penis envy" as from envy of the special power and privilege that societies awarded to men. Moreover, any envy that girls might have of the male sex organs (and Mead believed that such envy sometimes did exist) was counterbalanced by the envy little boys often exhibited for the remarkable reproductive organs of the female sex. In contrast to Lundberg and Farnham's tales of penis envy, Mead reported primitive societies in which male ceremonials imitated gestation and childbearing in an obvious display of "womb envy." American society's attempt to confine women to the home could be understood, from this primitive perspective, simply as a male attempt to prevent women from having too much power.

Mead, Thompson, and Komarovsky were fighting a strong current in their effort to maintain a feminist tradition in intellectual life. Even Mead and Komarovsky's students at Barnard did not share their view that women belonged in the public sphere. All but a few anticipated a life of domesticity, although most intended to work between graduation and marriage. "Work experience is beneficial because it gives some insight into the husband's world," a student observed.

The domestic ideology that permeated American culture remained powerful until the early 1960s. In 1962 a Gallup poll found that women across the country were committed to living through their husbands and children. "Being subordinate to men is part of being feminine," an Arizona mother declared. "Women who ask for equality fight nature," said a former career woman from New Jersey. "I want to be the kind of woman who gives her children emotional security," another mother stated. "That's one of the reasons why I don't think a mother should work." A staggering 96 percent of the respondents declared that being a housewife had made them extremely happy or fairly happy; and yet, most women interviewed wanted their daughters to have more education and to marry later.

These hopes for the next generation suggest that beneath the happy face that these housewives turned to the outside world lurked doubts about the choices they had made, doubts born of the conflicting expectations to which the women of their generation were subject. They felt torn between the egalitarian ideals taught in school and the reality of their subordination in the home; between the importance that Americans attached to money in a consumer society and their own exclusion from the wage-labor force; between the respect accorded specialized accomplishments in the larger world and the reality of their varied tasks within the home. The extraordinary success of the American economy in the postwar years exacerbated these tensions. As washing machines, dryers, televisions, and dishwashers flooded the market, the definition of middle-class status changed. As housewives, women were supposed to be the principal consumers of these new goods. But, increasingly, women found that they could not fulfill their role as the family consumer, unless they boosted the family's earnings through work outside the home. For a time the romance of post-Depression and postwar family life sustained women, but even in the 1950s there was clearly an undercurrent of discontent. Social scientists found it among housewives of all classes and ethnic backgrounds, but it seemed most pronounced among highly educated women, as Betty Goldstein Friedan began to discover in 1957 when she reviewed her Smith College classmates' responses to questionnaires circulated in anticipation of their fifteenth reunion.

Of the two hundred women who responded to Friedan's survey, 97 percent had married and 89 percent were housewives; only 3 percent were divorced. Most of the mothers had planned their children's births and had enjoyed their pregnancies. They found that sex "gets better with the years" but was "less important than it used to be." As their children had grown older, the great majority had become involved in community activities. But as they faced forty they regretted one thing—"that they had not taken their education seriously enough, that they had not planned to put it to serious use." These women seemed happy in their domesticity, gratified by motherhood, and satisfied sexually, but they had been denied the opportunity to fulfill their potential as human beings. As Friedan concluded a few years later in *The Feminine Mystique*, "We can no longer ignore that voice in women that says: 'I want something more than my husband and my children and my home.' "

The Government Rediscovers "Womanpower"

Even as Betty Friedan pored over her questionnaires, trying to plumb the discontent of her homebound college classmates, millions of women, including unprecedented numbers of wives and mothers, were joining the work force. Between 1940 and 1960 the proportion of women who worked rose from 25 to 35 percent, while that of married women doubled, jumping from 15 to 30 percent in just two decades.

Some married women worked for the same reasons that poor wives always had—because men's wages were too low to cover the cost of food, clothing, and shelter. In Los Angeles, Chicanas worked in the canneries to earn basic living expenses. "My father was a busboy," the daughter in one family recalled, "and to keep the family going . . . in order to bring in a little more money . . . my mother, my grandmother, my mother's brother, my sister and I all worked together at [California Sanitary Canning Company]." Working-class wives who were better off often worked to bring their families middle-class comforts. Margarita Salazar, whose Mexican parents had immigrated early in the century, could afford to stay home when she began having children, but she took a part-time job in a bakery when her sons reached school age to help pay for the family's new house. "When you bite off such a large bill, you need a little help," she later explained. And some women worked because married women in their culture always had. Margaret K. Pai, a Korean-American wife living in Hawaii, continued to work in her father's drapery business even after the birth of two children, as her mother had before her.

Most of these women were not reacting to Friedan's "feminine mystique." According to Mirra Komarovsky's study of white working-class wives, "The mere fact of working is not apparently associated with consistent or striking differences between working mothers and homemakers." Most wives sought employment to bolster the family budget, not to disrupt domestic power relationships. The "feminine mystique" did affect them, however. The reality of their daily existence, in which they struggled to balance work and motherhood, stood in such sharp contrast to the image of domestic serenity evoked by the mystique that they inevitably felt guilty as they struggled to balance PTA bake sales and workplace demands. One irritated working wife wrote to Friedan, soon after the publication of *The Feminine Mystique*, that she objected to

the false emphasis that is placed on the entire matter of women fulfilling themselves through a career. The vast majority of working women don't have careers. We have jobs, just like men. We work for money to buy things that our families need. If we're lucky, we like our jobs, and find some satisfaction in doing them well, but it is hard to hold a commercial job, raise a family and keep a house. Most of us would be delighted to chuck the wage earning back in our husband's laps and devote ourselves exclusively to homemaking and community projects. We worry about the children while we are at work. We don't really like to throw the last load of clothes in the washer at 11:30 p.m., and set the alarm at 6:00. . . . It just makes us tired, very tired.

Most married women sought work for the same reasons they always had—because they needed the money to survive or to achieve middle-class comforts.

An acute labor shortage in the postwar years gave growing numbers of women the opportunity to work. In the face of this shortage, the conventional wisdom among employers that married women workers were inherently less productive gave way to praise for their maturity, reliability, and neat appearance. All in all, the best female employee, according to a Sears Roebuck officer, was "a married woman with a mortgage on her home and her children partially raised." To attract mothers, employers had to change their policy on hours. Those who had long argued for the absolute right to work their employees however many hours they deemed necessary finally accepted the eight-hour day, five-day week. They even accepted part-time work. Without these changes employers could not have hired as many married women as they did. Two-thirds of women who worked did so either part-time or part of the year.

Black women also benefited from the labor shortage. Department stores who had never hired black saleswomen began to do so in the 1950s, while office managers began hiring black clerical workers. Although the majority of black women continued to work in domestic service, where they derived no benefits from protective labor legislation, and although the average black woman earned only half what the average white woman did each year, black servants were able to make five times as much as they had during the 1930s, and were increasingly able to bargain for better hours and working conditions.

While a labor shortage heightened the demand for married women workers, technological, medical, and educational advances increased their supply by making it easier for women to combine traditional tasks with outside employment. Contraception and the trend toward early marriage permitted women to complete their childbearing by the time they were thirty years old and to send their youngest off to school by the time they were thirty-five. When the government began to subsidize hot lunches in the schools (a practice aimed at helping farmers), large numbers of women found themselves with at least six hours each day available for wage labor. Antibiotics began to reduce the time spent on nursing sick children, while household appliances made it possible to cut back on housework. While women who did not work outside the home still put in fifty-five hours a week on domestic tasks, women who took jobs were able to cut that figure to thirty. Finally, rising levels of education prepared women for better jobs than their mothers could have claimed. Women whose mothers had been limited to agricultural labor, domestic service, or factory jobs were increasingly able to enter white-collar jobs that were both cleaner and more consonant with middle-class status.

For the first half of the twentieth century the best way for a woman to raise her family's standard of living was to invest her time in achieving better nutrition and health. By the middle of the 1950s, however, the majority of housewives had achieved these goals. The next step was to earn extra income, so that the family could raise its standard of living in other ways—through better housing, higher education, braces for the children's teeth, and family vacations. Nothing in this shift suggested any significant change in women's motivation. Women still went to work for the same reasons they always had. Polls of employed wives revealed that half were working "to buy something" while a mere fifth labored to fill "a need for accomplishment." Jane Addams's "family claim" held sway, even as women left home.

It was possible for postwar Americans to celebrate homebound mothers and working mothers, too, simply because by mid-century women could be both, at different times in their lives. The popular magazines that celebrated the domesticity of the suburban housewife at home with her children were looking at young women with children still under six years of age. Only 10 percent of these women were employed after World War II. They still made up less than 20 percent in 1960. The major increase in employment took place among mothers whose children had all entered school, rising from 25 percent at the end of the war to 39 percent in 1960. Ironically, high birthrates were leading to more working mothers, because families' income needs tended to balloon as a cluster of children at similar ages reached their teenage years. Given this concentration of economic pressure, even in suburbia 25 percent of women worked.

Although employers accepted the fact that they had to hire married women, they usually did not believe that women could be serious about careers, an attitude that had harsh consequences for ambitious, educated women. As an agent for the Insurance Company of North America told investigator Miriam Hussey in 1956, "Most girls who apply don't expect to have a career and of the few who do, many change their plans within a few years. . . . For this reason the company does not recruit women who are college graduates for career jobs." Ironically, other women faced the reverse situation. Firms geared women's jobs to those with less education, leading college-educated women to leave out of boredom. As a spokesman for the Tradesman's Bank and Trust told Hussey, "The bank has tried to use college women in positions as tellers, but . . . after a few months they begin asking themselves what they're doing counting money all day . . . training a teller is expensive so the personnel department looks for people who will stay longer than . . . college women." In short, educated women were often not hired for "women's jobs" for fear that they would be bored, and they were not hired for "men's jobs" out of fear that they would not remain.

In addition to the prejudices of employers, women who tried to chart new occupational terrain often faced resistance from customers, clients, and other members of the public, including other women. One woman told Mirra Komarovsky that she used to have so little confidence in the first women bank tellers that she "counted money received at their windows with special care."

Husbands posed an ever bigger problem for working wives. Half of all working-class husbands (as compared to one-third of their wives) expressed unconditional opposition to their wives' working. Middle-class husbands were no more enthusiastic. As one middle-class husband told his working wife, "A couple of well-planned dinner parties a month would be worth more to our income than what you earn a year." Women who overcame their husbands' opposition had another worry—that they might "emasculate" their husbands by being too successful at work. As one woman explained to Komarovsky, if she earned more than her husband, "He would shrink a little in my estimation."

Even Betty Friedan was not immune. "Carl's vision of a wife was one who stayed home and cooked and played with the children. And one who didn't compete," Friedan remembered. "I was not that wife." As her children started growing up, she returned to journalism, working as a free-lancer. "In some of those early years, I made more money a week than he did, and I took to doing stupid things like losing my purse so we wouldn't have a fight." Such strategies and fears inevitably limited women's ambition.

As Friedan struggled with domestic worries, world events were conspiring not only to accelerate women's exodus from the home but also to challenge some of Americans' most deeply held beliefs about what work women should be allowed to do. On October 4, 1957, the Soviet Union stunned the United States by launching Sputnik, the world's first artificial satellite. Though it weighed only 184 pounds and carried little more than a radio transmitter to signal its position, Sputnik represented a major victory for the Soviets in the Cold War.

The launching of Sputnik coincided with the publication of a report by the National Manpower Council, which had been investigating ways to improve the "development and utilization of the country's human resources" since 1951. Entitling its study *Womanpower*, the council recalled the importance of women to the war industry during World War II, when the term was coined. The council emphasized "the extent to which [the] nation's strength and security [depends] upon its manpower resources." Deploring the nation's failure to utilize women's talents fully, it called for training women in subjects long stereotyped as masculine, especially math and science. Responding to those who argued that education was wasted on future mothers, the council reported that "the more education [a woman] has, the more likely she is to work. Among women aged 25–

64 in 1952, fewer than 30 percent of those who had no more than elementary school, 37 percent of those who were high school graduates, and 47 percent of those who were college graduates were in the labor force."

Another investigator, Mary Bunting, underscored the council's dismay at America's failure to take full advantage of women's talent. Bunting, a Vassar graduate in physics, had earned a Ph.D. in agricultural bacteriology in 1934 at Wisconsin. After teaching at Bennington for a year, she married a fellow scientist and spent the next two decades raising a family. Following her husband from job to job, she picked up what work she could. In 1954 her husband died and she took a job as dean of Douglass College, the women's division of Rutgers University. While there she entered the debate over "womanpower."

As a member of a National Science Foundation committee investigating ways to increase the number of the nation's scientists, Bunting discovered that no one was paying any attention to women as a possible resource. At the committee's first meeting, the members decided to find how many bright high-school students did not go on to college. "It was surprising to me," Bunting recalled, "that according to the Education Testing Service and other national data 98 to 99 percent of the bright young people who didn't go to college were female." More surprising still was the reaction of her male colleagues on the committee. Having reviewed this data, they wanted to go on to the next item on the agenda, "instead of thinking about what should be done to encourage the women." Bunting suddenly realized "that there was something going on that I had not been aware of, and that we had to do something about it." She devoted the rest of her career to changing "the climate of unexpectation in the country" with respect to women.

The Soviet Union, Bunting taunted her colleagues, took women's abilities more seriously than America did. In engineering, for example, a quarter of all Soviet engineers were women, while engineering in the United States could claim only one woman for every one hundred men. If the U.S. was to close the space gap, it was going to have to break down old gender divisions and encourage women to do men's work.

No woman better illustrates the difficulties talented women

faced in reaching their potential in this country than Maria Goeppert Mayer, the first woman to win the Nobel Prize for theoretical physics. Born in 1906, the only child of a distinguished academic family in Germany, Maria Goeppert trained as a mathematician and physicist at the University of Göttingen, where she studied with several of the greatest physicists of the day and won a Ph.D. Her dissertation on the theory of double emission and absorption of light quanta was regarded as a fundamental contribution to the field.

At Göttingen she met and married an American chemist, Joseph Mayer, who had come to study on a Rockefeller fellowship. In 1930 the couple left for Baltimore, where Joseph Mayer joined the physics department at Johns Hopkins. Normally, a physics department in this country would have been delighted to hire a scientist of Maria Mayer's accomplishments, but rules forbidding nepotism precluded that possibility at Hopkins. She turned instead to research, collaborating with her husband and other male scientists without holding a university post. During World War II scientists at Columbia University, where Joseph Mayer was then a professor, asked her to join the Manhattan Project to build an atomic weapon. By this time Maria was the mother of two young sons, and she was reluctant to work full-time, especially since her husband was away five days a week on war-related research. She agreed, however, to work part-time.

In 1946 the Mayers moved to the University of Chicago, he as a full professor, she as an associate professor without salary. There she developed a theory for the movement of electrons in the atom, but not having had a conventional scientific career, she hesitated to publish. When, on the urging of her husband, she finally did so, other physicists were publishing the same results. In 1963 she shared the Nobel Prize in physics with them. Maria Goeppert Mayer triumphed despite the obstacles to her professional advancement. Most women scientists were not so fortunate.

If Americans had been as concerned about their scientific standing as such books as *Womanpower* urged them to be, they would have given greater encouragement not only to white women like Maria Goeppert Mayer but also to educated black women. The black women who reached college were more likely to finish than were their white classmates. Moreover, they were more likely to pursue a career after graduation, even if they married and became mothers. But even the most talented black women faced obstacles at every step. When Margaret Lawrence, a Columbia Medical School graduate with a degree in public health, began looking for work in New York in 1942, she met only discouragement. Married to sociologist Charles Lawrence and obviously pregnant with her first child, she was never sure whether she failed because she was black, because she was a woman, or because she was pregnant.

Only when her husband was recruited for a position at Fisk University in Nashville, training ground for some of the finest Negro scholars in the country, did a faculty position for her at neighboring Meharry Medical School save her career. Meharry's president, eager for the prestige that Lawrence's credentials would bring to his small black medical school, worried nonetheless about the effect that motherhood might have on her work. Moreover, he did not want to pay the $2,400-a-year salary that was the minimum she thought her due. But in the end, his anxiety over his school's status overcame his doubts. He agreed to her salary demands and accepted on faith that the motherhood issue would somehow be worked out.

The motherhood issue was worked out, but only with great difficulty. Before moving to Nashville, Lawrence did some work in pediatrics with Benjamin Spock at the Kips Bay–Yorkville Child Health Station in New York. "His exciting and well-integrated vision of the child, the family, the community, and society never left me," she later recalled. Nurtured all her life by a working mother and working aunts and encouraged by her husband (the son of two teachers), she took from Spock his "respect for the ordinary intuition and common sense of mothers" without accepting his dictum that mothers impelled by a desire to work should consult a psychiatrist. Nevertheless, she worried. "A mother could not expect her baby to appreciate her other endeavors," she later told her daughter. So Lawrence struggled to find just the right caretaker for her first baby, and then the two that followed. She struggled also to make a place for herself in a middle-class black community where friendships between men and women rarely developed outside marriage. At the medical school she felt isolated from the men, who did not know how to act toward her. In social gatherings, she felt isolated from the women, who seethed with resentment at the woman doctor who seemed to combine being a doctor and a mother so successfully. Conflicts and tensions such as these made Lawrence's pioneering efforts to advance pediatric public health in the South seem almost herculean.

The accomplishments of women like Maria Goeppert Mayer and Margaret Lawrence did much to vindicate the work of Mary Bunting and the National Manpower Council. They also confirmed the beleaguered staff of the Women's Bureau in their view that women were being underutilized. As the Cold War heated up, Women's Bureau literature argued that just as the country was preparing to stockpile weapons, so, too, should it stockpile expertise in the form of bright women. Those whose children no longer needed them full-time should return to school, and young women not yet married should prepare for careers. If America was to win the Cold War it would have to make the most of the available talent, even if it was female. In 1955 the Women's Bureau sponsored a conference on "womanpower" at the White House, where most of the issues explored in the report of the National Manpower Council two years later were aired.

Concrete, if indirect, support for the training of more women scientists came three years later, in 1958, when Congress passed the National Defense Education Act (NDEA)—the biggest bonanza for education since the GI Bill in 1944. NDEA provided $1 billion in student loans and fellowships in science and foreign languages (especially Russian), and new financial support for expanded vocational guidance at all levels. If the Americans failed to beat the Russians in science and technology, it would not be for lack of funds.

The GI Bill of 1944 helped college men almost exclusively, but the National Defense Education Act helped everyone from high school on. Schools had expanded enormously after the war to take care of the GIs, but once the GIs graduated the new students who came to take their places were increasingly female. The GI Bill set one generation of women back, but the educational expansion that the GIs led opened college doors to younger women much more widely than had ever been true in the past. In fact, by 1965 the expansion of higher education was enabling women to earn more Ph.D.'s each year than men had been earning at the end of World War II.

Despite this expansion of opportunity, advocates of careers for women fell far short of urging equality. A careful reading of *Womanpower* reveals that the authors expected women trained in science and language to teach high school, thereby freeing men for the more lucrative research positions in universities and industry. In the end, therefore, "womanpower" represented an expansion of women's traditional roles more than the creation of new opportunities.

And yet the Cold War set in motion forces that could not be indefinitely contained. By urging women to stay in school longer and by expanding the educational opportunities available to them in order to help America win the Cold War, the government was making it increasingly likely that women would one day demand opportunities commensurate with their increased training. Ironically, in doing so they would inevitably subvert the traditional family idyll, which, according to Richard Nixon in his 1959 Moscow "kitchen debate" with Nikita Khrushchev, represented capitalism's most shining monument.

Bringing Back Rights Talk

The boom years of the 1950s should have created an ideal climate for women to demand equality within the work force, but the crisis years of the Depression and World War II had seriously undermined the sense of entitlement that so many women had embraced early in the century. For women to unite around a demand for equal rights with men required a change in their thinking, a willingness to assert once again the legitimacy of "rights talk." A century before, the abolitionist movement had served as a vehicle for the first discussion of women's rights in America. Ironically, America's Cold War preoccupation with security created conditions that allowed a similar process to take place in the 1950s. By celebrating the virtues of the "free world," leaders in the United States all but invited civil rights leaders to ask how secure could that world be if a significant minority could legitimately claim not to have equal rights? Once blacks had asserted their right to full equality in American society, it was only a matter of time before women began claiming equality for themselves. In this process black women played a pivotal role.

The roots of black women's protest stretched far back in American history—to slave resistance in the antebellum South and later to Ida B. Wells-Barnett's turn-of-the century campaign against lynching. Protest grew in force, however, during World War II, when America's rhetorical support for equality inspired blacks to renewed fervor in demanding equality for themselves. One especially important activist during the war years was Pauli Murray, the woman who more than any other would link the movements for black rights and women's rights in the early 1960s.

Born in 1910, the fourth of six children, Pauli Murray was orphaned as a young child and reared by aunts in Durham, North Carolina. "My aunts were 'race women' of their time," Murray recalled. "They took pride in every achievement of 'the race' and agonized over every lynching." Copies of the NAACP publication "The Crisis" arrived regularly at their home, and Pauli learned that segregation was an evil against which every self-respecting black person should protest whenever possible. She walked rather than submit to segregation on a bus, and she refused to go to the movies rather than suffer the indignity of segregation in the balcony.

Graduating from high school in 1926, she persuaded her Aunt Pauline to take her to New York to live with cousins in Brooklyn while she completed the additional course work required to attend Hunter College, the elite public women's college in Manhattan. Of Hunter she later wrote, "The school was a natural training ground for feminism." But Hunter's academic excellence could not get her a job upon graduation in 1931. Racism and the Depression conspired to keep her out of work, until the New Deal saved her with a job at Hilda Smith's racially integrated camp for women, set up in Bear Mountain Park through the influence of Eleanor Roosevelt. From Smith's camp Murray moved to the WPA's worker-education project and became active in the labor movement, and through that in the civil rights struggle. Working on behalf of sharecroppers and other disadvantaged blacks, Murray discovered an ally in Eleanor Roosevelt, who took an active interest in her work.

In 1941, believing that she could fight more effectively with a legal education, Murray won admission to Howard Law School, the elite school for blacks in Washington, D.C. Having enjoyed the comparative freedom of New York, she found the racial segregation of the nation's capital "repugnant." Just as troubling, after her years of feminist confidence-building at Hunter, she encountered frank sexism. "Ironically, if Howard Law School equipped me for effective struggle against Jim Crow," she later reflected, "it was also the place where I first became conscious of the twin evil of discriminatory sex bias, which I quickly labeled Jane Crow." She remembered no overt hostility; in fact, the men were friendly. "But I soon learned that women were often the objects of ridicule disguised as a joke. I was shocked on the first day of class when one of our professors said in his opening remarks that he really didn't know why women came to law school, but that since we were there the men would have to put up with us. His banter brought forth loud laughter from the male students. I was too humiliated to respond." Her response came in working her way to the head of her class.

Murray found valuable support in Howard history professor Caroline Ware. A pioneering social historian, Ware was one of the few white faculty at Howard University. She and her husband, economist Gardner Means, were, according to Murray, "part of the leaven working in wartime Washington to change the racial atmosphere and provide a basis for more frontal attacks on Jim Crow." In 1943 and 1944 Murray and other Howard students conducted a series of sit-ins in Washington restaurants. They won a few isolated victories, but congressmen, who controlled Howard's purse strings, brought pressure on school administrators to force an end to the protests before they could abolish segregation throughout the capital.

Murray suffered a second defeat when she was denied the opportunity to continue her legal studies at Harvard Law School (a tradition among Howard's best graduates) because of her sex. She went instead to Berkeley, where she completed work, begun at Howard, which was to play an important role in the NAACP's briefing of *Brown* v. *Board of Education of Topeka, Kansas* (1954). For years the NAACP had worked with the 1896 ruling in *Plessy* v. *Ferguson*, which held that states might impose separate racial facilities as long as they were equal. Murray believed that the time had come to overturn *Plessy*, and she urged that lawyers work to persuade the Supreme Court that segregation was a violation of the Fourteenth Amendment equal-protection clause. Challenging the "separate but equal" doctrine, she argued that the effect of this rule was "to place the Negro in an inferior social and legal position," and "to do violence to the personality of the individual affected, whether he is white or black." Since there was virtually no legal precedent to which she could point to support this position, she relied on social scientific data to support her argument.

At first her former teachers at Howard did not think much of her approach, believing it far too risky. One of her teachers, Spotswood Robinson, even bet her that *Plessy* would not be overturned within the next twenty-five years. Within the next decade, however, Murray was vindicated. In 1954 the Supreme Court held in *Brown* that "in the field of public education the doctrine of 'separate but equal' has no place." Speaking of children in grade school and high school, the Court declared that to separate Negro children from others "of similar age and qualifications solely because of their race generates a feeling of inferiority as to their status in the community that may affect their hearts and minds in a way unlikely ever to be undone."

Murray did not realize how important her paper had been to the *Brown* decision until 1963, when, visiting Spotswood Robinson at Howard (and collecting on her bet), she asked if he knew what had happened to her paper. He promptly recovered it from his files, gave her a copy, and told her that, while he had not thought much of it in 1946, he had liked it much better upon rereading it in 1953 while working on the NAACP brief in the *Brown* case. "In fact," he told her, "it was helpful to us."

For all of Murray's legal creativity, the NAACP did not recruit her to work on any of its cases. Cornell offered her a research position in the early fifties, but in the McCarthyite atmosphere of the day, her labor work in the 1930s prevented her from winning a security clearance. Instead, she eked out a living during the 1950s in private practice in New York, working for clients, mostly women, too poor to pay her. Not until the early 1960s would she again play an important role in national politics. In the wake of the *Brown* decision, the center of civil rights activity moved, for the first time in nearly a century, to the deep South.

It is difficult to pinpoint a beginning, an exact time, when the fire storm of civil rights activity sparked a new wave of feminism. For some women the embers had been smoldering for a long time. That was certainly the case in Montgomery, Alabama, where three women, two black and one white, took action in December 1955 to end the segregation of buses. The women were Jo Ann Robinson and Rosa Parks, the granddaughters of slaves, and Virginia Durr, the granddaughter of a prominent slave owner. All were born early in this century in the deep South; all were caught in the tangle of racial and sexual inequality that typified their region; all were determined to do something to change their lives. These women are usually accorded little more than a passing reference in histories of the civil rights movement, but their historical significance goes well beyond what is conventionally acknowledged.

Virginia Foster Durr had grown up in Birmingham, Alabama, the bright and outspoken daughter of a preacher. With some misgivings and great financial hardship, her parents sent her north to Wellesley College, where she first learned to live with blacks on terms of equality. Unable for financial reasons to finish college, she returned to Birmingham, became a librarian (to the mortification of her proud father), and married a young lawyer, Clifford Durr. With the coming of the Depression the Durrs followed Virginia's brother-in-law Hugo Black to Washington to work in the New Deal. While rearing four children, Virgnia worked for Molly Dewson at the Democratic Women's Committee. Virginia was especially interested in abolishing the poll tax, which since 1900 had limited the voting rights of women, poor whites, and blacks in the South. All was well for the Durrs until 1947, when, as the Cold War heated up, Pres-

ident Truman demanded that all government employees submit
to loyalty checks. Clifford Durr, who by this time was serving
on the Federal Communications Commission, resigned, refusing
to enforce such a program on the grounds that it violated the
First Amendment. For a few years Clifford Durr defended those
who lost their jobs because of McCarthyism, but by the early
1950s the Durrs were penniless. They decided to move to Montgomery, Alabama, where Cliff's family still lived. Making a
living proved difficult, however. Not only had Clifford Durr
defended people accused of being sympathetic to Communism,
but in their years in Washington both Clifford and Virginia had
become supporters of integration and the work of the NAACP.

The Durrs had two friends in particular at the NAACP. One
was Mr. E. D. Nixon, a Pullman porter who was head of the
local chapter. The other was Rosa Parks, a seamstress at Montgomery Fair (a local department store), who was secretary of
the organization. Though working class in background, Parks
had the bearing, speech, and dress of a middle-class woman.
She wore rimless glasses, spoke quietly, wrote and typed fault-
less letters, and was admired by poor and well-to-do blacks
alike. A Methodist, she served as a teacher and mother figure
to the children of the NAACP youth council. In the summer
of 1955, Virginia Durr arranged to send Rosa Parks to the
Highlander Folk School in Tennessee for a couple of weeks on
a scholarship. The Durrs had helped found the Highlander Folk
School during the Depression, and for twenty years it had been
one of the only places in the South where blacks and whites
mixed freely. Eleanor Roosevelt sat on the board, as did Reinhold Niebuhr. The Durrs' association with the school led Mississippi senator James Eastland to drag them both before his
Internal Security Committee in 1952, where he charged their
school with being freakish, mongrelized, and basically Communist. Virginia Durr, never one to mince words, called Eastland a "nasty polecat." Rosa Parks returned from Highlander
more committed than ever to the civil rights movement.

The third woman was Jo Ann Robinson. Born in Cullendon,
Georgia, the twelfth and youngest child of landowning black
farmers, Robinson was the first member of her family to graduate from college, an achievement that catapulted her firmly

into the middle class. Having earned a B.A. from the all-black
Fort Valley State College, she took an M.A. in English at black
Atlanta University, and taught for a year at a black college in
Texas. In 1949 she moved to Montgomery to teach at the black
Alabama State College. She also became an active member of
the Dexter Avenue Baptist Church, which many Alabama State
professors attended, and she joined the Women's Political
Council, a black professional women's civic group. Robinson
owned a car and had no occasion to ride the city buses. However, at the end of the first term, intent on visiting relatives in
Cleveland, she took a bus to the airport. Ignorant of Montgomery's segregation practices, she took a seat in one of the
front ten seats reserved for whites. Immersed in holiday
thoughts, she did not hear the bus driver reprimand her, until
he was standing over her shouting, "Get up from there! Get up
from there!" with his hand drawn back to strike her. Without
thinking, Robinson fled, but the humiliating experience stayed
with her for years, and laid the foundation for her decision to
overturn Montgomery's segregation laws at the opportune time.

There were a number of opportunities between 1949 and
1955, times when black passengers ran afoul of white bus drivers
by refusing to give up their seats. The ordinances actually did
not require a black to surrender a seat if there was no other
seat farther back in the bus, but drivers routinely ignored this
technicality and forced blacks to stand so that whites might sit.
Again and again blacks threatened to take action, but they were
never able to act in common cause. In March 1955 a black
teenager, Claudette Colvin, was arrested for not giving up her
seat, and there was talk of retaliation, but when it was discovered that she was pregnant, Robinson and the other members
of the Women's Political Council concluded she would not be
a good symbol.

That was where matters stood on December 1, 1955, when
Rosa Parks left the Montgomery Fair department store for the
ride home. The bus filled up quickly, and Parks soon heard the
bus driver demanding that she give up her seat, which was in
the black section, to a white person. She refused, was arrested,
and jailed. E. D. Nixon, who routinely served as bail bondsman
for poor blacks arrested for drinking and fighting, could make

no progress with the white police on this matter. He therefore turned to Clifford Durr, who, accompanied by Virginia and E. D. Nixon, bailed Rosa Parks out and then talked about what to do. Cliff advised her that they could get the charges dismissed, since, technically, drivers could not ask blacks to give up seats to whites unless there were seats farther back in the bus for them to take, and there had not been any for Rosa Parks to move to. Or, they could test the constitutionality of segregation. Rosa Parks's husband, a barber, was deeply afraid, and wanted to get the charges dismissed. As the others debated he chanted in the background, "Rosa, the white folks will kill you. Rosa, the white folks will kill you." But Rosa Parks was determined to test Montgomery's Jim Crow laws. She had had enough.

Four days later, on Monday, Rosa Parks was brought to trial. In the meantime Jo Ann Robinson had been at work. As soon as she heard of Parks's arrest she mobilized a few trusted students at Alabama State to help her draft and duplicate on the college mimeograph machine tens of thousands of fliers, urging Montgomery blacks to stay off the buses that Monday. By early morning they were distributing packages of the fliers to checkpoints around the city, where other members of the Women's Political Council saw to their distribution. On Monday no black person road the bus. Parks was tried and convicted, and that looked like the end of it. But she decided to appeal, and the boycott, which was supposed to last just one day, looked as though it might continue. That night over ten thousand people turned up for a mass meeting at Holt Church. Young Reverend Martin Luther King, Jr., who had just moved to Montgomery, gave an impassioned speech that electrified the crowd. He urged them to continue their protest and spoke of the power of nonviolent resistance. The boycott continued.

That night King became the leader of a nonviolent civil rights movement in America, and much has been written about his part in the development of nonviolent resistance. Less has been said, however, about the black women like Rosa Parks and Jo Ann Robinson who formed the backbone of the civil rights struggle. Black women played a key role in the civil rights movement for several reasons. First, high male mortality rates and higher rates of out-migration left the South with a surplus of black women. Second, there was a long tradition of informal, female leadership in the South, going back to slavery. Third, women were the bulwark of the church in the South. And, finally, women were sympathetic to nonviolence, the favored method of the powerless. Convinced of the righteousness of their cause, black women became foot soldiers in the long war to win equal rights. In the Montgomery bus boycott, in particular, they demonstrated what it meant to be a foot soldier. For an entire year they walked to work. "My feet is tired, but my soul is rested," one elderly black woman put it. Since black women formed the larger part of the bus ridership in Montgomery, their participation in the boycott proved critical to the boycott's success. It wasn't easy for them. Not only was it tough walking in all kinds of weather, they had to face the hostility of Montgomery's white leaders, who tried everything they could to break the boycott.

In the end the federal judges in Montgomery and then the Supreme Court ruled that Montgomery's Jim Crow law violated the Constitution by depriving blacks of the equal protection of the laws guaranteed by the Fourteenth Amendment. And by Christmas time the following year, 1956, the buses of the capital of the Confederacy were integrated. It had been a year that testified to the power of the NAACP, the Southern black church, the tactic of nonviolence, and especially to the solidarity of poor black workingwomen.

As the black women of Montgomery savored their victory, the NAACP redoubled its efforts to win legal rights for blacks. But progress was maddeningly slow. It took forever for cases to wind their way through the courts. Not all judges were as liberal as those in Montgomery, Alabama. It seemed it would take another century before integration was achieved in fact as well as in theory in the South.

Seeking to mobilize black Southerners, Martin Luther King, Jr., and other ministers joined together in 1957 to found the Southern Christian Leadership Conference (SCLC), but they made little progress until they hired Ella Baker, the head of the New York chapter of the NAACP, to bring order to the organization. According to several of King's advisers, Baker, a fifty-four-year-old veteran of the civil rights struggle, was the most qualified person in the country to serve as director of the SCLC, but King refused to grant her that authority, restricting her instead to the role of administrative assistant. Baker understood the simple sexism involved: "As a woman, an older woman, in a group of ministers who are accustomed to having women largely as supporters, there was no place for me to come into a leadership role." Nevertheless, Baker did more to marshal the resources of black Southerners than any other person, with the possible exception of King himself, and possibly more even than he. Far more than King's oratory, Baker's organizing skills pushed the movement forward.

The granddaughter of a minister, and daughter of a waiter, Baker grew up in rural North Carolina and graduated from all-black Shaw College. In 1927 she moved to New York City to live with relatives and look for work. Despite her college degree she could get work only as a waitress and in factories. In the thirties she worked for the WPA and the NAACP, where she served as a field secretary, recruiting blacks throughout the South, visiting churches and schools, trying to overcome the terror of the poor and the snobbery of the middle-class blacks so that they could make common cause. During World War II she helped set up youth groups in Greensboro, North Carolina, the scene of student sit-ins in 1960. The year the Supreme Court decided *Brown* she became president of the New York City branch of the NAACP and worked to integrate the public schools.

In 1959, as acting director of the SCLC she made a special trip to the Highlander Folk School to talk to one of its best-known teachers, Septima Clark, about how to enable Southern blacks to exercise their right to vote. Clark, the sixty-year-old daughter of slaves, taught illiterate adults to read and barely literate adults to become teachers. In intensive training sessions she turned sharecroppers and unschooled blacks into potential voters. Baker felt drawn to Clark because, unlike so many of the male ministers in the civil rights movement, she seemed able to work both sides of the gaping class divide between Southern blacks. Two things impressed Baker about Clark's school. First, most of the teachers were black women, the people Baker considered to be the South's most valuable, untapped resource. Second, Clark's program was aimed at poor, rural blacks, who made up the vast majority of the population that needed registering. Baker knew, however, that the very aspects of Clark's program that appealed to her would raise doubts among the SCLC preachers. They would surely object to the tedious work of teaching illiterate blacks, a job that lay outside both their interest and their control. Also, the focus of the schools on widespread black ignorance did not fit with the preachers' image of the New Negro, ready to assume his rightful place in the modern world.

A combination of Clark's success and her persecution by Tennessee officials enabled Baker to bring the preachers around. Clark's quiet teaching so alarmed officials in Tennessee that in the summer before Baker's October 1959 visit the local prosecutor led a surprise raid on one of Clark's workshops, hoping to put a stop to what he considered Communist subversion. Blocked by the facts and the Constitution from convicting Clark of being a Communist, he charged the teetotaling teacher with selling liquor without a license, using as evidence the washtub full of ice, soft drinks, and beer, plus a jar of coins, which Highlander officials set out to encourage guests to help pay for their drinks. Within two years Highlander was closed down and all its property auctioned off. Acting to avoid the demise of Clark's citizenship school, Baker persuaded the SCLC to move her school to Dorchester, Georgia, and to seek funding from major foundations.

Baker also worked to move the civil rights movement in a more populist direction by helping found the Student Nonviolent Coordinating Committee (SNCC) in 1960. King wanted students to work under the leadership of ministers, but Baker, always the grass-roots organizer and skeptical of strong leaders, encouraged the students to take off on their own. "Strong people don't need strong leaders," she said.

The students threw off the tentativeness of older leaders like King. In February 1960 they began openly violating segregation statutes, breaking the law by sitting in at lunch counters, wading in at swimming pools, praying in at churches—determined to take the battle for civil rights into their own hands. Following Baker's advice that blacks should be fighting for "more than a hamburger," many SNCC workers turned next to voter-registration projects in the deep South, places where blacks had been barred from voting by a combination of local law and intimidation for sixty years. One of SNCC's most effective registration workers was Fannie Lou Hamer, a product of Septima Clark's citizenship-school program. Born in 1918 to sharecropping parents, Hamer was the youngest of twenty children. Her attempt to vote in 1962 cost her her job as a cotton picker and her house. She turned to SNCC, for which she became field secretary. In the summer of 1963 she and several other women workers were beaten in a county jail.

In Mississippi in those years, blacks were still informally barred from the state Democratic Party, so all delegates to the Democratic Convention in 1964 were white. Black and white civil rights workers held separate elections to elect their own slate of delegates to the Democratic Convention that year. Calling themselves the Freedom Democratic Party, they made Hamer their leader. At the convention, Hamer called on the Democratic Party to seat her group rather than the regularly elected white Democrats. She lost, but the power of her presence played an important role in passing the Voting Rights Act the following year.

The struggle for black rights did not, at first, appear to have any relevance for women. Though women like Virginia Durr, Rosa Parks, Jo Ann Robinson, Ella Baker, Septima Clark, and Fannie Lou Hamer served as important models for younger women, showing them how to stand up to powerful men, their importance in fostering a new wave of feminism was not at first apparent. The first woman to make an explicit link between race and gender was, instead, Pauli Murray.

In 1960 Murray won a fellowship to Yale Law School to do graduate work. While she was there, two of her old friends and mentors, Caroline Ware and Eleanor Roosevelt, called on her to make what would be her most important contribution in her lifelong battle against discrimination. They wanted her to serve on a new commission, just established by President John F. Kennedy, to study the status of women in American life and ways of improving it. They wanted her advice on how to deal with the most sensitive issue the commission faced, the controversy surrounding the proposed Equal Rights Amendment. Given her knowledge of constitutional law, perhaps she could find a way around the four-decade-old rift over the ERA.

6

Feminism Reborn
1961–73

The Lady Vanishes

As of the early sixties, compromise in the conflict over the Equal
Rights Amendment looked impossibly difficult. Arrayed on one
side of the battle line stood the affluent, business-oriented, politically conservative amendment supporters, committed to absolute equality with no exceptions. On the other side stood the
poor, union-oriented, and politically liberal opponents, fearful
that the ERA would destroy all of the reform legislation they
had fought so long to secure. Each viewed the other side as the
enemy of women's best interests. Neither seemed ready to make
concessions.

Though active membership in the National Woman's Party,
the group most committed to the Equal Rights Amendment,
had dwindled over the years to a few hundred aging, mostly
conservative women, the group's influence greatly exceeded its
numerical strength. Working out of the Alva Belmont House
on Capitol Hill, these dedicated women concentrated all their
energies on one issue, equal rights; in one place, Congress.
Moreover, the shifting composition of the female labor force
from blue-collar to white-collar and professional occupations
brought it steadily increasing alliances with other, more numerous women's groups, most prominently the American Federation of Business and Professional Women. By 1960 the
women's groups that had endorsed the ERA had a combined
membership of several million members, and included such

prominent women as Margaret Mead, Margaret Sanger, Helen Hayes, and Katharine Hepburn. With the exception of a brief moment in 1946, when a majority of the U.S. Senate (led by conservative Republicans and Southern Democrats opposed to protective labor legislation) voted in favor of the ERA, the Amendment remained stalled in congressional committees.

The amendment made no headway, because pro-union, liberal members of Congress, together with the Women's Bureau and its allies (including the National Consumers' League, the Young Women's Christian Association, the American Association of University Women, the national councils of Jewish, Catholic, and Negro women, and the women's affiliates of the AFL-CIO), fervently believed the ERA would do more harm than good. Large numbers of women, ERA opponents believed, still needed the protective laws that the ERA threatened to abolish. The Fair Labor Standards Act of 1938, which extended minimum wages and maximum hours to men as well as women, covered fewer than half of all workers. The act had been written to apply only to businesses actually "engaged in" interstate commerce. Moreover, the FLSA did not actually prohibit employers from demanding that their employees work long hours, it simply required them to pay overtime when they did so. State laws, therefore, remained an important source of protection for women workers. In addition to concerns over the protective umbrella of labor laws, social reformers continued to fear that the ERA would eliminate laws that required husbands to support their wives.

The possibility of ending the stalemate came finally in 1960 with the election of John F. Kennedy, and President Kennedy's appointment of labor advocate Esther Peterson as head of the Women's Bureau. Born in Provo, Utah, to a Republican Mormon family, Peterson discovered the labor movement at Columbia University's Teachers College in 1929. In the 1930s she taught in schools for workers and joined the Amalgamated Clothing Workers Union, for whom she worked as a labor lobbyist in Washington. Through her lobbying work, she met Kennedy in 1947. A freshman representative from a working-class district in Massachusetts, Kennedy proved, despite his wealthy background, to be a strong advocate of labor. Peterson followed his career with interest, signing on as a campaign worker when he declared his candidacy for the Presidency, and winning the directorship of the Women's Bureau as a reward for her loyalty.

The narrowness of Kennedy's margin of victory over Richard Nixon in 1960 gave Peterson an opportunity that she immediately exploited. The Democrats needed desperately to broaden their electoral base, Peterson observed, and the best way of doing so would be to pay attention to the problems of women. The President should begin, she urged, by appointing a commission on the status of women, which would explore ways of winning greater economic equality without sacrificing the protections for which reformers had fought so long and so hard. Hoping to win cooperation, if not endorsement, from the National Woman's Party, Peterson recommended that the new commission be broadly inclusive in its membership and examine all questions relating to women's status objectively, including the ERA.

Notwithstanding this recommendation, Peterson, who served as executive vice chairman of Kennedy's Presidential Commission on the Status of Women (PCSW), selected commissioners who, by and large, shared her views. They included representatives of the Women's Bureau and the groups that supported it, the chairman of the Civil Service Commission, several cabinet officers, and two labor-union representatives. Two college presidents—Mary Bunting (recently named president of Radcliffe), and Henry David of the New School for Social Research (and formerly head of the National Manpower Council)—along with Caroline Ware represented educational institutions. Peterson's one concession to ERA supporters was to include Margaret Hickey, former president of the pro-ERA National Federation of Business and Professional Women's Clubs, and attorney Marguerite Rawalt, a member of many pro-ERA groups.

To minimize conflict, Peterson established seven committees, only one of which—the Committee on Civil and Political Rights—would deal with the issue of constitutional equality. Many feared that nothing would come of the Committee on Civil and Political Rights until Pauli Murray suggested a way of winning constitutional equality for women without an Equal Rights Amendment. The Fourteenth Amendment, she reminded fellow committee members, guaranteed the "equal protection of the laws" to all "persons." What this meant in practice was that laws must treat everyone the same unless there was some "reasonable" justification for not doing so. States, for example, could discriminate against children in their laws governing driving on the "reasonable" grounds that those under a certain age lack the maturity to drive safely. Most laws restricting women's economic and political rights rested on similar reasoning. The time had come, Murray believed, to challenge the idea that women were essentially children and to demonstrate that "Jane Crow" was just as repugnant to the spirit of the Constitution as "Jim Crow." While conceding that the ERA would accomplish the same end, Murray cautioned that the difficulty of winning passage in three-quarters of the states should not be underestimated. Constitutional litigation offered a much surer route to equality. Murray's suggestion saved the commission from yet another ERA standoff. Though doubts remained on both sides, her strategy suggested a way of narrowing the gap. The Women's Bureau endorsed constitutional equality for the first time, while ERA supporters agreed, for the moment, to an alternative route to that end. The possibilities in Murray's approach became apparent within three years in an Alabama jury case brought by the American Civil Liberties Union (ACLU).

Lowndes County, Alabama—known locally as "bloody Lowndes"—had a long history of violence. A small minority of white men terrorized black men and kept all women in their place by killing anyone who challenged their power. In the rare event that a murderer reached trial, an all-white male jury inevitably voted to acquit. In 1965 lawyers for the ACLU, including Murray, challenged white male supremacy by attacking the Alabama jury system. In *White* v. *Crook* they charged that the jury selection system violated the equal-protection clause of the Fourteenth Amendment by barring all black men through discrimination and all women by statute from the jury rolls. In 1966 federal judges in Montgomery accepted their argument.

For the first time, a federal court agreed that the Fourteenth Amendment's guarantee of "equal protection" to "all persons" should apply to women as well as blacks.

While Murray wrestled with the issue of constitutional equality, members of the six other committees of the PCSW confronted the ways in which current policies limited women's opportunities. The commission's report, submitted in 1963, recommended a series of changes in employment policies, state laws, and in the provision of social services. Changes should begin, the commission asserted, with the federal government, which should act as a showcase for the nation by leading the assault against discrimination. In 1962, even before the commission filed its report, J.F.K. ordered an end to separate civil service lists for men and women. No longer would agency heads be allowed to specify that they wanted a man for a particular job. The commission recommended the extension of the FLSA to cover smaller businesses, to outlaw industrial homework, to endorse gender-neutral legislation with respect to limits on how much weight an employee could lift, to protect union membership, and to assure "equal pay for comparable work." The only sticking point was on the question of maximum hours, since some commissioners were unwilling to limit hours for men. Yet, on most issues the commissioners had endorsed the approach Alice Paul had been advocating since the 1920s—extending the laws that protected women to include men.

The commissioners maintained tradition by endorsing the belief that it was the responsibility of husbands to support their wives and by refusing to advocate a change in social security legislation that would permit a widowed man to stay home and care for his children. But they did recommend paid maternity leaves, tax deductions to cover child-care expenses, wider availability of health services, an increase in widows' benefits, and an extension of unemployment insurance to include domestics and agricultural workers. Most boldly, they endorsed the policy of extensive child-care services for children of all income groups, a recommendation that the National Manpower Council had thought too unpopular to consider making six years earlier.

The PCSW report brought early action in some quarters. Congress finally passed the Equal Pay Act in 1963, though its supporters failed to win all they had hoped for. The bill was narrowly written to apply only to businesses actually "engaged in" interstate commerce (rather than "affecting it"), and the wording was changed from "equal pay for comparable work" to "equal pay for equal work," prompting some supporters to worry that employers could easily circumvent the law by giving women slightly different responsibilities to justify different wage scales. But courts interpreted the act broadly to include jobs where the skills and responsibilities were substantially the same, even if not identical. Though the sex segregation of the work force inevitably limited the act's reach, between 1963 and 1973 171,000 employees won $84 million in back pay under the Equal Pay Act. Congress also acted to equalize health benefits in the civil service, raise the income level for tax deductions for child care, eliminate quotas on women officers in the armed forces, and extend the coverage of the FLSA to include 85 percent of all workers.

Perhaps the most significant outcome of the commission's work was its decision to create an institutional structure to continue its efforts. In its final recommendation to the President the commission urged the appointment of two bodies, an interdepartmental committee and a citizen's advisory council to "evaluate progress made, provide counsel, and serve as a means for suggesting and stimulating action," once the commission itself had disbanded. Led by government bureaucrats, including Catherine East of the Labor Department and Mary Eastwood of the Justice Department, these groups quietly engineered a semiofficial Washington women's underground, which coordinated activities and disseminated information of interest to women throughout the country. Women had been working their way into the government bureaucracy since the Progressive Era, but not until the 1960s did they achieve both the critical mass and the common purpose necessary to force a dramatic change in policy regarding women.

In addition to creating an underground network in Washington, the President's commission prompted the eventual establishment of fifty state commissions to carry on its work at the state level. The National Federation of Business and Professional Women's Clubs initiated the idea in 1962 as a way of

ensuring that the commission's work would not be forgotten.
State commissions laid the groundwork for future change, first,
by bringing together many knowledgeable and politically active
women to deal with matters of direct concern to women, and
second, by adding to the evidence already presented by the
PCSW of women's unequal status, especially their legal and
economic difficulties. Across the country married women faced
restrictions in their ability to sign contracts, to sell property, to
have access to credit, to serve on juries. In many states women
who became pregnant had to quit their jobs and yet were barred
from unemployment benefits. Women who worked for the government did not have the same right to benefits as men did.
Married women had to accept their husband's decisions with
respect to domicile. In most states women could not work overtime or night shifts in heavy industry. As the evidence of wom-
en's disadvantages mounted, the commissions created pressure
to fight for greater equality.

Despite the apparent success of national and state commissions in drawing attention to discrimination against women,
Alice Paul could not forgive their failure to endorse the ERA.
The Presidential Commission on the Status of Women represented the most prestigious group ever to consider the issue of
equality for women, and its only concession to the National
Woman's Party was Murray's recommendation of constitutional
litigation and the committee's statement that an Equal Rights
Amendment "need not now be sought." That might be enough
for ERA supporters on the commission, but it was not enough
for Paul. Perhaps in revenge, perhaps just grasping at the one
available opportunity to win a broad endorsement of equal
rights, Paul turned to the civil rights legislation pending in Congress in 1964. The Kennedy Administration's civil rights agenda
had been stalled in Congress for several years, held up by Southern senators. The assassination of the President in 1963, however, produced a sudden surge of support, and the ascendance
of Lyndon Baines Johnson to the Presidency brought powerful
political clout to the campaign. Though a Southerner from
Texas, Johnson was convinced of the importance of racial justice, and as a former majority leader of the Senate, he knew
how to twist arms.

The chance to win equal rights for women at the same time struck Alice Paul and her supporters at the National Woman's Party as obvious. Paul had recommended including "sex" in civil rights legislation as early as the late 1950s, but her suggestion was always rebuffed because it was considered too great a burden on what was, at best, a politically controversial measure. The heightened possibility of passage in 1964 prompted her to try a more indirect route. In what was surely the most Machiavellian gesture of her long career, Paul urged two NWP members from Virginia to contact Representative Howard Smith, chair of the House Committee on Rules, which was preparing to consider the most comprehensive civil rights bill in the history of the nation for clearance to the floor. This bill would prohibit segregation in stores, restaurants, theaters, and hotels; bar discrimination in employment; and increase the power of the government to file suits on behalf of school integration. Representative Smith, one of the South's most influential conservatives, was a longtime friend of the National Woman's Party and Alice Paul. Indeed, he had sponsored the ERA in Congress since 1945, and two of Alice Paul's lieutenants, Butler Franklin and Nina Horton Avery, both from Virginia, had worked with Smith in the past. Neither had much sympathy for civil rights, and they suspected that Smith would welcome the opportunity to subject the civil rights bill to ridicule by adding "sex" to the section of the bill prohibiting discrimination in employment. And then, who knew, it might just pass. As Butler Franklin wrote to Smith on December 10, 1963, "This single word 'sex' would divert some of the high pressure which is being used to force this Bill through without proper attention to all the effects of it." Five days later Nina Horton wrote a similar letter.

Commentators have debated ever since about why Smith rose on February 8, 1964, and moved to amend Title VII of the civil rights bill, the title that barred discrimination in employment, to include sex. His motives seem to have been mixed. On the one hand, Smith found his back to the wall and may have seen in the "sex" amendment an opportunity to take a swipe at the civil rights bill and possibly defeat it. That was the reading of Esther Peterson and other Democratic liberals, who rose as one to rally opposition to the amendment, fearing not only the threat to the underlying legislation but also the possible loss of protective legislation for women. On the other hand, as a chivalrous Southern gentleman, Smith also believed that it was only fair that women, specifically white women, be granted the same legal protections that the government was about to extend to black men.

The bill did pass, in part because Democratic representative Martha Griffiths of Michigan, a member of the NWP, who was prepared to add sex to Title VII if Smith did not, fought so successfully for it as amended. The final vote on the amendment was 168 to 133, a vote in which, ironically, most of the support came from Southerners and Republicans. Once the bill had passed the House Peterson and the Administration dropped their opposition to the "sex" amendment, not wanting to risk a joint committee that would have to resolve any differences between the versions passed by each chamber. In addition, Pauli Murray circulated a memo maintaining that the omission of "sex" would weaken the civil rights bill by once again dividing the interests of oppressed groups in the society and by neglecting the problems of black women. The bill passed and Johnson signed it on July 2, 1964.

Despite the addition of "sex" to Title VII, all hope of its improving economic rights for women were dashed at the outset by the very agency set up to administer it. Title VII established the Equal Employment Opportunity Commission (EEOC), an independent agency, to enforce the provisions of the civil rights bill. Herman Edelsberg, the first head of the EEOC, publicly refused to enforce the sex provision of Title VII. The provision was a "fluke," he declared, "conceived out of wedlock," and he would play no part in denying "female secretaries" to men. Edelsberg's public position prompted Martha Griffiths to blast the agency in a June 20, 1966, speech on the House floor. She declared that the EEOC had "started out by casting disrespect and ridicule on the law" and that their "wholly negative attitude had changed—for the worse."

Not everyone within the EEOC was opposed to the sex provision. There was a "pro-woman" faction, but they could do nothing without a greater show of support from women themselves, perhaps through "some sort of NAACP for women," as one official suggested, to put pressure on the government. As government employees they could not organize such a group, nor could members of the "feminist underground," with whom they were in contact. Catherine East, for one, was sure she would be either fired or reassigned if anyone in the Labor Department heard she was plotting such a thing. Only someone outside the government could do it, someone independent, someone with national visibility. "You, Betty, have got to do it," Catherine East told Betty Friedan, who had come to Washington to do research on a new book on patterns in women's lives.

The occasion to take such action came on June 30, 1966, on the last day of the Third National Conference of Commissions on the Status of Women. The preceding evening Betty Friedan, attending the conference as a journalist, had met with about two dozen women, including Pauli Murray, some members of the Washington underground, and representatives of state commissions around the country. They gathered in Friedan's hotel room to discuss the possibility of a civil rights organization for women, but decided that they should give the government one more chance. They formulated a resolution instead, urging the EEOC to treat sex discrimination as seriously as race discrimination. To their immense distress, leaders of the conference refused even to consider their resolution the following day. Meeting again over lunch they decided that the time for conferences was over. On a paper napkin, Friedan scribbled ". . . to take the actions needed to bring women into the mainstream of American society, now, full equality for women, in fully equal partnership with men, NOW. The National Organization for Women."

By the time NOW held its organizing conference in October 1966, three hundred men and women had declared themselves charter members. Among them was a representative of the United Auto Workers Women's Committee, but most came from state commissions on the status of women and the professions. Electing Betty Friedan as their first president, they then set forth their Statement of Purpose. Clearly inspired by the civil rights movement the document deplored "tokenism" and called for "a fully equal partnership of the sexes, as part of the worldwide revolution of human rights." In addition to combating occupational segregation, pay disparities, and discrimination in education and the professions, NOW demanded a national system of child care, a new "concept of marriage," which would include "an equitable sharing of the responsibilities of home and children," and an end to all policies and practices, which, "in the guise of protectiveness, not only deny opportunities but also foster in women self-denigration, dependence, and evasion of responsibility, undermine their confidence in their own abilities and foster contempt for women." Denying that men were enemies of women, the NOW statement stressed that men, too, were "victims of the current system of half-equality between the sexes," and that freedom for women would benefit society as a whole.

Through a skilled use of the media, NOW made itself appear bigger than it really was. Lawyers in NOW began developing litigation strategies to win more rights for women. Academics embarked on research that eventually created new subfields in the study of women throughout academia. Business leaders began to talk about ways of opening up opportunities to women in business. Journalists wrote hundreds of stories on women's lives.

NOW officials believed that the best way to achieve immediate results was not through legislative lobbying but by bringing direct pressure on the executive branch. In 1965 Johnson had set up the Office of Contract Compliance, with orders to ensure that those doing business with the government not only refrained from discriminating against workers on the basis of race, religion, or national origins but also undertook affirmative-action programs to correct the effects of past discrimination. Federal contracts affected one-third of the American labor force, and the new affirmative-action plans promised the possibility of greatly expanding opportunities for minority workers. NOW persuaded Johnson to amend his order in 1967, through Executive Order 11375, to include "sex" as an impermissible ground for discrimination and a justification for affirmative action.

NOW's second effort at administrative arm-twisting took

place at a meeting in the office of EEOC executive director Herman Edelsberg between NOW representatives and EEOC administrators. There Betty Friedan excoriated the assembled officials for having so few women in responsible positions at the EEOC. "Why, I'm interviewing girls right now for an opening as Assistant General Counsel," one of the commissioners responded. "I hope, Commissioner," retorted Friedan hotly, "that you're not interviewing girls for such an important job." Her colleagues from NOW laughed. "Did I say something wrong?" the commissioner asked. Friedan informed him that since the lawyers applying for such a job would surely be over twenty-five, calling them girls would be like calling a forty-five-year-old black man a boy.

"That was the first time, in public," Friedan later recalled, "a government official got a lesson in sexist language. He tried 'ladies'—and we wrinkled our noses—and he began to sweat. 'What do you want to be called?' 'Women,' we said."

No more would professional women settle for being demeaned as "girls." Nor would they accept the honorific "ladies" and thereby be relegated to some symbolic pedestal. They wanted full and equal partnership with men, and they wanted it without further delay. In creating a new women's movement NOW led the assault on discrimination against women in American society. Within a year, that assault had expanded to include two new demands: the Equal Rights Amendment and the decriminalization of abortion. These demands represented a stunning historical reversal. Only a few short years before supporters of the ERA had been predominantly elderly, elite, conservative; now the country's leading liberals were endorsing it. Not that the shift took place without controversy. Labor leaders, still worried about the impact of protective labor legislation, left now, as did women opposed to abortion. The issue of abortion also troubled those members of NOW who wanted to focus on legal and economic issues, and they finally left to form the Women's Equity Action League. But to growing numbers of women, equal rights could only be assured if control over fertility could be guaranteed. By the end of 1967 NOW's membership had topped one thousand members.

NOW stood for the right of each woman to rise as high as

she could in a competitive, free-market economy, unconstrained by legal barrier or biological accident. Within a year, however, the new feminist vanguard found itself challenged by a younger wave of dissident women. Less genteel even than Betty Friedan, they called not just for full equality for women but for social revolution.

The Personal Becomes Political

On the afternoon of September 7, 1968, a startling sight flashed across the television screens of millions of viewers tuned into the annual Miss America Pageant in Atlantic City, New Jersey. Roughly one hundred women, mostly young, dressed variously in jeans and miniskirts, with hair flying in the ocean breeze, were marching up and down the boardwalk singing and chanting: "*Atlantic City is a town with class. They raise your morals and they judge your ass!*" Some of the women were waving their arms, others were carrying placards that read "No More Beauty Standards—Everyone Is Beautiful," and "Welcome to the Miss America Cattle Auction."

Suddenly the marchers began tossing objects into a large container marked Freedom Trash Can. Television viewers could not make out exactly what was happening, but press reporters standing close by had a clear view. The women were jettisoning dishcloths, girdles, false eyelashes, curlers, high-heeled shoes, copies of *Playboy, Vogue, Cosmopolitan*, and the *Ladies' Home Journal*, and bras. "Instruments of torture," one marcher explained, symbols of the American woman's subject status. The women had hoped to burn it all, but the city, fearing another fire on its flammable boardwalk, had barred them from doing so.

Robin Morgan, a former child actress best known for her role as Dagmar in CBS's hit show *I Remember Mama*, coordinated the activities of women converging from Boston, Detroit, New York, Washington, D.C., Florida, and New Jersey. They were drawn by a flier calling them to protest the "degrading, mindless, Boobie-girl symbol" that Miss America represented. "Women in our society [are] forced daily to compete for male approval," the flier declared, "enslaved by ludicrous 'beauty' standards we ourselves are conditioned to take seriously." Though a veteran of political protests, neither Morgan nor any of her women friends had ever had the chance to organize one. The men had always taken charge of that; the "chicks" were expected "to volunteer for cooking duty." Sleeping only three hours a night for days, Morgan argued with the company that chartered the buses, persuaded the mayor of Atlantic City to grant a permit, notified the press that protestors would speak only to women reporters, and helped letter signs. It all made her feel "well, *grown up.*"

"We were doing this one for ourselves, not for our men," Morgan later wrote, "and we were consequently getting to do those things the men never let us do. . . . We fought a lot and laughed a lot and felt very extremely nervous."

From behind the police barricades, set up on each side of the boardwalk, hundreds of hecklers taunted the marchers: "If you got married, you wouldn't have time for all this," one yelled. The marchers were called Lesbians, and "screwy, frustrated women." But the women marched on, shouting their scorn for the contest taking place in the convention hall behind them, and singing songs that ridiculed not only the pageant but the contestants themselves: "*Ain't she sweet? / Makin' profit off her meat. / Beauty sells, she's told / So she's out pluggin' it. / Ain't she sweet?*"

For the afternoon finale, they led a live sheep, with a bow strapped to its tail, out onto the boardwalk. Inspired by the Yippies, who had nominated a pig for President the week before at the Democratic Convention in Chicago, the protestors draped the sheep with a banner and crowned *it* Miss America.

That night, at the official pageant, a few of the protestors managed to smuggle in a great, white bed sheet, emblazoned with the words WOMEN'S LIBERATION. As the outgoing Miss America read her farewell speech, these women unfurled the banner from the balcony and shouted, "Freedom for women! No more Miss America!" Police quickly hauled them off to jail, followed by black civil rights lawyer Flo Kennedy, who had been standing by all day in case of trouble. "It was," she would write, "the best fun I can imagine anyone wanting to have on any single day of her life."

That day had been years in the making. During the early 1960s, while professional women in their forties and fifties like Esther Peterson, Martha Griffiths, and Betty Friedan were bringing pressure on the government to grant women equal opportunity in American economic and political life, a group of younger women, mostly in their twenties, committed themselves to the civil rights movement, the student movement, and a variety of other New Left causes. As a group they were well-off, well educated, mostly white. Some were writers and academics. Others worked in the female clerical- and service-sector ghetto. Religion often played an important part in their lives, nurturing in them faith that people of goodwill could make a better world. A few were "red-diaper babies," whose parents had been driven from their jobs during the height of McCarthyite hysteria. Many more came from liberal homes in which McCarthy was quietly condemned as a threat to American democratic principles. Unlike older activists, who had come to maturity during the Depression and war, these young women had grown up in an era of unprecedented affluence, many of them in the spreading suburbs where mothers like Betty Friedan had hoped to make them feel secure and happy. But by the time Friedan declared the suburban home to be a trap, preventing women from full participation in the business and political world, these younger women were beginning to question not just the trap but the world to which Friedan wanted entry.

They were, even among their peers, a minority, alienated from the sorority and fraternity life on America's expanding campuses, disheartened by the lack of intellectual community around them, offended by the crass materialism abundance had produced. They debated intellectual issues, listened to folk music, and grew restive under the Victorian restrictions that continued to govern campus social life. Everywhere they looked, reality made a mockery of American ideals. The civil rights movement dramatized the stark contrast between America's formal commitment to equality and the reality of American racism. The spreading poverty in the ghettoes that surrounded universities in cities like Chicago and New York cast doubt on the scope of America's vaunted abundance. The increasing facelessness of modern bureaucratic life put the lie to the American tradition of individual autonomy. The Cold War, and especially the escalating war in Vietnam, brought home to them the discrepancy between America's espousal of democracy and the reality of an increasingly centralized federal power imposing its will on others.

Students for a Democratic Society (SDS), formed in 1960, embodied these new perceptions. Formed as the youth group of the League for Industrial Democracy (LID), an Old Left group whose politics were social-democratic and anti-Communist, SDS fashioned what it called New Left politics. Its manifesto, the Port Huron Statement, drafted in 1962 by Tom Hayden, lamented the decline of American political traditions and called for "participatory democracy." SDS envisioned a society in which stifling bureaucratic structures would be replaced by new institutions that would allow "the individual [to] share in those social decisions determining the quality and direction of his life." Small-scale institutions would give an outlet to "feelings of helplessness and indifference, so that people may see the political, social, and economic sources of their private troubles and organize to change society." While the Old Left focused on "class-based economic oppression," SDS stressed "how late capitalist society creates mechanisms of psychological and cultural domination over everyone."

Though no one appreciated it at the time, SDS helped lay the foundation for the resurgence of feminism by expanding political discussion to include the subject of personal relations. If personal problems could be understood as part of larger systems of power relations, then marriage, the family, even sexuality could be seen as legitimate topics of political analysis. The Old Left had always maintained a formal opposition to "male supremacy," but since members were expected to set aside personal needs in order to work for a new economic order, women rarely succeeded in resolving "private" grievances against men. The New Left, however, opened the door for a large-scale reconsideration of personal relations by legitimizing its members' right to seek personal fulfillment through the movement. During the early 1960s, however, racism, not problems between the sexes, seemed to most young people, both in and outside SDS, the country's most pressing social issue.

In the North thousands of students picketed chain stores whose Southern branches refused to serve blacks, while in the South hundreds more answered the call of Ella Baker to help the Student Nonviolent Coordinating Committee to desegregate the South and set up voter-registration projects. Women, in particular, felt drawn to SNCC's statement of purpose: "Through nonviolence . . . the redemptive community supersedes systems of gross social immorality." At first the women (blacks and whites) were mostly from the South, but by the summer of 1964, growing numbers of college students from the North and West had joined SNCC. Following Ella Baker's precept that strong people don't need strong leaders, SNCC tried to ensure "participatory democracy," in which the "people" would decide their fate, all voices would be heard, and meetings would be run by consensus, not by the will of an elite.

Within SNCC young women achieved positions of importance, leading demonstrations against segregation and organizing voter-registration projects. Ruby Doris Smith Robinson, SNCC's black executive secretary, was one of the most revered figures in the entire organization. According to one SNCC volunteer, she was "the nearest thing I ever met to a free person. I mean really free, free in the sense that be you black or white, you could not commit a great indignity or injustice about Ruby and have it go undealt with. . . . Ruby just stood up to anybody. . . . As a result, she made you stand taller." The widely publicized successes of the black struggle inspired other groups to take action.

Chicana farm workers like Jesse Lopez De la Cruz had labored for decades as migrant laborers in the grape, apricot, beet, and cotton fields of the Southwest and West. Though they shared the fieldwork with the men in the family, they still lived under the patriarchal authority of their husbands and fathers. The growing power of women in American society, together with the civil rights protests of the 1960s, proved infectious. When De la Cruz joined the staff of the United Farm Workers in 1967, she viewed her chief responsibility as that of bringing women into the union and bettering their lives. "It's way past time when our husbands could say, 'You stay home! You have to take care of the children! You have to do as I say!' "

The sense of democracy and community that informed these protests, however, proved difficult to sustain. That sense began to disintegrate in SNCC as early as the summer of 1964. Part of the reason was sexual. In the intimacy and fear of the Mississippi freedom houses, black men and white women began sleeping with each other, testing the limits of racism, but also generating massive resentment on the part of black women, who felt denigrated by their black coworkers' choice of sex partner. At the same time, this interracial sex fostered anxiety among the white women, who began to feel that they were being used as symbols of men's sexual prowess. Added to this undercurrent of sexual tension was the constant danger under which the civil rights workers labored, and the growing resentment felt by Southern blacks, who had founded SNCC, toward the whites who had come to help them. Most of the whites were comfortable and secure Northern students who got most of the publicity that summer, while suffering the least danger. These tensions undermined the commitment to participatory democracy and led to a level of masculine posturing that offended many women (black and white). The women saw massive hypocrisy in men's espousal of democratic ideals, given their discriminatory treatment of women volunteers. Women were expected to do the housework and were shielded from the more dangerous work assignments, while the men took an increasingly assertive role in the organization.

At the end of the summer two white women, Mary King and Casey Hayden, wrote an anonymous paper on the subordination of women within SNCC, and tucked it in among the dozens of "position papers" assembled for a SNCC staff retreat in November 1964 held in Waveland, Mississippi, on the Gulf of Mexico. A woman in SNCC, they wrote, "is often in the same position as that token Negro hired in a corporation. The management thinks it has done its bit. Yet, every day the Negro bears an atmosphere, attitudes and actions which are tinged with condescension and paternalism. . . ." They went on to say that SNCC men's relegation of women to clerical work, their insistence on calling them "girls," "their assumption of male superiority," was "as widespread and deep rooted and every much as crippling to the women as the assumptions of white

supremacy are to the Negro." The paper prompted little response when it came up for discussion, apart from some spec-
ulation on its authorship (most believed that Ruby Doris Smith
Robinson had written it). Later that day, however, after hours
of acrimonious discussions on a wide range of issues, especially
on the role of whites in the movement, the woman issue came
up once more. As the staff relaxed and traded barbs on the
dock at Waveland, each trying to outdo the other in outra-
geousness, black leader Stokely Carmichael easily took first
prize. Recalling the sexual gymnastics of the summer past, he
declared, "The only position for women in SNCC is prone."
Carmichael's aphorism became a kind of in-joke among civil
rights workers, summing up the sexual dynamics of "freedom
summer," but for the white women, who were feeling increasingly unwelcome, it came gradually to stand for the chauvinistic
attitude of many men in the movement.

King and Hayden left SNCC the following year and turned,
instead, to the Students for a Democratic Society, where they
joined in organizing community projects in inner-city ghettoes,
laying the basis for the welfare rights movement led by black
women in the next decade. But as the war in Vietnam redirected
attention to American militarism, women encountered the same
kind of conflict they had experienced in SNCC between male
idealization of participatory democracy and the reality of male
aggrandizement. Ruefully, some women came to realize that
the New Left had turned its back on more than the centralized
political control accepted by the Old Left; it had abandoned as
well the Old Left's opposition (in rhetoric if not always in reality)
to "male supremacy." When SDS women objected to their
treatment, only those with ties to the Old Left took them seriously. As the war heated up, competition pushed out community in SDS. Women long active in the organization found
themselves relegated to that precursor of the photocopier, the
mimeograph machine, while the men did all the speaking. The
women protested, calling men to account for their hypocrisy in
treating women no better than American society treated blacks
and Asians, but they met only ridicule. Women gained valuable
political experience in the male-led political movements of
which they were a part. But the time came when they could

grow no further within the constraints that those movements imposed on their female members. In 1967 the SDS publication *New Left Notes* featured a cartoon of a girl, with earrings, polka-dot minidress, and matching panties, holding the sign "We Want Our Rights and We Want Them Now." As activist Sara Evans later commented, "SDS had blown its last chance."

Outraged women started setting up small groups of their own, first in Chicago, then in New York, Washington, D.C., and Boston, and from there across the country. They declared that the time had come for them to fight their own oppression as women, to work for what they began to call women's liberation—the freeing of women from all the restrictions that cramped their lives, politically, socially, economically, and psychologically.

Of those who joined, few came from minority groups. Pauli Murray had long insisted that race and gender oppression in America were two sides of the same coin, but others were beginning to doubt that she was right. By 1967 the civil rights movement's turn toward Black Power was putting black women in the awkward position of having to choose between race and gender. On the one hand, they found themselves attacked by Black Power advocates for robbing black men of their "manhood." On the other hand, they found white women's blanket claims of female oppression to be insensitive to racial realities. Though black women's long-standing concern for legal rights made them even more likely than whites to support the ERA, when it came time to decide where to focus their energies, most black women chose civil rights over the women's movement. As one young woman told Betty Friedan in 1966, the important thing for black women was "for black men to get ahead." In view of that priority, she declared, "We don't want anything to do with the feminist bag." Many other minority women shared that view. Apart from a few leaders like Pauli Murray, who stayed with NOW, and Jesse Lopez De la Cruz, who served on the California commission on the status of women, most minority women felt uncomfortable with feminist demands. The needs of their families and community seemed more important than the individualistic aspirations of most feminists.

Even within feminist ranks, many women were reluctant to

break away from the protest movements in which they had long been active. Many of the white women who helped form the proliferating women's liberation groups called themselves politicos and continued working within the New Left. To them, women's liberation had to be part of a larger human liberation, and women had to work within the New Left to force men to be true to their own egalitarian, communitarian ideals. Men's oppression of women, they believed, derived from men's privileged position in an economic order based on private property and class oppression. Once that privilege disappeared, so, too, would men's subjugation of women.

To a growing number of others, however, patriarchy, not private property or class, posed the primary problem. Calling themselves radical feminists (to distinguish themselves both from the old suffragists and those older contemporaries content with mere legal reform), they argued that all oppression, be it racial, class, or religious, derived from the template of men's subjugation of women. Only with the overthrow of patriarchy could other forms of inequality be combated.

Disagreements over their relationship to the New Left influenced debates over proper tactics. Politicos favored action; radical feminists wanted to talk. They called it consciousness-raising, a discussion format modeled on early SNCC meetings but never before so successfully employed. By sharing personal experiences, a group would learn to regard personal problems as common problems with social causes and political solutions. *Newsweek* researcher Susan Brownmiller, a Cornell graduate who had gone to Mississippi in 1964 only to return because of the growing furor over Black Power, first learned of consciousness-raising from a friend, who told her there were "rap sessions" on women going on at the New York office of the Southern Conference Educational Fund. "It was absolutely amazing," she would remember. "They were talking about things that we had never dared say out loud." There, and increasingly across the country, small groups of women were asking themselves questions like "Have you ever felt that men have pressured you into sexual relationships?" and "Do you ever feel invisible?" In consciousness-raising, Brownmiller wrote, "A woman's experience at the hands of men was analyzed as a *political* phenomenon." Sexual relations were simply another form of power relations, and therefore rape, according to Brownmiller, was not an isolated crime but an extreme example of men's efforts to dominate women.

The meaning of sexual relations was the subject of continuing debate by the late 1960s. Not since the 1920s had attitudes toward sex been in such flux. In 1969, a Gallup poll reported that 74 percent of all women believed that premarital sex was wrong; four years later only 53 percent still held that view. The Pill, which became widely available in the mid-1960s, gave women unprecedented control over their bodies. And the youth movement of the 1960s brought with it a revolt against the sexual proscriptions of the older generation. Within a few years parietal rules, which set curfews for female (but not for male) students, were wiped from the books; rules against women's wearing slacks were abolished; and women began living with men without benefit of marriage. Helen Gurley Brown, publisher of *Cosmopolitan*, instructed her young female readers on how to "have it all"—a job, glamour, romance, sex. The allure of suburban domesticity weakened dramatically. The change was in many ways liberating. But it also led to exploitation. As *Ms.* magazine put it in 1972 (in words reminiscent of Charlotte Perkins Gilman), "The sexual revolution and Women's Movement are at polar opposites. Women have been liberated from the right to say 'no.' "

Consciousness-raising groups soon spread throughout the country. As women talked about their personal experiences they began to see a pattern they began calling "sexism," which operated in much the same way that racism did in restricting the lives of blacks. Robin Morgan summed up the importance of consciousness-raising in coming to this new understanding: "You begin to see how all-pervasive a thing is sexism—the definition of and discrimination against half the human species by the other half."

Beginning in 1968 a flurry and then a flood of articles and books began appearing that explored the meaning and workings of sexism. The most famous was Kate Millett's *Sexual Politics*, published in 1970. Born in 1934, Millett grew up in St. Paul, Minnesota, the daughter of a Catholic family. Her father was an alcoholic who abandoned his wife and children, consigning them to a life of genteel poverty. Despite hardship at home, Millett excelled at parochial school and attended the University of Minnesota. After graduation a wealthy aunt sent her to study at Oxford University, a gesture that had less to do with the aunt's respect for Kate's intellectual gifts than with the family's discovery that Kate was in love with another woman. In the years that followed, Millett married Japanese artist Fumio Yoshimura, lived in New York in the Bowery, worked in the civil rights and peace movements, joined NOW, and taught English at Barnard College.

In *Sexual Politics* Millett argued that sexism permeated society. It was not simply a function of misguided public policy, as NOW often seemed to be suggesting, but rather part of a patriarchal system that affected every aspect of social relations. Sexism was institutionalized in the family, the schools, the church, the economy, the government, and the legal system. It ensured that men and women would develop different personalities and play different social roles. "Male and female are really two cultures, and their life experiences are utterly different," Millett wrote. Sexism guaranteed that men would rule and that women would remain subordinate. Women would depend on men, define themselves in relation to men, and develop contempt both for themselves and for other women as well. The elimination of sexism, like the elimination of racism, therefore called for a drastic transformation. It meant changing values and attitudes, behavior and institutions. Seeing women's personal relations with men as, at root, political, young feminists like Kate Millett dismissed the legislative lobbying of NOW as unequal to the task of dismantling the patriarchal order. Only a social revolution that brought about true democracy and the abolition of sex roles could hope to liberate all women. Not since Emma Goldman had feminists called for such far-reaching change.

At its founding and for several years thereafter, NOW gave little sign of endorsing the radical worldview. Betty Friedan dismissed consciousness-raising as just so much "navel gazing," while younger women, according to Susan Brownmiller, viewed Friedan as "hopelessly bourgeois." Brownmiller later recalled that when she tried to join NOW in 1966, she was rebuffed with the explanation that the group was to be "a lobbying committee of no more than 100 women." How much change could a lobbying committee be expected to produce, the young radicals wanted to know. According to Chicago activist Jo Freeman, "Women's liberation does not mean equality with men," for "equality in an unjust society is meaningless."

However "bourgeois" its founding intentions, NOW began moving to the left, as hundreds of younger, more radical women joined its ranks. It all started with Betty Friedan's introduction of Ti-Grace Atkinson to the New York chapter of NOW. Atkinson came from an upper-class Republican family in Louisiana. Married at seventeen in 1957, she received a degree in fine arts in 1961 from the University of Pennsylvania and a divorce the same year. In the mid-sixties she moved to New York, enrolled in Columbia's program in political philosophy, and, inspired by Simone de Beauvoir's *The Second Sex*, joined NOW in 1967. Betty Friedan pushed her into NOW's leadership, because, as she later commented, "Atkinson's Main Line accent and ladylike blond good looks would be perfect . . . for raising money from those mythical rich old widows we never did unearth." In December of 1967 Atkinson was elected president of New York NOW, a chapter with 30 percent of the organization's total membership.

Still a registered Republican when she joined NOW, Atkinson quickly turned into a radical feminist and began attracting a younger contingent to the staid organization. By early 1968 she was calling publicly for the abolition of the family and the communal raising of children. In June, she rushed to the defense of counterculture actress, feminist, and writer Valerie Solanis, who had just shot Andy Warhol, the director of a film in which she had appeared. The reason for the shooting, Solanis claimed, was that Warhol had stolen her ideas. Besides her work as an actress, Solanis was also the author of a twenty-one-page feminist tract entitled "The SCUM [Society for Cutting Up Men] Manifesto," in which she called on women to "overthrow . . . the government" and "destroy the male sex." To Atkinson, Solanis embodied the new feminist revolutionary spirit. To Betty Friedan's alarm and in the face of her vigorous opposition,

Atkinson turned the Solanis case into a major NOW cause. Then in October she proposed that NOW eliminate all leadership positions. When the NOW membership rejected her proposal on October 17, she walked out, joined by Flo Kennedy and Kate Millett (who would later return). Together they formed the October 17 Movement, which soon became, simply, The Feminists.

The Feminists regarded themselves as the radical vanguard, but they were not alone. In 1969 radical feminist groups proliferated. The Redstockings, WITCH, Cell 16, and Boston's Bread and Roses led the way. By the end of the year there were thirty-five groups in the San Francisco Bay Area, thirty in Chicago, twenty-five in Boston, fifty in New York. Radical feminists disagreed on how best to bring about change. Robin Morgan believed that change had to start with women themselves— women like the Miss America contestants who allowed a patriarchal society to use them. Others like Shulamith Firestone, author of *The Dialectics of Sex* (1970) and a founder of the "pro-woman" Redstockings, insisted that the enemy was not the contestants but men. Only when men stopped oppressing women could women feel free not to pander to their desires. Whatever their approach, however, all radical feminists agreed that nothing short of a social revolution would liberate all women.

Some groups continued to concentrate on consciousness-raising, using it as a recruitment device as well as a resocializing tactic. But most began moving on to some form of action, such as organizing a women's health collective or day-care center, forming an abortion counseling center or publishing a newsletter. Group projects reflected the range of topics that had contributed to consciousness-raising—from sexual relationships and reproduction to child care and housework. "[Men] recognize the essential fact of housework right from the beginning," wrote Pat Mainardi in one famous position paper, "which is that it stinks." Robin Morgan asserted her flair for the dramatic with the Miss America Pageant protest and the formation of WITCH (Women's International Terrorist Group from Hell). Descending on Wall Street in the fall of 1968 to pronounce an incantation, WITCH members watched in jubilation as the stock market dropped five points.

NOW quickly caught the confrontation spirit. Betty Friedan led a sit-in at the all-male Oak Room Bar at the Plaza Hotel on February 12, 1969. That same year, NOW joined the Redstockings in sponsoring speak-outs on abortion. Abortion reform was not, in its early stages, a feminist issue. It had begun in the early sixties as an effort by doctors and lawyers who wanted to allow abortions for specific reasons. Such reasons might include the danger of a severely deformed fetus or the threat to a woman's mental or physical health. Through their efforts twelve states had adopted some form of abortion-law reform by the end of the decade. But when feminists took up the abortion issue in the late sixties, they demanded that laws recognize abortion as a basic woman's right. Abortion speak-outs dramatized the importance of this right in the lives of a wide array of women.

At one 1969 speak-out, held at Judson Memorial Church in Greenwich Village, Friedan asked Barbara Seaman to come along. Seaman, the wife of a psychiatrist, mother of three, and coauthor with her husband of a woman's column, was not yet ready to call herself a feminist, but she believed in the importance of abortion reform. Friedan suggested that she represent the women's magazines and give some statistics on abortion. But at the church, before the meeting started, Seaman fell to talking with a black woman from the Harlem Consumers Council about abortions they each had had. Hers, undergone while a student at Oberlin, had been paid for by her educated young lover and, though emotionally traumatic, had been safe. The experience of the black woman had been life-threatening. Overhearing their conversation, Friedan urged them to set aside their statistical reports and describe their own experiences. Though Seaman had never told another soul of her abortion, and had not again seen her young lover, she soon found herself telling the thirty to forty women who made up the audience the details of her experience, about how she had learned the name of a doctor from a friend, how her lover raised the extraordinary sum of $500, how she had lain on the couch at home later and told her mother she was having menstrual cramps. Seaman was aware that there were cameras in the room, but she was nonetheless stunned when she saw herself on the television screen later that night. The news media, which had ignored the abortion-reform campaign, found the very private revelations of a well-to-do psychiatrist's wife highly newsworthy.

Suddenly, the unspeakable became the center of public debate. Both Redstockings and NOW members testified before New York state legislative committees considering reform of state abortion laws. Women who had thought that their experiences had been unique found many others who had shared them. The state of New York made abortion available, essentially on demand, in 1970 (following Hawaii and Alaska). California quickly followed.

Agreement on the abortion issue did much to enable the women's movement to maintain a fragile unity. Betty Friedan decided to celebrate that unity on August 26, 1970, the fiftieth anniversary of the winning of women's suffrage, with a massive women's strike. "Don't Iron While the Strike Is Hot" read one of the placards that swayed above the heads of the thousands of women and men who marched down Fifth Avenue in homage to those who had marched decades earlier for the right to vote. In Boston ministers turned their pulpits over to women. In Chicago women demonstrated against the "male chauvinism" of *Playboy*. In San Francisco, Baltimore, and Miami women marched, broke teacups, and, in a few cases, dropped their kids on their bosses' laps. Regrettably, this grand unity was not to last. Within a few months the women's movement foundered over the issue of sexual preference.

In 1955 a small group of lesbians in San Francisco had formed the Daughters of Bilitis, named for a Greek lesbian poet, to work with other homosexual organizations to advocate homosexual rights. But the homosexual rights movement remained a small, professionally dominated group until June 27, 1969, when a police raid of the gay bar at the Stonewall Inn in Greenwich Village turned into a riot in which gay men and lesbians lashed back at their tormentors. The Stonewall riots led directly to the formation of the Gay Liberation Movement, which united gays and lesbians in common protest against the homophobia that pervaded American society. Despite their shared oppression, however, lesbians often found working with gay men difficult, and by the end of 1969 many were turning to radical feminism. One group, the Radicalesbians, proclaimed that women's liberation would only be complete when women identified with one another. "It is the primacy of women's relations to women," wrote one Radicalesbian, "which is at the heart of women's liberation and the basis of cultural revolution." The implication was that the only true feminist was a lesbian. If the personal was political, then the most personal act (sex) was also a political act. Women who slept with men were therefore consorting with the enemy. The logical conclusion of this idea was that in order not to betray women and the feminist movement, women must give their full love and commitment to women and become lesbian feminists.

According to William Masters and Virginia Johnson's *Human Sexual Response* (1966), women wouldn't be sacrificing any sexual enjoyment from choosing women rather than men as sexual partners. In contrast to Freud, who had argued that the female orgasm took place within the vagina, Masters and Johnson's clinical studies confirmed what lesbians had long known, that the orgasm took place in the clitoris. Women didn't need men to be satisfied sexually.

Most lesbian feminists adhered to the radical view that sex roles are the arbitrary product of social forces and should be abolished. Men and women are essentially the same, stripped of their sex roles. Some lesbians, however, were shifting toward a position that would soon be called "cultural nationalism" or "essentialism." In their view, biology was indeed destiny. Women, because they knew their own bodies, made better lovers of other women than did men. They were inherently more nurturing and less aggressive.

The lesbian issue split the feminist movement wide open in December 1970, when Kate Millett, suddenly famous for her book *Sexual Politics*, was asked at a public lecture at Columbia University whether she was a lesbian. Millett had never discussed her sexual preference openly. She was, indeed, living with her husband, Fumio Yoshimura, at the time. Unwilling to deny her sexual attraction to women, however, she responded that she was. Lesbianism suddenly became the major public issue in feminism. Betty Friedan, apoplectic at what she considered the radical lesbian threat to the future of the women's movement, wanted lesbians out of the movement. NOW could not survive, she fervently believed, if feminism was identified with lesbianism and what she deemed its inevitable corollary—a wholesale attack on men and the family. She labeled lesbians the "lavender menace." Many other feminists, in turn (heterosexual as well as homosexual), viewed Friedan as the menace—a bourgeois liberal who was willing to settle for minor meliorist legislative goals in the face of the enormity of sexism. Within days of Kate Millett's going public on the subject of her sexual preference, women in NOW, both lesbian and straight, were wearing lavender armbands in a defiant show of sisterhood and solidarity, sweeping disagreements under the rug for the time being. Friedan refused to join them, thereby ending her position of leadership within the movement. NOW never fully recovered from the tumult.

By the early 1970s schisms plagued the women's movement. Despite all of these battles, however, important similarities continued to unite liberals and radicals. Both factions were dominated by "achievement-oriented," middle-class, white, educated women. Both shared the common goal of combating a male power structure. Since 1966, moreover, NOW had been transformed by its growing membership and, accordingly, had enlarged its demands to suit its constituency much as suffragists had been forced to do early in the century as a new generation of suffragists became active in the women's movement. In 1966, the emphasis had been on legal equality, on winning women access to the male world. By 1970, even liberals were talking about sexism and the need to transform the male world. Indeed, despite splits like that between gays and straights, despite the proliferation of new groups, despite the fierce sectarian quarrels, despite the absence of any unified organization, policy, or headquarters, the women's movement continued to grow.

Feminism Comes of Age

By the early seventies the new women's movement in America had clearly come of age. A national newsletter in 1973 listed several thousand women's groups around the country working in various ways for change. In 1970 the Women's Equity Action League filed a complaint with the U.S. Department of Labor, demanding a review of all colleges and universities holding federal contracts to determine whether they were complying with antidiscrimination regulations. By the end of the year women's organizations and individual women had brought more than 160 institutions of higher education into court. The National Women's Political Caucus, started in 1971, concentrated on getting women elected to office. At an early meeting black activist Fanny Lou Hamer announced that she had suffered more discrimination as a woman than as a black. New York congresswoman Shirley Chisholm said the same. In 1972 five women, including Pat Schroeder, Elizabeth Holtzman, and Barbara Jordan, joined New York representatives Bella Abzug and Shirley Chisholm and Michigan veteran Martha Griffiths in Congress, and more women than ever ran for political office. In that one year women's representation in state legislatures jumped by 28 percent. Other organizations included Human Rights for Women (an abortion rights group), the Coalition of Labor Union Women, the National Black Feminist Organization, hundreds of professional associations and caucuses, and hundreds of radical collectives, which created research libraries, publishing groups, rape crisis and battered-women centers, and health clinics.

The impact of feminism was broadened further by the attention of the media. At first journalists reacted to the new movement with constant reports of its early demise, but by 1970 women reporters who were not merely feminists but radical feminists were beginning to write feature articles on the movement, and to draw inspiration from it to claim equality in their own work. Women at *Time* and *Newsweek*, restricted for years to jobs as researchers, filed suit against their employers in 1970. Susan Brownmiller led a sit-in at the editorial offices of *Ladies' Home Journal*, demanding an issue devoted to feminism. Most dramatic of all, a new magazine, dedicated to the movement, appeared: *Ms.*, edited by Gloria Steinem.

Steinem, born in 1934, was a relative latecomer to the movement. The stunningly beautiful daughter of a ne'er-do-well, show business entrepreneur father and a psychologically troubled mother, Steinem led a peripatetic childhood, settling down only at the age of twelve, after her parents divorced, in a rundown house in East Toledo, Ohio. There she cared for her disturbed mother, until rescued in her senior year of high school by an older sister in Washington, D.C.

Encouraged by her sister, Steinem applied to Smith College, from which she graduated in 1956 with honors and a graduate fellowship to India. Like Friedan many years before, Steinem had a boyfriend; unlike Friedan, she accepted the fellowship and said goodbye. She got as far as England, where she was reduced to working as a waitress and at other odd jobs in the long months that it took for her Indian visa to come through. Partway through the winter Steinem discovered she was pregnant. "I had no money. It was awful. I saw my whole life going, the total value in my life would be over." After much frantic searching, she found a doctor willing to perform an abortion: a wire inserted into her womb, an ancient technique, but performed under sterile conditions, with anesthesia. "Enormous relief" was all that she felt when it was all over, relief that she could continue her life.

Steinem continued on to India, and after a year she returned to New York to get started in journalism. She wrote for *Esquire, The New York Times*, a humor magazine called *Help!*, and a new magazine called *Show*. It was for *Show* that Steinem achieved fame, going "undercover" to work as a Playboy Bunny in 1963. Done up in bunny ears, a tight strapless costume with a white cotton tail, black stockings, and high heels, she spent nearly three weeks serving drinks. The piece she wrote was both amusing and revealing of the sordid conditions under which Bunnies worked. She did not think of herself as a feminist, but she felt slightly schizophrenic about her work; most of the assignments she had been getting (on textured stockings, Zsa Zsa Gabor's bed, lounging at the beach) did not interest her. In 1968, however, with the founding of *New York* magazine by her friend Clay Felker, Steinem's writing and her political interests began to coincide in a column in which she discussed and gave legitimacy to the political protests of the sixties, to the peace movement, migrant farm workers, and civil rights. Women's liberation was, of course, part of that protest, but Steinem thought feminism too narrow, and public demonstrations like the Miss America protest embarrassing. She wanted to be a "humanist" and an observer. Remaining detached proved difficult, though; the issues raised by women's liberation cut too close to her own life.

In 1970 she published a piece called "What It Would Be Like If Women Win" in an issue of *Time* magazine that featured Kate Millett on its cover. *Time* editors described Steinem as someone who "admits to being not only a critical observer but a concerned advocate of the feminist revolt." In a deft blending of radical prophecy and comforting reassurance, she made women's liberation sound problem-free. Yes, the movement would bring women greater power, homosexuals the right to marry, single women the right to refuse sex "arranged on the barter system"; but it would also bring an end to men's being "the only ones to support the family, get drafted, bear the strain of power and responsibility." Indeed, she concluded, "if Women's Lib wins, perhaps we all do." A media star, admired by women, alluring to men (though she never married), Gloria Steinem had the uncanny ability to make the most radical proposals seem overwhelmingly sensible.

The word *Ms.* had been circulating around the women's movement for some time. Someone had come across it in a 1930s secretarial handbook, listed as the proper form of address if one was unaware of a woman's marital status. Here was a word that would help eliminate sexual discrimination in language, the perfect name for a feminist magazine. *Ms.* began as a section in *New York* magazine in December 1971, and then in January it was published as a "one-shot." In eight days the issue's 250,000 copies had sold out. These first two issues included articles entitled "Welfare Is a Woman's Issue," "The Black Family and Feminism," "How to Write Your Marriage Contract," "Can Women Love Women?" and "Down With Sexist Upbringing." There was also a list of women who had undergone illegal abortions, which included Gloria Steinem, Susan Brownmiller, Barbara Tuchman, Nora Ephron, and Lillian Hellman. By 1973 *Ms.* had a subscription list of almost 200,000 and a long list of advertisers. For the first time feminists had a mass publication, one that carried the message of feminism far beyond the activists. Indeed, a 1973 poll revealed that almost three-quarters of *Ms.* readers were not members of feminist organizations.

The popularization of feminism quickly passed beyond publishing to the entertainment industry. Actress Marlo Thomas had been looking for a book for her three-year-old niece, something to replace *Sleeping Beauty*, with its message of passive damsels and savior princes. She later remembered being on a plane, campaigning for George McGovern during his ill-fated 1972 Presidential bid. "I was reading *Ms.* and Letty [Pogrebin] had done an article, something to do with what she called 'Stories for Free Children.' " Struck by the possibility of reaching kids, Thomas turned to friends in show business—Mel Brooks, Harry Belafonte, Dick Cavett, Carol Channing, and Diana Ross—and with their help she produced the record *Free to Be You and Me*, eighteen charming, consciousness-raising songs for kids—about girls who were athletic and boys who played with dolls. In an ultimate assault on gender and racial stereotyping, black football star Roosevelt Grier sang, with feeling, *"It's all right to cry. Crying gets the sad out of you."*

The pressure of feminist organizations and media coverage hastened the process of legal change that swept the country in the decade after passage of the Civil Rights Act of 1964. In October 1971 the House of Representatives passed the ERA with a vote of 354 to 23; the Senate approved it 84 to 8 in March 1972, and sent it to the states for ratification. In 1972 alone Congress banned sex discrimination in health-profession training; passed the Child Development Act (vetoed by Richard Nixon), which would have established a national system of day care; prohibited sex discrimination in all federally aided education programs; enabled working couples to claim income-tax deductions for child care; and broadened employment benefits for female government employees. Most of these bills, in addition to about twenty others on issues relevant to women, were sponsored by either Bella Abzug or Martha Griffiths. Their energy and success demonstrated the overwhelming importance of electing women to Congress. Legislative enactments brought important gains for women, but the most dramatic changes took place out of the limelight, through the judicial system and in the federal bureaucracy. A small group of dedicated women lawyers, trained in the civil-rights litigation strategy of the day, won decisive victories in the courts, while the so-called Washington women's underground proved a critical force in advancing the idea of affirmative action through federal agencies.

One of the questions left unanswered by the Civil Rights Act of 1964 was whether Title VII would nullify the protective labor laws that social reformers had fought so long to secure. The question was ultimately answered by the courts, as individual women brought challenges to state laws that barred them from good jobs. One of the first women to do so was Leah Rosenfeld, a married woman worker in Thermal, California, who sued the Southern Pacific Company in 1966 for denying her a job as an agent-telegrapher solely because of her sex. Southern Pacific invoked California's protective labor laws, which prohibited women from, among other things, working over ten hours a day (which telegraphers must do in peak seasons). This prohibition, the company concluded, prevented them from considering female applicants. But in *Rosenfeld* v. *Southern Pacific* (1968), the judges of the Ninth Circuit did not agree. Title VII, they held, overruled state protective laws that discriminated against women.

As of 1964, forty states and the District of Columbia had maximum-hours laws. By 1974 only Nevada had neither repealed nor severely restricted their applicability. Testimony in Congress on the probable impact of the ERA had, over the years, sought to reassure opponents that the courts would likely extend protective laws to men, rather than deny them to women, should equality ever be required. But to the surprise of many, that did not happen. Quietly, in the high-ceilinged chambers of the American judicial system, protective laws for women simply disappeared. A few commentators objected. Leo Kanowitz, an expert on women's legal issues, warned Congress in 1970 that this trend "not only removes limitations upon women's rights

to work extra hours . . . but also means that those women who
do not wish to . . . work excessive hours—and I would suggest
that they are many if not in the majority—can henceforth be
forced to do so." But hardly anyone was listening. Male workers
had lost interest in further reducing their hours of work after
World War II, and many depended on the right to work overtime to keep up with inflation. The professional women who
now dominated the women's movement worked hours as long
as any man's. And although more than four out of five employed
women told pollsters throughout the 1970s that they did not
want to work longer hours even if doing so brought more pay,
their views were ignored.

While attacks on protective legislation made their way
through the courts, disciples of Pauli Murray at the ACLU
Women's Rights Project in New York were constructing a legal
strategy to win equal rights for women under the Fourteenth
Amendment's equal-protection clause. The principal architect
of the Fourteenth Amendment strategy was a junior colleague
of Murray's on the ACLU—Ruth Bader Ginsburg. Ginsburg,
born in 1933, graduated from Cornell in 1954, and then like so
many of her peers she married and had a baby. Unlike most
young mothers, however, she did not settle into full-time motherhood. Instead, she became one of the first female students at
Harvard Law School, which began admitting women in 1951.
There she endured "Ladies' Day," the one day each year on
which professors deigned to call on women students, and exclusion from the library's periodicals room—the school's last
male preserve. This latter indignity proved more than irksome
the following year, when she became an editor of the *Harvard
Law Review*; without access to the periodicals room, she could
not fulfill her editorial responsibilities.

Ginsburg transferred to Columbia for her third year, when
her husband accepted a job in New York. She graduated in
1959, tied for first in her class. Unable to find a job with a law
firm, she settled for a clerkship with a federal district court judge
and then became a law professor at Rutgers Law School. When
she became pregnant again in 1965, she kept her pregnancy
secret for as long as possible. In 1955, before attending law
school, she had been denied a managerial position with the

Social Security Administration because she was three months pregnant. She did not want to lose another job. "It never entered my mind to think of claiming benefits for it," she later recalled. "I just didn't want to get thrown out."

In 1971 Ginsburg began building on Pauli Murray's victory in the Lowndes County, Alabama, jury discrimination case, *White* v. *Crook* (1966), to test the limits of the Fourteenth Amendment's equal-protection clause with respect to women. Since Alabama's lawyers had decided against appealing their case, the Supreme Court had not yet confronted the ACLU argument that sex should be treated like race under the Fourteenth Amendment, when Ginsburg brought them *Reed* v. *Reed* in 1971. Sally Reed was living in Ada County, Idaho, with her adopted son, Richard, when he died in 1967. She had been married when Richard was adopted, but had since separated from her husband. When Sally petitioned to be named administrator of her son's estate, however, the state denied her the right, granting it instead to her husband, who, as a man under Idaho law, had a superior claim. Sally took the case to the Supreme Court. And with Ruth Bader Ginsburg writing the brief and arguing the case, Sally Reed won. The Court found the law's preference for males over females in this matter "arbitrary" and thus unjustifiable.

The following year Ginsburg took another case to the Supreme Court. *Frontiero* v. *Richardson* concerned Lieutenant Sharron Frontiero of the United States Air Force, who was stationed in Montgomery, Alabama. Lt. Frontiero had sought an increased allowance for housing and additional health benefits to cover her husband. If Lt. Frontiero had been a married man, she would have won these added benefits automatically. But as a married woman, she could not claim them unless she could show that her spouse was actually dependent on her. The government's justification for this rule was that it was too expensive to investigate every male officer who claimed dependency benefits to see whether his wife was truly dependent. Most wives were. Married women officers, however, usually had husbands capable of supporting themselves. For them to claim benefits, they should have to prove dependence. Objecting to what struck her as unequal treatment, Frontiero brought her grievance to the Southern Poverty Law Center in Montgomery, Alabama, which first represented her and then called on Ginsburg.

With this case Ginsburg took a big risk. She decided that it was time to argue that the Supreme Court should give sex the same strict scrutiny that it had long given race. In having different rules for male and female officers, she argued, the state was drawing a distinction that, while perhaps rational from the point of view of administrative expediency, perpetuated the stereotype of men as the natural breadwinners and women as dependents. This distinction denied to women the equal protection of the law. In January 1973 Ginsburg won.

At about the same time that Ginsburg was arguing *Frontiero*, another young woman lawyer, Sarah Waddington, was presenting the first abortion case to reach the Supreme Court: *Roe* v. *Wade*. Arguing on behalf of Jane Roe, a pseudonym for a pregnant, single woman in Texas, and "all other women," Waddington argued that Texas's antiabortion law abridged women's right to privacy. Unlike Ginsburg's cases, which reflected a strategy of seeking careful, incremental progress, Waddington's case came out of the blue. The only precedent having any relevance to abortion was *Griswold* v. *Connecticut* (1965), a case in which the Supreme Court decided that the right to privacy, guaranteed by the "penumbra" of the Bill of Rights, barred states from legislating against the use of contraception. Moreover, the abortion reform movement had as yet made only modest headway. To the surprise of almost everyone, however, on January 22, 1973, Waddington won. Indeed, not only did she win women greater rights to abortion, she won more than all but four states in the country then allowed—the right of a woman to a medically safe abortion, before the third trimester, for whatever reason she and her doctor deemed appropriate. Abortion, the Supreme Court held, was a fundamental right, guaranteed by the right to privacy and the due-process clause of the Fourteenth Amendment.

Not all change came through the courts. Much of the most far-reaching change came through the federal bureaucracy. In the five years following Betty Friedan's denunciation of an EEOC commissioner for saying "girls" and "ladies" when he meant "women," a sea change took place at the EEOC. The commission began hiring attorneys sympathetic to, and in some instances even active in, the National Organization for Women. At first these lawyers simply worked to process cases brought to them by aggrieved women, but by 1970 there was a growing conviction among them that something more had to be done.

Women in the Washington underground had been talking about how to speed the pace of social change for some time. Case-by-case progress was maddeningly slow, and hardly seemed equal to the enormity of the problem that radical feminists had persuaded them existed in institutionalized sexism. Catherine East of the Citizen's Advisory Council on the Status of Women sponsored meetings that brought NOW members and EEOC attorneys together to talk about this problem. What they needed to do, she urged, was to think big. Sexism was not going to be ended by winning individual women equal pay for equal work or the equal right to work. Sex roles had to be uprooted. Employment practices in the country's largest companies had to be changed so that distinctions between men's jobs and women's jobs would disappear. Women had to be hired for jobs long held by men, while men had to be hired for jobs held by women. Only then would sexism disappear.

A review of the Equal Employment Opportunity Commission's caseload revealed that 7 percent of their cases came from workers at American Telephone and Telegraph (AT&T). Rather than fight AT&T one case at a time, the EEOC decided to conduct a frontal assault. In 1970 it moved to block AT&T's request before the Federal Communications Commission for a rate hike on the grounds that AT&T's discrimination against women and minorities was not in the public interest.

David Copus, an attorney at the EEOC, as well as a member of the board of directors of NOW, took the initiative in the attack on AT&T. "[W]e were advancing the really revolutionary view of sex discrimination. We took more or less hook, line and sinker the feminist view as espoused by the National Organization for Women—their view of institutionalized sex discrimination—and we said we wanted to attack it at its roots in the Bell System. Not just equal pay for equal work, etc. We wanted to present the whole sociology and psychology of sexual stereotypes as it was inculcated into the Bell System structure."

The impact of the meetings between NOW leaders and EEOC lawyers was evident in the final settlement with AT&T. Previously, the orientation of the EEOC had been solely to advance minorities and women into better jobs, while ignoring those poorly paid jobs held primarily by members of those groups. But NOW leaders persuaded them that any job category that remained solely female (or black) would contribute to the maintenance of sex-role and race stereotypes and with that the psychological aspects of discrimination. AT&T agreed to a broad affirmative-action plan that required not only the hiring of women as linemen to work on telephone poles but also the hiring of men to work as operators. Companies around the country quickly adopted similar plans. With the passage of the Equal Employment Opportunity Act in 1972, Congress broadened the powers of the EEOC still further, allowing it to go into court on its own. Within six months EEOC had filed 5 suits against companies; by the end of 1973, it had filed 147 more.

Beyond its impact on government policy, the women's movement transformed the lives of millions of American women. Schools began integrating their shop and cooking classes; military academies began accepting women; Ivy League schools that had long been single-sex began going coed (though the reasons for doing so had less to do with feminism than concern over a shrinking applicant pool); women's colleges that decided not to change took new pride in their single-sex status; by 1974 five hundred colleges were offering two thousand women's studies courses; and academic disciplines were being reshaped by new research on women. In the years of feminism's rebirth, 1961–73, women's educational aspirations rose markedly. Their percentage of B.A.'s rose from 35 percent to 45 percent; of medical school degrees, from 5 percent to 9 percent; of law degrees, from 2.6 percent to 8 percent; and of Ph.D.'s, from 10 percent to 18 percent. Across the country gender barriers fell in the most unlikely places. A casino in Las Vegas hired its first female blackjack dealer; a group of women in Manhattan formed a moving company called the "Mother Truckers"; AT&T began hiring women to climb poles and string telephone lines; and the airlines began hiring men as flight attendants. On

September 20, 1973, tennis star Billie Jean King responded to the taunts of 1939 Wimbledon champion Bobby Riggs that women tennis players did not deserve the greater opportunities King was seeking. "You insist that top women players provide a brand of tennis comparable to men's," Riggs charged. "I challenge you to prove it. I contend that you not only cannot beat a top male player, but that you can't beat me, a tired old man." In Las Vegas the odds were five to two for Riggs, but in the nationally publicized "battle of the sexes" King trounced Riggs 6–4, 6–3, 6–3. Across the country women who had never had any confidence in their athletic ability gained a new pride, and among both women and men a new respect for the women's movement developed. The growing acceptance of feminism can be tracked in the public-opinion polls of this period. In 1971 a majority of the public disapproved of "efforts to strengthen and change women's status in society," but four years later 63 percent of the public endorsed those efforts. Never before had the American public given such strong support to improving women's lives.

7

The Family Claim Revisited
1973–91

Right Turn

In the spring of 1973 Martha Griffiths predicted, "ERA will be part of the Constitution long before the year is out." There seemed no reason to doubt her judgment. In the brief year since she had ushered the amendment through Congress, thirty-two state legislatures had ratified it, only a half dozen short of the required thirty-eight. But trouble was brewing. The political and social turmoil, out of which feminism had emerged, was destroying the liberal coalition on which continued success depended. The civil rights movement produced the first defections. The antiwar movement brought more. Other issues, like law and order, the sexual revolution, and the feminist attack on traditional roles, added to the disenchantment. To many Americans these protest movements challenged deeply held values, like morality, patriotism, order, motherhood, and local autonomy. Angry and resentful, conservative groups unleashed a backlash with devastating consequences for feminism. By the end of the 1980s the ERA would be dead, the right to abortion imperiled, social welfare policies dismantled, and feminists forced to reconsider their agenda.

The backlash had been building for several years. George Wallace, the segregationist governor from Alabama who railed against Washington interference in local affairs, achieved remarkable support in northern industrial towns like Gary, Indiana, when he ran as a third-party candidate for President in

1968. A more effective attack gathered energy within the Republican Party, where Richard Nixon, vowing to represent what he called "the silent majority" of "Middle America," captured the Presidency with the promise that he would return America to its traditional values, bring "victory with honor" in Vietnam, get tough with criminals, and pare down the government.

Nixon fulfilled this promise most notably in 1972, when he vetoed the Comprehensive Child Development Bill. The bill, Nixon charged, represented a "communal approach to child-rearing" and had "family-weakening implications." Most feminist-inspired legislation extended basic rights to women at little cost to the taxpayer, but the Comprehensive Child Development Bill, which would have funded a nationwide system of day-care centers, threatened to cost billions of dollars. The problem feminists faced was not merely economic. Many opponents regarded child care as bad for children, and most child-development specialists agreed. Nursery-school programs in which children spent a few hours each week of educational play won wide praise, but child care, whose principal aim seemed to be freeing mothers to work, did not.

Despite growing popular support for improving the status of women in America, many remained suspicious of the image of the independent, assertive, equal, liberated woman. As late as 1980 half of all married women remained outside the work force, and many housewives viewed their role as more satisfying than the most likely alternatives, factory work or service jobs. As Congresswoman Barbara Mikulski explained in 1976, "We and our mothers and grandmothers and great-grandmothers were the women of the sweatshops. The women who died in the Triangle Shirtwaist fire. And I can tell you something: when World War II was over . . . my aunts and other relatives wanted to get out. . . . They wanted to be 'ladies' . . . and they wanted their daughters to be 'ladies.' " To these women, Mikulski concluded, the ideas of women's liberation were "very threatening" and "very confusing."

Even the majority of the public sympathetic to the idea of equal rights often harbored traditional beliefs about gender roles. Indeed, much of the apparent support for the Equal Rights Amendment that public-opinion surveys consistently revealed came from a sympathetic response to the concept of "rights," not from a commitment to actual changes in women's roles. For instance, in 1977 the National Opinion Research Center's General Social Survey asked a representative sample of Americans how they felt about women's roles and whether they favored or opposed the ERA. They found that 62 percent of the sample thought that married women should not hold jobs when jobs were scarce and their husbands could support them. Astonishingly, of those who held this view, two-thirds also supported the ERA. Men were slightly more supportive of the ERA than women, but they were also more opposed to married women's working. What these numbers reveal is that Americans were ambivalent regarding the appropriate role for women. There was substantial support for formal equality, but lingering opposition to substantive change. In short, a majority of men and women approved the principle of equal rights only as long as it did not change much in practice.

The person most responsible for tapping this ambivalence over gender roles and the growing fear of government intrusion into private life with which it was frequently associated was Phyllis Schlafly. In 1971 she began one of the most successful conservative political campaigns in American history, a campaign to organize American women against the Equal Rights Amendment. College-educated, with a master's degree in government from Radcliffe College, Schlafly was intelligent, attractive, self-confident, articulate, and the mother of six children, all of whom she had taught to read before they entered school. During the 1950s she became an influential activist in Republican Party politics and established a national reputation as an expert on the Soviet Union, the arms race, and defense policy. In 1964 she propelled Arizona senator Barry Goldwater to the head of the Republican Party with her book, *A Choice, Not an Echo*, which was a right-wing, populist attack on Eastern "kingmakers" like Nelson Rockefeller who dominated Republican Party politics. By the end of the 1960s, however, Goldwater's ignominious defeat by Lyndon Johnson and her own loss in a 1967 race for the presidency of the National Federation of Republican Women had pushed her to the periphery of party politics. There she became the heroine of a loyal band of supporters who provided the base for her campaign to stop the ERA.

So incongruous did ERA supporters find the juxtaposition of Schlafly's self-confident intelligence and her traditionalist views that they nearly all assumed she was simply a tool of right-wing men who must be paying her to say things she did not really believe. But Phyllis Schlafly had been bred to a conservative worldview from early childhood. Born in 1924 to Bruce and Odile Stewart of St. Louis, Missouri, Phyllis attended a Catholic girls school, where nuns instilled in her a deep respect for hard work and family, while giving her the confidence to believe she could do anything. This confidence in individual initiative made her highly suspicious of government-sponsored social welfare.

Unlike many conservatives, Schlafly did not come to her views from a position of material comfort. Her father lost his job at Westinghouse in 1930, and her mother became the family bread-winner, working seven days a week to feed her two daughters and keep them in school. After graduating from high school in 1941, Phyllis Stewart took a night job in a wartime ammunition plant to pay her way through Washington University, and managed to go to graduate school only by winning a fellowship to Radcliffe. In the five years between completing an M.A. and marrying lawyer Fred Schlafly, she supported herself, sometimes by working at several jobs at once. She concluded from these experiences not that women should be independent but that they should work hard to help their families. She taught all of her children to excel, but she instructed the boys that careers came first, while teaching the girls that the family took priority. If her daughters were disciplined enough to be both housewives and have careers, fine; she had always succeeded in combining domesticity with work outside the home. But husbands were the natural head of the family, and their needs, as well as those of the children, came first.

The various threads of Schlafly's religious and moral upbringing intertwined into a fairly consistent conservative set of positions on issues ranging from foreign policy to family life. She opposed big government, Communism, the SALT treaties on arms limitation, welfare, abortion, and the women's liberation movement. To Schlafly, women's liberation was "destructive of family living" and feminists were "selfish and misguided." In 1970–71, when the ERA was being debated in Congress, however, Schlafly took no special interest in it; she was much more concerned with the upcoming SALT agreements and Nixon's policy of detente, which she opposed. "I figured ERA was something between innocuous and mildly helpful," Schlafly later recalled. Then, in 1971, in response to the exhortations of a friend who wanted her to take part in a debate against the amendment, she did some reading on it and changed her mind. The ERA was far from innocuous, she concluded; it must be stopped.

Stop ERA

Schlafly's goal of stopping the amendment seemed ludicrous in 1971. Endorsement in Congress was assured; ratification by the states almost certain. But Schlafly was able to capitalize on two important political realities. First, she understood, as only Pauli Murray before her truly had, the difficulty of winning ratification. Most state legislatures require a two-thirds vote to ratify, and that supermajority must be won in at least three-quarters of the states. Second, though the crescendo of feminist strength in the early 1970s persuaded many state legislators that ratification was inevitable and that they might as well be on the winning side, the ambivalence that the majority of the public felt about changes in gender roles provided an opening wedge for organized opposition. If Schlafly could persuade legislators that the ERA would endanger gender roles, she could defeat the amendment. Trying out her theory, she testified before the state legislatures in Georgia, Virginia, Missouri, and Arkansas. All four states rejected the amendment.

In late 1972 Schlafly established the National Committee to Stop ERA, and by January 1973 the committee had several thousand members in twenty-six states. Soon a predictable list of conservative groups, including the Daughters of the American Revolution, the National Council of Catholic Women, and the Conservative Cause, came out against the ERA. In addition, a host of groups dedicated specifically to defeating the amendment formed. These included WWWW (Women Who Want to Be Women), HOW (Happiness of Womanhood), and FLAG

(Family, Liberty, and God). Schlafly believed in the same highly decentralized, grass-roots organizing that radical feminists had relied on in spreading consciousness-raising across the country. Bowling clubs, church groups, neighborhood block associations formed the divisions in her well-organized army; she was the general. In Illinois, for instance, she could mobilize twenty thousand supporters through a network of telephone calls and have them at the state legislature within days, presenting homemade bread, jams, and apple pies to their representatives and bearing signs that read "From the Breadmakers to the Breadwinners," "Preserve us from a congressional jam; Vote against the ERA sham," and "I'm for Mom and apple pie."

Schlafly's greatest concern was one that had worried opponents of the amendment as far back as the 1920s, the amendment's demand for absolute equality, without exception. If states had to treat men and women identically, Schlafly warned, the security of the middle-aged, full-time homemaker with no job skills would be at serious risk. No longer could courts require husbands to support their wives; no longer could wives count on alimony after divorce. As Schlafly delighted in reminding her audiences, the ERA did not have a "grandmother clause."

The fact that the ERA would allow no reasonable differences in treatment of the sexes, Schlafly charged, would affect a large number of institutions. Women's colleges that received federal funding (almost all did) could not continue as single-sex schools. Protective labor laws for blue-collar women would be unconstitutional. Although federal courts were striking down maximum-hours laws and weight-lifting restrictions under Title VII, even as Schlafly spoke, no one could be sure how much further the protective rollback might go under the ERA. Hearing Schlafly's warnings on the radio and TV, many blue-collar women began to worry.

Economist Sylvia Ann Hewlett discovered just how worried they were one cold and rainy December morning in 1979 on the outskirts of Atlanta, Georgia, when she and some friends tried to distribute ERA literature to women coming off the night shift at a textile plant. Most of the tired workers just pushed by, but one black woman stopped to talk. "You know, I've heard of you 'libbers' and your ERA. I've seen that Schlafly person on TV and she says that equal rights for women is a bad deal because we would lose a whole lot. Like us girls get an extra break in the shift, and management can't force us to work overtime the way they force the men." When Sylvia Ann Hewlett replied that men needed special benefits, too, the textile worker retorted, "I've got two kids under five and a husband who doesn't lift a finger. . . . Why shouldn't I get some breaks on the job?"

To Schlafly, threats to women's colleges and protective labor legislation were troubling but minor when compared to the ERA's potential effect on the military. The ERA, Schlafly warned, would render unconstitutional federal laws exempting women from the draft and excluding them from combat. America was still at war with Vietnam in the early 1970s and Schlafly's warning that the ERA would force the military to draft women and send them to fight raised widespread concern. Eighty percent of the public was strongly opposed to sending women into combat, partly out of chivalry, partly out of fear that America's fighting strength would be thereby reduced.

To Schlafly the ERA's promise of equal rights was disturbingly vague. But it was the amendment's grant to Congress of power to enforce those rights "by appropriate legislation" that struck her as truly dangerous. The laws regarding family relations—marriage, divorce, child custody, and adoption—represented one of the last sectors of the law over which states continued to exercise autonomy in the American federal system. When Schlafly pointed out to state legislators that the ERA would transfer some 70 percent of their remaining power to the federal government, she won decisive negative votes.

Having identified the parade of horribles one could expect from the ERA, Schlafly delighted in emphasizing what the ERA would not do. It would not equalize men's and women's wages. It would not prevent employers from discriminating against women. It would not, in short, bring women any new rights. Schlafly labeled the ERA the "men's liberation amendment" on the grounds that it would transfer substantial old rights from women to men without giving women any substantial new rights in return. She had a point. Since the ERA acted only on state and federal governments, it could not reach private employers.

In fact, by the mid-1970s the combination of Ruth Bader Ginsburg's Fourteenth Amendment litigation strategy and Title VII of the Civil Rights Act of 1964 had improved women's lives more substantially than the ERA could be expected to do if it were passed. Test cases under the Fourteenth Amendment had proven highly successful in winning women equal rights under state and federal law. In addition, test cases and administrative initiatives under Title VII had won women employment rights and wage increases that the ERA could never have effected. Though inequalities remained—in pension rights and in opportunities in the military—the gains that had been won tended to take much of the wind out of pro-ERA sails, leaving only potential losses from the ERA as subjects for debate. In the face of these changed circumstances, Phyllis Schlafly whipped her troops to ever greater outrage.

In 1979 the time allotted for ratification ran out. A three-year extension, passed by Congress, proved no help to ERA supporters. In 1982, Schlafly and her supporters could boast that not a single state had ratified the amendment since 1977, and five had voted to rescind their initial endorsement. The ERA was dead.

The Abortion Struggle

Many of those who opposed the ERA rejected women's right to abortion as well, but feminists were not initially concerned. In their view, the Supreme Court's decision in *Roe* v. *Wade* had settled the question. They were wrong. Instead of quieting controversy, the Court's decision inspired the organization of a small but exceptionally well-organized grass-roots "right-to-life" movement. Like ERA opponents, those who opposed abortion tended to be regular churchgoers. The movement drew its most fervent support from Catholics, but also gained adherents among Mormons and fundamentalist Christians. Anti-abortion activists tended to be housewives who regarded traditional family values as central to their lives. In their view abortion, like equal rights, seemed to set selfish individualism above family responsibility and to challenge women's traditional conception of themselves as nurturing caretakers. Abortion served as a symbol for the devaluation of motherhood, and as a threat to the social guarantees that a woman with children will be supported by the child's father. It was also, most foes contended, a form of murder. Fetuses, they claimed, had a "right to life" from the moment of conception. The struggle over abortion was based on a religious debate about when life began and a battle over the significance of reproduction in American culture.

Throughout the 1970s and 1980s only a minority of the public, about 20 percent, supported the Supreme Court's decision granting abortion essentially on demand. On the other hand, only about 20 percent opposed abortion in virtually all instances. In between these two positions stood the majority of the public, supporting abortion under some conditions. Neither side of the abortion struggle had much impact on public opinion, which remained ambivalent over the entire period. Most people supported abortion when a woman's health was endangered, but less than half supported it when the reasons for terminating the pregnancy were economic or the woman was not married and did not wish to get married.

No single individual ever emerged to lead the antiabortion movement, but a series of groups, the biggest of which was the Catholic-based National Right to Life Committee, came into existence after the Supreme Court's 1973 decision in *Roe* v. *Wade*. These groups sought to influence local and national elections in the hope of returning the country to the antiabortion stance that had characterized it between the end of the nineteenth century and 1973. Phyllis Schlafly also contributed the influence of her Stop ERA campaign to the abortion fight. In addition to all of her other charges, she warned that the ERA would secure the right to abortion and allow lesbians to marry one another, both of which she viewed as positions opposed to motherhood. Few legal scholars agreed with her analysis, but it won favor in the right-to-life movement.

Abortion opponents enjoyed little success in changing public opinion, and they failed in their effort to win a constitutional amendment to ban abortions, but they were nevertheless able to take advantage of the prevailing ambivalence and the public's desire to cut government spending to win some important political victories. In 1976 Representative Henry Hyde of Illinois secured passage of an amendment barring the use of Medicaid funds to pay for abortions for poor women, even if doctors asserted that the abortions were medically necessary. Two years later the Supreme Court declared the amendment constitutional, and Congress cut off federal funding of abortions for government employees, Peace Corps volunteers, and members of the military and their dependents.

Despite their relatively small numbers, pro-life activists achieved even greater influence during the 1980s because of their role in the conservative wing of the Republican Party. In 1980 conservatives rose to dominance when Ronald Reagan, one of their number, became President. With Reagan in power, the pro-life movement gained access to the federal bureaucracy and began issuing rulings that threatened the funding of all clinics that performed abortions or even counseled women about the availability of abortion. In addition, Reagan was able to use his power to appoint federal judges to influence abortion rulings in the courts. By the end of the 1980s Reagan had appointed more than half of the federal judges in the country, and his appointment of three new Supreme Court justices had guaranteed a conservative majority there. Reagan's appointees did not always vote as he would have liked, but the conservative shift in judicial thinking from 1973 to 1992 was unmistakable.

The changing composition of the Supreme Court increased the right-to-life movement's hopes of reversing *Roe* v. *Wade*. In 1989 the Court upheld a Missouri law that forbade any institution receiving state funds from performing abortions, whether or not those funds were used for abortions. This case, *Webster* v. *Reproductive Health Services*, triggered legislative battles across the country to pass ever more restrictive anti-abortion statutes in the hope of eventually winning from the Court a ruling that would overturn *Roe*.

Throughout most of the 1970s and 1980s between 25 and 30 percent of all pregnancies ended in abortion, a rate that made abortion a critical element in women's attempt to control their fertility. Supporters of abortion rights fervently hoped that *Roe* v. *Wade* would continue to protect women's right to terminate their pregnancies. But as the right-to-life movement won suc-

cessive victories, supporters of abortion rights began to envision
a return to the back-alley abortionists of the years before 1973.
Unwilling to face that possibility, supporters of abortion rights
began to organize, too. They called themselves "pro-choice" to
emphasize that they were not calling for abortions but rather
for women's right to *choose* whether to have one. Picking up
where feminists had left off in the early 1970s, pro-choice advocates demonstrated by the end of the 1980s that they were
just as strong, if not stronger, than their opponents. They realized, however, that the conservative backlash had achieved
such power and that abortion was so divisive an issue that they
could no longer make a "pro-choice" position a litmus test of
feminism. In 1989, a *New York Times* poll revealed that roughly
half of all women who said that America needed a strong wom-
en's movement also favored more restrictions on abortion than
existed under current law. Mindful of the ERA defeat, black
professor Eleanor Holmes Norton of Georgetown University
Law School told the National Women's Political Caucus in the
same year, "You must not allow any issue, however important,
to displace all others. Otherwise, you and others who must take
leadership on choice will risk resentment and backlash both
from within the women's movement and from our allies who
consistently lend their support to our issues."

Attacking the Welfare State

The strength of the conservative backlash could be seen as well
in the efforts of conservatives, beginning with Richard Nixon
in the early 1970s, to pare down social welfare services. This
strategy had disproportionately harsh consequences for women,
especially minority women. Women's low wages and primary
responsibility for children always made them more subject to
poverty. The still lower wages of minority women, trapped by
racism and inadequate education into low-skilled, service jobs,
meant that minority women were even more likely to be poor,
especially if they had children. Social welfare programs did
much to alleviate this poverty during the 1960s. In 1961 Congress
extended Aid to Families with Dependent Children (AFDC) to
cover families with unemployed fathers. Four years later it

adopted health care for the elderly through Medicare, health
care for the poor through Medicaid, and rent supplements for
the poor. Together with the economic expansion of the postwar
years and a steady increase in social security benefits, these
programs reduced poverty to an all-time low of 11 percent by
the end of the 1960s. Since the poor were disproportionately
single mothers with children and older women, this reduction
helped women in particular. One beneficiary was Ruby Lee
Daniels.

When Ruby Lee Daniels arrived in Chicago in 1949 at the
age of thirty-three, she believed she was leaving the poverty
and violence of the Mississippi Delta behind her, and for a
couple of decades her dream seemed close to coming true. The
work she found as a janitor paid four times what she could make
in Mississippi, and in 1962, when she married Luther Haynes,
a factory worker and the father of four of her eight children,
she was able to move into a brand-new public housing project.
When Luther left her in 1965, Aid to Families with Dependent
Children came to her rescue. When her children entered school,
they attended nine months a year, rather than the three months
common in the South when she was a child. When she had
problems with public services, she took them to the Democratic
Party, as she had never been able to do in Mississippi; she even
became precinct captain for the Democratic Party in her housing
project.

But despite these advances beyond the life she had known as
a sharecropper, Ruby Daniels Haynes never realized the dream
of seeing her children rise above poverty. As a growing black
middle class managed to escape the housing projects of Chicago's South Side, poor, single mothers like Ruby Haynes remained trapped, with a declining level of public service and a
growing level of violence, drug addiction, and disease to contend
with. Despite these problems, as her children grew up, Ruby
Haynes returned to work, laboring nights in hospitals and hotels
when she could, and subsisting on state public assistance ($78
a month in 1978) when she could not. Then in 1978 she won a
small victory. Reaching the retirement age of sixty-two, she
became eligible for Social Security. At about the same time her
youngest child, Kevin, who was retarded, reached eighteen and

became eligible for supplemental security income. Suddenly, she entered a whole new economic class. Welfare, generally associated with the undeserving (and mostly black) poor and therefore unpopular, had been steadily cut through the 1970s. Social Security, in contrast, had always been regarded as an insurance policy from which every working American would one day profit. The benefits, always much higher than welfare's, were legally tied to inflation during the Nixon Administration. Ruby Haynes started receiving two $300 checks each month, almost eight times what she had received under welfare. With Kevin she returned to Clarksdale, Mississippi, where she found a new apartment, to live at last in safety and relative ease. In short, the federal government had addressed the problem of poverty among the elderly and disabled fairly successfully by the 1970s, but it continued to regard single mothers and their children as unworthy of comparable assistance.

The problems faced by Ruby Haynes and her children through the 1970s only intensified for those who remained poor in the 1980s. Arguing that family assistance programs had fostered "indolence, promiscuity, casual attitudes toward marriage and divorce, and maternal indifference to child-rearing responsibilities," President Reagan decided to cut social welfare programs still further. He pared funding for food stamps, unemployment insurance, child nutrition, vocational education, the Jobs Corps, and AFDC, and he ended public-service employment. The Administration also eliminated cash welfare assistance for the working poor and reduced federal subsidies for child-care services for low-income families. As low-skilled jobs began to disappear from inner-city ghettos in the 1970s and 1980s, ill-educated women found themselves increasingly unemployed, with no way out.

Of course, not all poor women were black. At least three-quarters lived outside the black ghetto. Their poverty most often derived from unemployment, low wages, costly illness, divorce, separation, single parenthood, or cutbacks in social programs. Many were part of the new wave of immigration that swept across America after the Immigration Act of 1965 dropped long-standing quotas, bringing women and men from the Caribbean, Latin America, and Asia. Their needs and views were to have an increasingly important influence as feminists struggled to respond to the conservative backlash of the 1970s and 1980s.

Reshaping the Feminist Agenda

The conservative emphasis on the family inevitably left a mark on the women's movement. Though the commitment to equality remained strong, new debates emerged over how best to achieve it. Feminists, both radical and liberal, had initially agreed that women's best chance of winning equality was to emphasize the essential sameness of the sexes and to advance women into male jobs. By the middle of the 1970s, however, some feminists were suggesting that such a strategy could not help most women—those who by virtue of personal taste, educational background, or domestic responsibilities could not easily enter many male jobs. For these women, comparable worth seemed more attractive than affirmative action; maternity leaves and quality day care more desirable than the ERA; and guaranteed child support more useful than no-fault divorce.

The first intimations of this shift from sameness to difference occurred in the early 1970s among radical feminists who were growing increasingly disenchanted with the failure of male radicals to treat women as equals, and who sought some way of overcoming the differences in class, race, and sexual preference that threatened to tear the women's movement apart. The most dramatic solution came in 1973, when Jane Alpert published "Mother Right: A New Feminist Theory" in *Ms.* magazine. Alpert was part of a revolutionary left-wing movement bent on destroying the military-industrial establishment by force. On March 6, 1970, the Weathermen, a violent revolutionary group, accidentally detonated a bomb in a Greenwich Village apartment, killing two of their own people. Shortly thereafter, twenty-three-year-old Jane Alpert was arrested, along with her lover, for bombing military and war-related corporate buildings in late 1969. After her arrest, she jumped bail and disappeared into the underground of Weathermen and other revolutionary groups. Disguised by bleached hair, makeup, and tortoiseshell glasses provided by Miss America Pageant protestor Robin

Morgan, Alpert became a committed feminist after going into hiding.

In "Mother Right," she detailed the sexism of the male revolutionaries with whom she worked. If she had done no more than cite male failings, Alpert would have attracted little attention, but she went further, condemning feminists for assuming that differences between men and women were the artificial product of roles imposed by patriarchal society. That argument, she countered, *"contradicts our felt experience of the biological difference between the sexes as one of immense significance"* [her emphasis]. Alpert traced the "power of feminist culture" and the "powers which were attributed to the ancient matriarchies" to female biology, specifically to women's reproductive capacity. She maintained that all women, not just mothers, possess maternal qualities because "motherhood" is a "potential which is imprinted in the genes of every woman." Alpert's appeal to a shared maternalism offered a means for solving the dilemma of how to maintain a unified women's movement, given women's vast differences from one another, for "motherhood," she declared, "cuts across economic class, race and sexual preference."

The emphasis on women's differences from men gained wider currency as feminist scholars began to explore the ways in which traditional values and expectations continued to affect women's lives and aspirations. Historian Carroll Smith-Rosenberg uncovered a distinctive woman's world through which women criticized the dominant male culture and won significant power for themselves. Psychologist Carol Gilligan studied the differing ways in which men and women form moral judgments. Literary critic Alice Jardine influenced by French theorist Jacques Lacan examined the symbolic construction of gender. Theologian Mary Daly explored the implications of God as a female figure. And legal scholar Catharine A. MacKinnon attacked the "sameness standard" for having "mostly gotten men the benefit of those few things [like child custody] women have historically had" without protecting women from rape, pornography, sexual harassment, and economic inequality. Though only a minority of feminists went so far as to argue that women were inherently different from men, many began to consider the possibility that socially constructed differences might indeed be deep-seated.

Concern over differences, both gender and cultural, was particularly evident among minority women, whose voices gained new authority within feminist circles in the 1980s. Writers Alice Walker and Toni Morrison explored the dual oppression of race and gender. Angela Davis analyzed the interplay of race and class. Audre Lorde wrote poignantly of homophobia among blacks. And they all revealed the strengths in black women's heritage. Gradually, other minority women entered the discussion. Chinese-American novelists Maxine Hong Kingston and Amy Tan explored the affinities and tensions between Chinese mothers and their American-born daughters. Native-American Mary Crow Dog wrote of her effort as a Lakota both to reclaim tribal traditions in South Dakota and to reject the aimless drinking, punitive missionary schools, and oppression of women that characterized her youth. And Latina scholars Edna Acosta-Belen, Vicki Ruiz, Patricia Zavella, and Sylvia Padraza-Bailey were a few of those who revealed the distinct experiences of women within the Puerto Rican, Cuban, and Chicano communities. Because they knew firsthand the protective power of female bonds in a racist society, these minority women tended to value gender and cultural differences more positively than many white feminists did. To them, equality did not necessarily mean the erasure of difference.

The shift in feminist thinking toward a greater respect for both gender and cultural differences did much to bridge the gap that had long existed between middle-class and working-class women. Among working-class women of diverse backgrounds, the belief that men and women were essentially the same had never carried much weight. Affirmative-action programs, which were based on this belief, seemed helpful to well-educated, younger women able to compete for managerial and professional positions. Indeed, during the 1970s alone women jumped from comprising 5 percent to 12 percent of all lawyers, from 25 percent to 33 percent of all accountants, and from 17 percent to 25 percent of all managers. But affirmative-action programs seemed less useful to unskilled, older women who found themselves trapped by limited education in low-paid women's jobs. They were working less for the self-realization that many feminists championed than for the money that seemed increasingly necessary to maintain their families' standard of living.

Between 1973 and 1989 male wages fell 19 percent. In addition, families faced sharply increased living costs. Housing and education costs both consumed significantly higher proportions of family budgets by the end of the 1980s than they had in the early 1970s. Most women entered the work force simply to keep their families from falling behind economically. In a national housing survey conducted by Chicago Title & Trust, the proportion of families that purchased a home on a single income fell from 47 percent in 1976 to 21 percent in 1989. At the same time, the proportion of families owning their own home began to fall. Under growing economic pressure millions of women took jobs for whatever they could get. Their big concerns were not occupational mobility but rather decent treatment and fair pay.

In 1974 clerical workers formed two organizations to defend their interests: Nine to Five, in Boston, and Women Employed, in Chicago. Through them women fought not to rise out of clerical work but to force their employers to stop treating them as servants. Secretaries took pride in their clerical skills, but they refused to make coffee for their bosses. The same year women in the labor movement formed the Coalition of Labor Union Women, which helped women overcome the isolation they felt in separate unions and signaled women's determination to make their particular concerns heard by male union leaders.

Women workers' greatest concern was their low wages. From 1950 to 1980 the average woman's wage had remained stuck at about 60 percent of the average man's. This difference was perplexing, given the fact that women were flooding the labor force in these years. Between 1950 and 1980, women's employment rose from 30 to 51 percent. The increase for married women was even more dramatic, jumping from only 24 percent to 50 percent in those same years. At the same time, minority women were abandoning the agricultural and domestic-service jobs, which had long been their mainstay, and moving into white-collar and service occupations. Between 1965 and 1978, for instance, the percentage of black women in white-collar jobs nearly doubled, from 23.5 to 45.5 percent. Women were also moving into occupations long dominated by men. By 1980, for instance, women made up nearly 50 percent of all bus drivers, up from 3 percent in 1950. Theoretically, women's increased work experience and assault on male-dominated occupations should have led to an increase in their earnings. The reason this did not happen is due to two additional facts. First, the women entering the work force between 1950 and 1980 were disproportionately older women, with little prior work experience and relatively fewer educational qualifications than male workers. Their entry into the work force tended to depress wages overall. Second, most women continued to work in a narrow range of female-dominated occupations. As late as 1980, half of all women worked in occupations that were 80 percent female. These included many clerical occupations (bank tellers, bookkeepers, cashiers, data-entry clerks, receptionists, secretaries, typists, and telephone operators) and service occupations (chambermaids, waitresses, practical nurses, child-care workers, hairdressers, and private household workers) as well as garment workers. The entry of relatively less-experienced women into a narrow range of jobs kept wages from rising relative to those of men.

The persistence of the wage gap raised doubts in the minds of many feminist labor leaders that affirmative action would ever raise enough women out of low-paying jobs to have a significant impact on women's economic well-being. Moreover, the prospect of moving into male-dominated occupations seemed unattractive and even unfair to many women, who professed to like their jobs but objected to how little they were paid for them. The low pay, they argued, had nothing to do with the value of the work they performed; it was the historical consequence of women being offered low wages because women had always earned low wages. Why should women now have to be truck drivers to win the pay that should rightfully have been theirs as clerical workers all along?

The idea that women deserved to be paid the same wages as men not only when they performed the same job but also when they engaged in work that required comparable skill and responsibility came to be known as "comparable worth." This approach gained widespread support in the 1980s among women in jobs where professional job evaluators had long set wage rates according to particular formulas. By comparing jobs on the basis of the relative skill, responsibility, and working conditions associated with them, evaluators could judge the fairness of pay schedules for very different kinds of jobs. In racially and ethnically mixed San Jose, California, for instance, job evaluators found that the female-dominated jobs in city government paid 15 to 20 percent less than the comparable male-dominated jobs. A nurse earned $9,120 a year less than a comparably rated fire-truck mechanic; a senior librarian made $5,304 a year less than a comparably rated senior chemist; and a legal secretary made $7,288 a year less than a comparably rated equipment mechanic. If women had traditionally worked as mechanics and chemists, and men had worked as secretaries, nurses and librarians, comparable-worth advocates believed, these figures would have been reversed.

Comparable worth met with little success in the courts; it was lambasted, in the mid-1980s, as the "looniest idea since Loony Tunes," by Clarence Pendleton, the conservative chairman of the Civil Rights Commission; and it was criticized by many economists as a dangerous interference with market forces that might raise wages for some women but only at the cost of their increased unemployment and the loss of talented men to better-paying jobs in firms not covered by comparable-worth plans. Nonetheless, comparable worth continued to win adherents. Comparable worth clearly represented a threat to the market economy, but it was far from the first such threat to be embraced by the American public. When the Equal Pay Act was being debated in Congress in the 1960s, one of the arguments used against it was that it would interfere with market forces, which had long enabled employers to cut their costs by replacing men with women at lower wages. After years of debate, Congress finally concluded that the government would no longer allow market freedom to produce that result. Comparable worth merely extended that principle.

Comparable-worth advocates won their greatest advances among labor unions and government workers. With blue-collar work in America declining ever since the 1950s, union membership contracted from a high of 35 percent to less than 15 percent of the work force by the end of the 1980s. Expansion into the white-collar and service sector seemed the only way to recoup those losses. This shift brought impressive gains. Women composed only 18 percent of all union members in 1960, but by the mid-1980s, if one includes employee associations, women's membership had reached 34 percent. To take advantage of women's increased presence, however, labor leaders had to consider women's growing support for comparable worth. Except for government employees, comparable worth had done little to improve women's wages, since most significant pay differences occurred between firms, not within them. In textile firms, where women predominated, all wages were substantially lower than in steel mills, where men predominated. Despite these limitations, belief in comparable worth continued to spread. In the 1980s, at least twenty states began to study the theory, and where it was adopted, comparable worth brought women wage increases of up to 15 percent over what they had previously earned.

Despite these gains, a significant wage gap remained for most female workers, because only part of women's wage disadvantage could be traced to being paid less for comparable work. There were many other factors, including, for example, discrimination, education, and length of experience, that contributed to women's lower wages. By the 1980s this last factor—experience—attracted growing attention from economists, who began to observe that a significant part of the wage gap could be traced to losses suffered when women workers left the work force to bear and care for children. A two- to four-year break in employment lowered average earnings by 13 percent, while a five-year break in employment lowered average earnings by 19 percent. Women who worked for employers who provided paid maternity leaves and job-back guarantees avoided this drop, but while such benefits were routine in all other industrial countries (and many developing ones), Americans had no statutory maternity leave.

Not only did the U.S. have no such protection for its women workers, but efforts by its state legislatures to provide maternity leaves (even unpaid leaves) ran into trouble from employers as well as many feminists. Employer opposition to maternity leave is understandable enough; holding a job open, even without paying benefits, is at best inconvenient, and at worst costly. But why were feminists opposed? Many contended that state-mandated maternity leaves were simply another form of protective legislation, whose long-term effect would be to encourage employers not to hire women. In 1987 the Supreme Court confronted this issue in *California Federal Savings and Loan* v. *Guerra*, a case that pitted bank receptionist Lillian Garland against her employer. When she returned to work, having taken advantage of California's mandated maternity-leave law, she discovered to her dismay that her job had been given to someone else. The bank argued that the California law conflicted with Title VII as amended in 1978 by the Pregnancy Discrimination Act, which holds that employers may not discriminate "on the basis of pregnancy." The National Organization of Women submitted an amicus brief in the case, arguing against special treatment for new mothers. The Supreme Court, however, ruled that the state was not compelling employers to treat pregnant workers better than other disabled employees. It was merely saying that all employers must provide maternity leaves. If they wished to provide leaves for other workers, they could, of course, do so.

Women workers' victory in *Guerra* prompted feminists to settle their differences by making parental leave, as opposed to maternity leave, a priority on the feminist agenda. Those in favor of the "sameness" approach thereby won gender neutrality, while those preferring the "difference" strategy moved women's family concerns to the forefront of feminist lobbying efforts. Congress passed a parental-leave bill in 1990, but President George Bush vetoed the plan, making the likelihood of federal statutory reform unlikely in the near future. Parental leave continues to gain adherents among private employers, however, and as families become increasingly dependent on two incomes, popular support for parental leave continues to grow.

The most generous maternity leaves in America, those granted by a few employers that provide up to six months of paid leave, have not addressed the problem that most new mothers face after recovering from childbirth: how to care adequately for their new child while returning to work. Before the mid-

1980s, the majority of mothers of children under six were not employed. Tradition, plus the widespread consensus of child-development experts that young children did best with their own mothers, discouraged most women from seeking employment until all of their children reached school age. The cumulative impact of inflation, declining male wages, and increasing opportunities for work, however, prompted growing numbers of mothers with preschool children to ignore tradition and the experts and seek employment. In doing so, they made a variety of ad hoc arrangements for the care of their children. As of 1990, roughly two-thirds of all children were cared for at home or in someone else's home, while less than a quarter were in day-care centers or preschools. This preference for home care over day care reflects the stigma that the latter continues to carry because of its historical association with poverty and welfare programs aimed at the poor. Families with sufficient resources have long sent their children to nursery school for a few hours several days a week, but they have generally avoided day care.

Because of its association with the poor, day care has remained underfunded and underregulated. In 1970 the National Council of Jewish Women began a study of day-care centers around the country. While they visited some superior centers, they rated over half as being either fair or poor. They found one center where children were kept in " 'cages'—cribs of double-decker cardboard—in one room with open gas heaters," and another "run by high school girls without any adults present. The children not allowed to talk. . . . Rat holes . . . apparent." Conditions did not improve much in the next decade, according to Marion Blum of the Wellesley College Child Study Center, who wrote a damning review of American day care in 1983. She condemned the use of cagelike cribs, harnesses, and leashes; argued that eight or more hours each day was a long time for a young child to be away from home; pointed out the high rates of colds, flu, diarrhea, and hepatitis A among children who attend day care; and condemned the limited training and pay available for child-care workers.

The demand for universal, quality child care has been on the feminist agenda ever since NOW's first statement of principles in 1967, but until the 1980s it was not as important to feminists as either the ERA or the right to abortion. Especially after Nixon vetoed the Child Development Act in 1972, it seemed too costly a goal to fight for, especially given the lack of sympathy for motherhood that pervaded the early women's movement. As Betty Friedan later admitted, "The women who started NOW had had their fill of child care, or they were young professional women who had no children. And some of these younger radical women were pushing a line that liberated women either should refuse to bear children or, as a revolutionary act, leave their own, refuse to bring them up." As young mothers flooded the job market during the 1980s, however, support for day care grew. Though knowledge about the impact of day care on children's intellectual, social, and emotional development remains limited, and expert opinions range from those who regard day care's effects as "neither salutary nor adverse" to others who warn that day care may interfere with "the formation of close attachment to the parents," over a quarter of working mothers of one- and two-year-olds today say they would switch to center-based programs with an education component if cost were no object and the centers were available.

Though the paucity of maternity leaves and adequate day care in America long created problems for women, the American legal system, in the event of divorce, often brought disaster. Divorce reform in America paralleled but was essentially unconnected to the growth of the women's movement. Beginning in the early 1970s, states across the country repealed their old divorce statutes, which typically allowed divorce only in the case of adultery, abandonment, or cruelty, and permitted, instead, divorce for any couple suffering from "irreconcilable differences," however defined. To a society in the full throes of discarding old moralistic restrictions, divorce reform was emancipating. But, as soon became clear, men, not women, were the principal beneficiaries of this emancipatory trend. Leonore Weitzman, studying divorced families in California in the 1970s, found that in the year after divorce the average ex-husband's standard of living rose 42 percent, while that of the ex-wife (and usually her children) had fallen 73 percent. Scholars have since criticized Weitzman's figures as too extreme, but few challenged her central point: the economic vulnerability of women in case of divorce. The rising rate of divorce made this vulnerability increasingly obvious. In 1940 there was one divorce for every six marriages. By 1980 there was one divorce for every two marriages. In the pre-reform days a woman whose husband wanted out of a marriage had some leverage over him—that is, she could bargain for support in return for granting him a divorce. That leverage disappeared when it became possible for either party to sue for divorce without cause. Although most states adopted a policy of equal or equitable division of family property, women gained little, because few families had any property apart from their homes and many did not have that. Divorce therefore usually led to the dependence of the ex-wife and her children on whatever low-wage job she could secure. As Betty Friedan conceded, "We had fallen into a trap, in the first years of NOW; when divorce laws began to be reformed in New York and other states, leading to the no-fault divorce law, we were so anxious to espouse full equality, that we repudiated the very concept of alimony. Now women who had been housewives, who hadn't worked in years, or who made very little money, found themselves divorced with no provision whatsoever for their maintenance or for training for a job to earn real money, and often with the whole responsibility for the children to boot."

Gradually, feminist lawyers began to look for ways to protect women and their children against the pauperization that too frequently attended divorce. One tactic was to expand the concept of property to be divided at the time of divorce to include future earning potential, frequently a couple's only major asset. Feminist lawyers argued that spousal professional degrees and nonvested pensions should be viewed as property to be divided in case of divorce. They also worked to raise the levels and guarantee the payment of child support, with some success. In 1988 Congress passed the Family Support Act, which required automatic wage withholding and state guidelines for establishing appropriate levels of child support. No longer would it be as easy as it once was for fathers to abandon their families, leaving women with the full financial responsibility for raising the children.

In the feminist challenge to divorce reform, as well as the pursuit of comparable worth, maternity and parental leaves, and improved day care, advocates returned to the strategy championed by reformers like Jane Addams and Florence Kelley early in the century and then abandoned in the 1960s—the strategy of seeking equality for women in American society by seeking to meet women's particular needs. Rather than making men's experience the model for change, feminists began once again to look to women's lives as a guide to a better social order. Those lives are very different now, because of women's increased employment, greater education, more accepting attitude toward sexuality, and improved health. Only in rare instances would any family presume to regard a daughter as a possession. And yet, women still bear the primary domestic responsibility in American society. For all of their bitter disagreements, conservatives and feminists reached a consensus by the end of the 1980s that this continuing fact had to inform all discussion of public policy.

Toward the Year 2000

The past nine decades have witnessed enormous changes in the lives of American women. In 1900 most women lived on farms or in small rural towns. Today, most live in cities and suburbs. As they enter the final decade of the twentieth century, they are entering higher levels of education, working more often, delaying marriage and childbirth, divorcing more frequently, heading households more regularly, and living longer than at any time in this century. Overall, these changes have resulted in the family exercising less power over women's lives than was true in 1900. Especially in recent years women have come to spend more of their lives as single adults, pursuing personal and occupational objectives. They devote less time to child care and housework and more time to employment. As women's opportunities have increased, their reliance on family ties has declined. More than ever, women today are on their own.

A few statistics reveal the extent of the change. Improvements in medicine and nutrition have increased women's life expectancy from forty-eight to seventy-nine years and greatly reduced the chances of their dying in childbirth or of losing an infant. The country's shift away from agriculture and heavy industry toward a service economy has led to greatly increased educational opportunities. Whereas few women had more than an eighth-grade education in 1900, today 85 percent finish high school and 22 percent complete college. Higher levels of education have expanded women's occupational opportunities. One in five doctors and one in five lawyers are now women, up from one in twenty and one in a hundred, respectively, at the turn of the century. Virtually all occupations are now open to women, including selected combat positions in the armed forces. Educational and work opportunities have prompted women to defer marriage, raising the average age of marriage to twenty-four (two years higher than the average in 1900 and four years higher than the average in the 1950s). These opportunities have also increased the likelihood of women's divorcing. Whereas one in ten marriages ended in divorce at the beginning of the century, today one in two does.

Changes in education and work have been so closely intertwined with changes in sexuality that it is virtually impossible to sort out cause and effect. The results, however, are clear. Today, only one in five women waits until marriage before becoming sexually active. Ninety-three percent of all women, including 87 percent of unmarried women, now use contraceptives. Abortion is safer, and the right to abortion, though threatened, is more widely available than in the past. And apart from a period of dramatically increased childbearing after World War II, women's fertility has continued its long decline since 1800. Today women are bearing 1.8 children each, lower than the level needed for population replacement.

Because women are having fewer children, because technological improvements have reduced the time needed for housework, and because fast-food purveyors have decreased the time spent cooking, women are devoting less of their life to domestic responsibilities. In 1900 only 6 percent of all married women worked outside the home; today over half do. Among mothers, two-thirds are in the labor force (though only 40 percent of mothers with children under eighteen work full-time). For the first time in history, the majority of women are employed virtually all their adult life.

Most importantly, the proportion of all women living in poverty has declined from somewhere over half of all women in 1900 to approximately 15 percent today. Although black women suffer a poverty rate twice as high, even they are far better off today than they were at the turn of the century. Roughly 40 percent of all black women have entered the middle class, working in white-collar jobs, and another 30 percent are in the working class, engaged in service and factory occupations. In sum, women are healthier, more independent, and more economically secure today than their grandmothers and great-grandmothers ever dreamed of being.

In many ways women's lives have come to resemble men's. In 1900 women made up 18 percent of the work force; by the year 2000 they are expected to make up almost half. Women's educational attainment, which lagged behind men's at the post–high-school level for many decades, is now virtually the same. And women's wages, which were stalled at roughly 60 percent of men's between 1950 and 1980, have begun to rise in the past decade as women's training and work-force participation have increased (and men's wages have fallen); they currently stand at 70 percent of men's earnings.

Despite this seemingly steady progress, women's overall economic well-being (as measured by income and leisure time) compared with that of men's has not improved in the past generation. While women's income has risen dramatically, most studies suggest that their leisure time has decreased while men's has risen. In addition, the increase in the number of unmarried and divorced women has made more women dependent on their own income, while increasing their financial responsibility for children. The one exception to this pattern of stagnation has been the experience of young, white, unmarried, well-educated women, who have made large gains relative to their male counterparts. Though the family determines women's lives far less than it once did, it remains a central institution in most women's lives. Today, as in 1900, nine out of ten women marry, and though women spend less time with husbands and children than they once did, they nevertheless devote far more of their life to domestic responsibilities than do men. Moreover, although women have significantly increased their access to high-paying occupations long dominated by men, those occupations have changed very little to accommodate women's continuing domestic responsibilities. As women approach the year 2000, therefore, significant barriers to gender equality remain.

The most pressing issue facing women today, and the most important obstacle to achieving equality with men, is their greater responsibility for children, which increasingly has come to mean raising children by themselves. Low life expectancy at the turn of the century meant that one in seven women was likely to face this eventuality, as a widow, even then. But with skyrocketing divorce rates and the high incidence of single motherhood, one out of five women is now raising her family alone. The women who are struggling to do so are far more likely to be poor than those who are married. Forty percent of white and 60 percent of black female heads of household fall below the poverty line, which is now roughly $10,000 a year for a family of three.

Take the case of Ruby Lee Daniel Haynes's daughter-in-law, Connie. Connie Haynes and her children are the only remaining members of the Haynes clan still living in Chicago's Robert Taylor Housing Project. Despite rising levels of drug-related violence, declining levels of social services, and the desertion of her husband, Johnnie, Connie Haynes has succeeded through sheer force of will in creating a home life that has allowed all of her five children to prepare for productive lives. Maxine, her oldest daughter, graduated from the local high school and a nearby community college and is today studying computer science. Marlo, the next daughter, studied at a secretarial college in downtown Chicago. Melanie, the third daughter, graduated first in her class from high school and went on to study psychology at the University of Illinois's Chicago campus. The youngest daughter, Melissa, had a baby at sixteen, to Connie's intense distress, but with Connie's help returned to school and finished high school in 1990. Connie's youngest child and only son, Melvin, is in high school outside the neighborhood; both he and his mother decided that he would be better off away from the Robert Taylor neighborhood, where the pressure on boys to display their masculinity in destructive ways is powerful. As her children were growing up, Connie tried from time to time to work, but she finally decided that given the dangers to which her children were constantly exposed, it was more important for her to stay home to supervise them than to earn the extra income they sorely needed. Lacking money, education, community support, and a husband, Connie Haynes's prospects of leaving the housing project are remote, though she would love to do so.

Many women share Connie Haynes's plight, but their problems are not theirs alone. Today, one in four children lives in a female-headed household. Because these families are more likely to be poor than two-parent families, the implications for the next generation are dire. The only way for the United States to prevent an escalating cycle of poverty for women and children is to provide the kinds of social services—education, job training, police protection, income maintenance, day care, after-school care, and health care—that will make single women's child-rearing task easier.

Most mothers still have the benefit of a partner to help them with the labor of raising their families. But that assistance is often limited at best. In a recent *New York Times* poll 62 percent of all women agreed with the statement "Most men are willing to let women get ahead, but only if women do all the housework at home." Men actually perform less housework and child care today than they did in 1960. Some, of course, do more, but because of rising rates of divorce, others do less, and in general men perform only 30 percent of domestic labor; women do all the rest. Even so, men feel aggrieved. In 1989 55 percent of men in one poll said they believed that the women's movement had "made things harder for men at home," citing housework and increased responsibility around the home as the two biggest changes. That was 13 percent higher than the number of men who thought that the women's movement had made life tougher for men on the job.

Feminists once predicted that as women's work-force participation increased, men would share the burden of domestic labor, but that has not happened. While men now do more housework compared with women than was the case twenty years ago, the reason is that women are doing less, not that men are doing more. Even with decreased attention to the bathroom floor than their mothers once gave, the average woman in America today works roughly fifteen hours longer each week than the average man. That adds up to an extra *month* of work each year. Women have largely acceded to this unequal burden, some because they were brought up to accept housework as their responsibility, others because it's the price they pay to remain married, still others because their lesser wages make them feel that they must do most of the housework to make an equal contribution to the household. This rough concept of economic justice seems to hold only for wives, however. In households where women outearn their spouses, sociologist Arlene Hochschild has found that women still do most of the housework, perhaps to compensate their spouses for their loss of male pride.

One of Hochschild's subjects is a woman she calls Nancy Holt. A thirty-year-old social worker in the San Francisco Bay area, Nancy Holt is married to Evan, also thirty and a warehouse furniture salesman, who makes about 50 percent more than she does. They have a four-year-old son, Joey. From the beginning of the study, Nancy told Hochschild that she is an "ardent feminist." She believes men and women should have equal power and that there should be a balance between their commitment to work and to homelife. Unfortunately, Evan does not share that view. He is content for Nancy to work, if she wishes, but he sees no reason that her personal decision to work outside the home should require him to do more within it. When Joey was still an infant, Nancy once raised the issue with Evan of the unequal burden. "I told him: 'Look, Evan, it's not working. I do the housework, I take the major care of Joey, *and* I work full-time. I get pissed. This is *your* house too. Joey is *your* child too. It's not all *my* job to care for them.' " She suggested that they split the cooking and the laundry, but the experiment soon ended in disaster. Evan usually forgot to do his part. Increasingly, Nancy turned her attention to Joey, and Evan grew more distant from them both. By the time Arlene Hochschild showed up they had formed an armed truce under which Nancy did virtually all of the housework and child care. It was a poor bargain from her point of view, but it was better than divorce. Not that Evan won, exactly. As Hochschild interviewed them separately, she learned that as Nancy Holt felt increasing discouragement over her failed dreams, she lost all interest in sex. As Hochschild read the meaning of all this, Nancy Holt was saying, "You win. I'll go on doing all the work at home, but I'm angry about it and I'll make you pay." Americans live in a period in which women are changing more quickly than men, in their behavior and in their attitudes. Until men catch up, inequality will persist and tensions continue.

Some married women—Hochschild estimates the figure at about 20 percent—have succeeded in persuading their husbands to share domestic responsibilities equally. For these women, and for the 12 percent of all women whom statisticians calculate will neither marry nor have children, the chief problem is not home but work. Women have been able to gain access to the public world to an extent their mothers only dreamed of. That world remains largely hostile, however, to their presence. Structured for men with wives, the workplace makes success for women, who do not have wives, extremely difficult. This is especially true in male-dominated occupations. Thirty-six percent of all medical students are now women, but the professional life of women as a group differs markedly from that of male doctors. Women are far more likely to choose specialties like dermatology or radiology that have more regular hours, or specialties like family practice and psychiatry that emphasize doctor-patient relationships. Women work fewer hours each week and see fewer patients.

Perri Klass, a physician, has written extensively about women in medicine and her own experience as a mother struggling in a male world. Klass attended Harvard College in the late 1970s, moved out to Berkeley to study zoology, and after two years decided she did not like the study of parasites so much as she did their human hosts. She took time off from school for a year, followed her friend Larry Wolff to Italy, where he worked on his doctoral dissertation in the Vatican archives and she worked in a lab and wrote. In September 1982 they both returned to Cambridge, Massachusetts, he to teach at Harvard, she to enter Harvard Medical School. Klass found medical school something of a shock. She was perplexed by the ease with which her male teachers and classmates seemed able to assume "the mantle of all-knowing, paternal medical authority," and distressed by their tendency to reduce medicine to a technological game. Though she learned the rules of the game and came to feel more comfortable in this male world, she found herself relying more on one-to-one relationships, taking time to talk to her patients, and treating health-care workers in a more egalitarian way. Her different approach to medicine was reinforced in her second year, when she and Larry decided to have a baby. Given the demands of medical school, this seemed like a rash decision. But Larry's academic schedule gave him a certain flexibility, and Perri calculated that she would have more time for motherhood in medical school than she would later as an intern and resident. She very much appreciated the way her fellow students rallied round, treating her unborn child as the "class baby." But she found the medical school curriculum's treatment of pregnancy highly distressing. Rather than treating it as a natural process that could be optimized through attention to proper nutrition, education, and exercise, her teachers treated pregnancy as a diseased condition, which could at any moment end in disaster. About nutrition and exercise, she and her classmates learned nothing at all. Today she is a pediatrician with two children. A woman who "has it all," she nonetheless continues to feel the extraordinary stress that life as a mother and doctor entails.

Studies of women doctors reveal that Klass's patient-centered approach to practice is widely shared among women doctors, a fact that surely benefits the medical profession. But women have yet to move into positions of leadership in the profession. In 1988 only 2 out of 187 medical schools had female deans, and out of the two thousand academic departments in those schools, only seventy-three had female chairs.

For many women, competing for academic leadership while fulfilling family responsibilities is impossible. Sarah Stark, a medical researcher in New York City, explains why. The "guys" in her department work from 7 a.m. to 9 p.m. every day. "The male model *is* the working model. It never lets up. If you take time off, you'll get behind—in technical expertise, in publications, in climbing the academic ladder. They think the more scared you are, the more productive you'll be. They want you to be scared." Stark and her husband, also a physician, have decided not to have children at all. "When a physician who is a mother is late for a conference, the men *always* comment!"

The situation for women in other male-dominated professions is not much easier. A recent survey in the *National Law Journal* indicates that 90 percent of the partners in the 247 largest law firms are white males. A study by the Boston Bar Association found that women were significantly more likely than men to be single or divorced, and without children. Several major firms have instituted the option of part-time work, but this arrangement often precludes becoming a partner. Even in the public sector, where nine-to-five jobs are more common and part-time jobs possible, choosing a part-time job limits one's chance of advancement. According to one lawyer, "Unless somebody acts like a man, she is not perceived as management material."

The story in business, politics, and academia is much the same. Women have moved into business in large numbers, but are now reaching a "glass ceiling." Working steadily and effectively is no longer enough, especially now that America is part of an increasingly competitive world economy. As Rosabeth Moss Kantor says of the corporate world, "Flex-time isn't going to help. We're talking about voluntary overtime, about people who think that anyone who just gets through his work isn't doing enough. Day care won't help. These people work at night."

In politics, women's gains have been largely limited to state office, and even there the numbers are low. The percentage of women in state legislatures stood only at 15.5 percent after the 1988 elections. Forty-two women held statewide office, twenty-five women were elected to the House of Representatives, and there were still only two women senators, Barbara Mikulski of Maryland and Nancy Kassenbaum of Kansas. Women have not risen higher in significant numbers.

In academia women now earn over a third of all Ph.D.'s, but their tenure rate lags behind that of men, as do their salaries. In scholarship, as in medicine, law, business, and politics, women must act in ways that have long been socially disapproved of in women if they are to succeed. They must be active, not passive; leaders, not followers. But even if women act as leaders they cannot be sure that their work will be judged fairly.

Numerous studies have shown that gender makes a difference in how work is evaluated. One experiment, for instance, asks groups of male and female subjects to rate the same résumés, professional articles, and artwork. For some groups the work is ascribed to women, for others to men. Repeatedly, researchers have found that if a group thinks a man was the creator, the group rates it more highly than if they think a woman produced it.

The situation for women in blue-collar occupations is more difficult still. Margaret Schaeffer, a twenty-eight-year-old electrician's apprentice in Chicago and the single mother of boys ages nine and seven, told an interviewer in 1990 a typical story. Male workers told her, "Women don't belong in a job like this," a remark she called grossly offensive. Of all the blue-collar occupations, construction has remained the hardest for women to enter. Over the past decade women's share of jobs in this field has hovered around 2 percent. But the wages are high, more than $40,000 per year in good times, and therefore women's advocates are pushing hard to overcome men's opposition. Slowly, through the courts and on the job, women have begun to challenge the sexual taunts and other abuse that they have long suffered in male-dominated jobs.

For all the gains that women have made in these demanding fields, the most common occupations for women continue to be elementary-school teaching, nursing, retail sales, and service and clerical jobs. In teaching and nursing, salaries start at only $20,000; salaries in other predominantly female occupations are still lower. Women in sales earn an average of $14,000; women in service jobs, $11,000. Women who are married to employed men can cling to a middle-class standard of living by working in such jobs. But given the frequency of divorce, the financial irresponsibility of many men, the lack of support services, and women's child-rearing responsibilities, these jobs offer little economic security.

Higher levels of education and expanding opportunity have drawn sharply increasing numbers of married women into the labor force in the past decade. But the jobs available to most women either pay too little to support a family or demand so much time as to make family life extraordinarily difficult. The typical woman ends up feeling like the character in the vaudeville act who spins plates for a living. No sooner does she get all of her plates spinning than the one marked "children" begins to wobble. She rushes over to deal with that problem, only to see that another plate, marked "demands at work," is gyrating wildly. Just as she gets that plate spinning again the plate marked "household maintenance" topples and breaks. Despite the valiant efforts of feminists, women are still far from achieving economic equality with men. And they still remain very much tied to their families, providing most of the social services that the family claim has always exacted and without which society could not function. "Women today don't have it all; they just do it all," observes feminist writer Elizabeth Janeway. The consequence has been overwork for most women.

If America is to prosper in the next century, if children are to flourish and marriages succeed, women and men will have to make changes in their lives that are still more fundamental than any discussed in this book. They will have to find ways to restructure work so that it can accommodate the needs of families. They will have to renegotiate domestic life to accommodate women's increased aspirations. And they will have to persuade policymakers that social services like health care, day care, education, and income maintenance are critical national needs. Only if they succeed will women no longer feel torn between the family claim, to which they feel a continuing attachment, and the claim to equality, which, according to this country's most fundamental ideals, should by right have been theirs all along.

BIBLIOGRAPHICAL ESSAY

A vast body of work on American women in the twentieth century has appeared in the past several decades. The following bibliographical essay does not cover it all, but includes all of the sources from which quotes have been taken, as well as the principal secondary works consulted. Several books provide especially useful background to anyone seeking an overview of American women's history and modern gender relations: Nancy Woloch, *Women and the American Experience* (1984); Peter Filene, *Him/Her/Self: Sex Roles in Modern America*, 2nd ed. (1986); Sarah Evans, *Born for Liberty: A History of Women in America* (1989); and William Chafe, *The Paradox of Change: American Women in the Twentieth Century* (1991), which updates his earlier, pioneering work, *The American Woman* (1972). I have drawn on a number of historical overviews on specific themes throughout this book. On sexuality the best survey is John D'Emilio and Estelle Freedman, *Intimate Matters: A History of Sexuality in America* (1988). For the history of birth control and abortion see Linda Gordon, *Woman's Body, Woman's Right: A Social History of Birth Control in America* (1977); James Reed, *The Birth Control Movement in America: From Private Vice to Public Virtue* (1978); and James Mohr, *Abortion in America* (1978). The best surveys of the family are Carl Degler, *At Odds: Women and the Family in America from the Revolution to the Present* (1980), and Steven Mintz and Susan Kellogg, *Domestic Revolutions: A Social History of American Family Life* (1988). Linda Gordon, *Heroes of Their Own Lives: The Politics and History of Family Violence* (1988), and Elizabeth Pleck, *Domestic Tyranny: The Making of American Social Policy Against Family Violence from Colonial Times to the Present*

(1987), discuss the history of family violence. Patterns of fertility among different groups are discussed in Wilson H. Grabhill et al., *The Fertility of American Women* (1958). On childbirth see Judith Walzer Leavitt, *Brought to Bed: Childbearing in America, 1750–1950* (1986). The history of housework is ably recounted in Ruth Schwartz Cowan, *More Work for Mother: The Ironies of Household Technology from the Open Hearth to the Microwave* (1983); Susan Strasser, *Never Done: A History of American Housework* (1982); and Glenna Matthews, *"Just a Housewife": The Rise and Fall of Domesticity in America* (1987). Claudia Goldin, *Understanding the Gender Gap: An Economic History of American Women* (1990), and Julie A. Matthaei, *An Economic History of Women in America: Women's Work, the Sexual Division of Labor, and the Development of Capitalism* (1982), offer the best introductions to the place of women in American economic history, as well as the historical roots of sex segregation in the work force and the wage gap. For the history of wage work see Alice Kessler-Harris, *Out to Work: A History of Wage-Earning Women in the United States* (1982), and Lynn Weiner, *From Working Girl to Working Mother: The Female Labor Force in the United States, 1820–1980* (1985). Part of the challenge of writing American women's history is the diversity of women's experience. Fortunately, a number of works have been written recently that deal specifically with different ethnic and racial groups. The best surveys of African-American women are Jacqueline Jones, *Labor of Love, Labor of Sorrow: Black Women, Work and the Family from Slavery to the Present* (1985), and Paula Giddings, *When and Where I Enter: The Impact of Black Women on Race and Sex in America* (1984). On white women in the South see Anne Firor Scott, *The Southern Lady: From Pedestal to Politics, 1830–1930* (1970), and Shirley Abbott, *Womenfolk: Growing Up Down South* (1983). Sarah Deutsch, *No Separate Refuge: Culture, Class, and Gender on an Anglo-Hispanic Frontier in the American Southwest, 1880–1940* (1987), offers a good introduction to the experience of Mexican-American women. Useful works on immigrants include Hasia R. Diner, *Erin's Daughters in America: Irish Immigrant Women in the Nineteenth Century* (1983); Virginia Yans-McGlaughlin, *Family and Community: Italian Immigrants in Buffalo, 1880–1930* (1977); Ronald Takaki, *Strangers from a Different Shore: A History of Asian Americans* (1989); and Sidney Stahl Steinberg, *The World of Our Mothers: The Lives of Jewish Immigrant Women* (1988). Little exists as yet on the lives of Native-American women, but I found useful Caroline Niethammer, *Daughters of the Earth: The Lives and Legends of American Indian Women* (1977).

Excellent document collections include Gerda Lerner, ed., *Black*

Women in White America: A Documentary History (1972); Maxine Seller, ed., *Immigrant Women* (1981); Susan Ware, ed., *Modern American Women: A Documentary History* (1989); and Mary Beth Norton, ed., *Major Problems in American Women's History* (1989). Edward T. James, Janet Wilson James, and Paul S. Boyer, eds., *Notable American Women: A Biographical Dictionary*, 3 vols. (1971), and Barbara Sicherman and Carol Hurd Green, eds., *Notable American Women: The Modern Period* (1980), provide invaluable biographical essays on many of the women discussed herein.

1. The Family Claim: 1900

On the centrality of the family in shaping women's lives see Jane Addams, "The College Woman and the Family Claim," *The Commons* (September 1898): 3–7; Leslie Woodcock Tentler, *Wage-Earning Women: Industrial Work and Family Life in the United States, 1900–1930* (1979); and the first chapter in Phyllis Rose's *Parallel Lives: Five Victorian Marriages* (1984). Zora Neale Hurston, *Dust Tracks on the Road* (1942), and Robert Hemenway, *Zora Neale Hurston: A Literary Biography* (1978), recount the life of Lucy Potts Hurston. On sexuality in the South see Christie Farnham, "Sapphire? The Issue of Dominance in the Slave Family, 1830–1865," in Carol Groneman and Mary Beth Norton, eds., *"To Toil the Livelong Day": America's Women at Work, 1780–1980* (1987), pp. 68–83, and Hortense Powdermaker, *After Freedom: A Cultural Study in the Deep South* (1939). Information on the Ozarks comes from D'Emilio and Freedman, *Intimate Matters*. On economic conditions in the South see Gavin Wright, *Old South, New South: Revolutions in the Southern Economy Since the Civil War* (1986), and Jones, *Labor of Love, Labor of Sorrow*. On alcohol consumption at the turn of the century see Ruth Bordin, *Woman and Temperance: The Quest for Power and Liberty, 1873–1900* (1981). Darlene Hine, *Black Women in White: Racial Conflict and Cooperation in the Nursing Profession, 1890–1950* (1989), describes racial barriers in health care.

Peter Kurth, *American Cassandra: The Life of Dorothy Thompson* (1990), includes a brief biography of Margaret Thompson. I have elaborated on Thompson's domestic tasks by drawing from the sources on housework and family life listed above. The best general treatments of women and the law are Michael Grossberg, *Governing the Hearth: Law and the Family in Nineteenth-Century America* (1985), and Leo Kanowitz, *Women and the Law: The Unfinished Revolution* (1969). Nancy Cott compares the marital contract to the law governing indentured servitude in *The Grounding of Modern Feminism* (1987). On divorce see Elaine Tyler May, *Great Expectations: Marriage and Divorce in Post-Victorian America* (1980). On the laws regulating contraception and abortion and the medical community's role in enforcing them see D'Emilio and Freedman, *Intimate Matters*; Gordon, *Woman's Body, Woman's Right*; and Mohr, *Abortion in America*. Margaret Sanger, *An Autobiography* (1938), describes the plight of immigrant women on the Lower East Side. On laws restricting women's political freedom see Eleanor Flexnor, *Century of Struggle* (1959). For useful analyses of Victorian sexual ideology see Carroll Smith-Rosenberg, *Disorderly Conduct: Views of Gender in Victorian America* (1985); G. J. Barker-Benfield, *The Horrors of the Half-known Life: Male Attitudes Toward Women and Sexuality in Nineteenth-Century America* (1976); Clelia Duel Mosher, *The Mosher Survey: Sexual Attitudes of Forty-Five Victorian Women*, edited by James Manhood and Kristine Wenburg (1980); and Kate Simon, *Bronx Primitive: Portraits in a Childhood* (1982).

The possibilities that urban America and the new consumer culture offered young women is analyzed in William Leach, "The Clown from Syracuse: The Life and Times of L. Frank Baum," introduction to *L. Frank Baum, The Wonderful Wizard of Oz* (1900; reprinted by the Wadsworth Publishing Company, 1991). On the city as a frontier for women see the classic essay by David Potter, "American Women and the American Character," in John Hague, ed., *American Character and Culture* (1964). For the life of Sadie Frowne see Frowne, "The Story of a Sweatshop Girl," *Independent* 55 (September 25, 1902): 2279–82, reprinted in David Katzman and William Tuttle, eds., *Plain Folk: The Life Stories of Undistinguished Americans* (1982). George Mowry, *The Era of Theodore Roosevelt and the Birth of Modern America, 1900–1912* (1958), compares standards of living in urban and rural America at the turn of the century. For conditions among the urban poor see Jacob Riis, *How the Other Half Lives* (1890), on New York; Robert Hunter, *Poverty* (1900), on Chicago; Margaret Byington, *Homestead: The Households of a Mill Town* (1910), on the steel mills of Homestead, Pennsylvania; and Jacquelyn Dowd Hall et al., *Like a Family: The Making of a Southern Cotton Mill World* (1987), on Southern textile mill towns. Diane K. Applebaum, "The Level of the Poverty Line: A Historical Survey," *Social Service Review* 51 (September 1977): 514–23, discusses the difficulty of determining poverty levels over time. Elizabeth Butler, *Women and the Trades, Pittsburgh, 1907–1908* (1909), describes the sex segregation of occupations in Pittsburgh early in the century. Martha May, "Bread Before Roses: American Workingmen, Labor Unions, and the Family Wage," in Ruth Milkman, ed., *Women,*

Work, and Protest: A Century of U.S. Women's Labor History (1985), describes the evolution of the idea that men should be paid enough to support a family. For descriptions of the different kinds of work in which women engaged see David Katzman, *Seven Days a Week: Women and Domestic Service in Industrializing America* (1978), on domestic service; Sheila Rothman, *Woman's Proper Place: A History of Changing Ideals and Practices, 1870–Present* (1978), and Susan Porter Benson, *Counter Cultures: Saleswomen, Managers, and Customers in American Department Stores, 1890–1940* (1986), on salesclerks; David B. Tyack, *The One Best System: A History of American Urban Education* (1974), Agnes Smedley, *Daughter of Earth* (1929), Deutsch, *No Separate Refuge*, and James D. Anderson, *The Education of Blacks in the South, 1860–1935* (1988), on teachers; Margery Davies, *Woman's Place Is at the Typewriter: Office Work and Office Workers, 1870–1930* (1982), and Lisa M. Fine, *The Souls of the Skyscraper: Female Clerical Workers in Chicago, 1870–1930* (1990), on clerical workers; and Barbara Melosh, *The Physician's Hand: Nurses and Nursing in the Twentieth Century* (1982), and Susan Riverby, *Ordered to Care: The Dilemma of American Nursing, 1850–1945*, on nursing. For the social life of working-class young women see D'Emilio and Freedman, *Intimate Matters*; Kathy Peiss, *Cheap Amusements: Working Women and Leisure in Turn-of-the-Century New York* (1986); Jane Addams, *The Spirit of Youth and the City Streets* (1909); and Joanne J. Meyerowitz, *Women Adrift: Independent Wage Earners in Chicago, 1880–1930* (1988). On prostitution see Ruth Rosen, *The Lost Sisterhood: Prostitution in America, 1900–1918* (1982), and Lucie Cheng Hirata, "Chinese Immigrant Women in Nineteenth-Century California," in Carol Berkin and Mary Beth Norton, eds., *Women of America: A History* (1979). Daniel Scott Smith, "The Dating of the American Sexual Revolution," in Michael Gordon, ed., *The American Family in Social-Historical Perspective* (1973), charts the rise in premarital intercourse in the general population, while Katharine Bement Davis, *Factors in the Sex Life of Twenty-Two Hundred Women* (1929), offers evidence on middle-class women.

For more on the life of Jane Addams one should consult Allen Davis, *American Heroine: The Life and Legend of Jane Addams* (1973), and Ann Firor Scott, "Jane Addams," in Scott, *Making the Invisible Woman Visible* (1984). Barbara Miller Solomon, *In the Company of Educated Women* (1985), provides the best overview of the history of higher education for women. For the women's colleges see Helen Lefkowitz Horowitz, *Alma Mater: Design and Experience in the Women's Colleges from Their Nineteenth-Century Beginnings to the 1930s* (1984), and Roberta Frankfort, *Collegiate Women: Domesticity and Career in Turn-of-the-Century America* (1977). The ambivalence of educators regarding women's roles is analyzed in Adele Simmons, "Education and Ideology in Nineteenth-Century America: The Response of Educational Institutions to the Changing Role of Women," in Berenice Carroll, ed., *Liberating Women's History* (1976). On higher education for black women see Jean Noble, *The Negro Women's College Education* (1956). Barbara Sicherman, "College and Careers: Historical Perspectives on the Lives and Work Patterns of Women College Graduates," in John Mack Faragher and Florence Howe, eds., *Women and Higher Education in American History* (1988), gives the best brief account of the work opportunities available at the turn of the century to women college graduates. For the experience of black women teachers in the South see Mamie Garvin Fields, *Lemon Swamp and Other Places* (1983). Lela B. Costin, *Two Sisters for Justice: A Biography of Grace and Edith Abbott* (1983), recounts Grace Abbott's early teaching experience, as well as both sisters' graduate training and careers in social work. Rosalind Rosenberg, *Beyond Separate Spheres: Intellectual Roots of Modern Feminism* (1982), analyzes the careers of early women social scientists. Margaret Rossiter, *Women Scientists in America: Struggles and Strategies to 1940* (1982), discusses the situation for women in science more generally. Virginia G. Drachman, "Women Lawyers and the Quest for Professional Identity in Late Nineteenth-Century America," *Michigan Law Review* 88 (August 1990): 2414–43, describes the difficulties women lawyers faced at the turn of the century. Regina Morantz-Sanchez, *Sympathy and Science: Women Physicians in American Medicine* (1985), is the best work on women doctors. On the emergence of social work as a career for women see Barbara Sicherman, *Alice Hamilton: A Life in Letters* (1984); Ellen Fitzpatrick, *Endless Crusade: Women Social Scientists and Progressive Reform* (1990); and Roy Lubove, *The Professional Altruist: The Emergence of Social Work as a Career* (1965). On settlements see Allen Davis, *Spearheads for Reform: The Social Settlements and the Progressive Movement, 1890–1914* (1967), and Kathryn Kish Sklar, "Hull House in the 1890s: A Community of Women Reformers," *Signs* 10 (Summer 1985): 657–77. Jane Addams describes her career in social work in her autobiographies, *Twenty Years at Hull House* (1910) and *The Second Twenty Years at Hull House* (1930). Christopher Lasch, ed., *The Social Thought of Jane Addams* (1965), is a useful collection of Addams's most important essays. James T. Kloppenberg, *Uncertain Victory: Social Democracy and Progressivism in European and American Thought, 1870–1920* (1986), surveys the intellectual debates that led social reformers to a new understanding of the causes of poverty. Edith Abbott and Sophinisba Breckenridge, *Truancy and Non-Attendance in the Chicago Schools* (1917), analyzes the economic basis of juvenile delinquency. The tensions that persisted between settlement workers and their neighbors are discussed in Seller, ed., *Immigrant Women*, chapter 5. Karen J. Blair, *The Club Woman as Feminist: True Womanhood Redefined, 1868–1914* (1980), describes the rise of the woman's club movement. For black women's success in building their own club movement see Gerda Lerner, "Community Work of Black Club Women," in Lerner, *The Majority Finds Its Past: Placing Women in History* (1979); pp. 83–93; Cynthia Neverdon-Morton, *Afro-American Women of the South and the Advancement of the Race, 1895–1925* (1989); and Giddings, *When and Where I Enter*. On Charlotte Perkins Gilman see Ann J. Lane, *To Herland and Beyond: The Life and Work of Charlotte Perkins Gilman* (1990). Jessie Taft, *The Woman's Movement from the Point of View of Social Consciousness* (1916), explains why many educated women preferred women to men as life companions. On "Boston marriages," see D'Emilio and Freedman, *Intimate Matters*. Davis, *Factors in the Sex Life*, describes the sexual practices of educated women in the early twentieth century. Estelle Freedman, "Separatism as Strategy," *Feminist Studies* 5 (Fall 1979): 512–29, analyzes the pivotal role of female communities in fostering change.

2. Domesticating the State: 1901–12

On the trend away from state responsibility for public welfare in the nineteenth century and women reformers' response see Paula Baker, "The Domestication of Politics: Women and American Political Society, 1780–1920," *American Historical Review* 89 (June 1984): 620–47. On early efforts to reassert state responsibility see William R. Brock, *Investigation and Responsibility: Public Responsibility in the United States, 1865–1900* (1984). For a good overview of progressive politics see David Kennedy, *Progressivism* (1971). William O'Neill, *Everyone Was Brave: A History of Feminism in America* (1969), remains a valuable source on women's organizing efforts in the early twentieth century. On the life and thought of Florence Kelley see Josephine Goldmark, *Impatient Crusader: Florence Kelley's Life Story* (1953), and Kathryn Kish Sklar, ed., *The Autobiography of Florence Kelley: Notes on Sixty Years* (1986). For organizing among immigrant Jewish housewives see Paula Hyman, "Immigrant Women and Consumer Protest: The New York City Kosher Meat Boycott of 1902," *American Jewish History* 70 (1980): 91–105. Leon Fink, "Labor, Liberty, and the Law: Trade Unionism and the Problem of the American Constitutional Order," *The Journal of American History* 74 (December 1987): 904–25, analyzes the role of America's judicial system in inhibiting labor organizing. Alice Kessler-Harris, "Where Are the Organized Women Workers?" *Feminist Studies* 3 (Fall 1975): 92–110, discusses the special problems associated with organizing women workers. On the Women's Trade Union League see Nancy Schrom Dye, *As Equals and As Sisters: Feminism, Unionism, and the Women's Trade Union League of New York* (1980), and Colette A. Hyman, "Labor Organizing and Female Institution Building: The Chicago Women's Trade Union League, 1904–24," in Ruth Milkman, ed., *Women, Work and Protest.* Meredith Tax, *The Rising of the Women: Feminist Solidarity and Class Conflict, 1880–1917* (1980), discusses the organizing work of Mary Kenney and Leonora O'Reilly, the shirtwaist-makers' strike, the strike at Lawrence, and the Wobblies. The best brief account of the shirtwaist-makers' strike is Nancy Woloch, "The Shirtwaist Strike," in Woloch, *Women and the American Experience* (1984). For the career of Rose Schneiderman see *One for All*, written with Lucy Goldwaite (1967). On the Wobblies see Ann Schofield, "Rebel Girls and Union Maids: The Woman Question in the Journals of the AFL and IWW, 1905–1920," *Feminist Studies* 9 (Summer 1983): 335–58, and Elizabeth Gurley Flynn, *The Rebel Girl: An Autobiography* (1955).

Robyn Muncy, *Creating a Female Dominion in American Reform, 1890–1935* (1991), offers a good overview of women's reform efforts. For the campaign against child labor, see Mary Field Parton, ed., *The Autobiography of Mother Jones* (1925); Viviana A. Zelizer, *Pricing the Priceless Child: The Changing Value of Children* (1985); and Michael Katz, *In the Shadow of the Poorhouse: A Social History of Welfare in America* (1986), chapter 5. Molly Ladd-Taylor, *Raising a Baby the Government Way: Mothers' Letters to the Children's Bureau, 1915–1932* (1986), and Nancy Schrom Dye and Daniel Blake Smith, "Mother Love and Infant Death, 1750–1920," *The Journal of American History* 73 (September 1986): 329–53, discuss the early years of the Children's Bureau. The history of protective labor legislation for women is recounted in Judith Baer, *The Chains of Protection: The Judicial Response to Women's Labor Legislation* (1978), and Susan Lehrer, *Origins of Protective Labor Legislation for Women, 1905–1925* (1987). Barbara Meil Hobson, *Uneasy Virtue: The Politics of Prostitution and the American Reform Tradition* (1987); Rosen, *The Lost Sisterhood*; and D'Emilio and Freedman, *Intimate Matters*, discuss reformers' reaction to prostitution. On the development of social welfare policies see Roy Lubove, *The Struggle for Social Security, 1900–1935* (1968), and James T. Patterson, *America's Struggle Against Poverty, 1900–1985* (1986); Edith Abbott and Sophinisba Breckenridge, *The Administration of the Aid-to-Mothers Law in Illinois* (1921); and U.S. Children's Bureau, *Mothers' Aid* (1931). On reformers' reluctance to extend mothers' aid to divorced women see Linda Gordon, *Heroes of Their Own Lives*. For Crystal Eastman's role in the passage of workmen's compensation legislation see Blanche Wiesen Cook, ed., *Crystal Eastman: On Women and Revolution* (1978); and Crystal Eastman, *Work Accidents and the Law* (1910).

Aileen Kraditor, *The Ideas of the Woman Suffrage Movement, 1890–1920* (1965), analyzes the changing arguments in support of suffrage. On the suffrage movement in the South see Scott, *The Southern Lady*. The best brief overview is Degler, *At Odds*, chapter 14. Anne F. Scott and Andrew Scott, *One Half the People: The Fight for Woman Suffrage* (1975), includes a fine collection of documents. On the radical heritage of the suffragists see Ellen Carol DuBois, "The Radicalism of the Woman Suffrage Movement: Notes Toward a Reconstruction of Nineteenth-Century Feminism," *Feminist Studies* 3 (Fall 1975): 63–71. Ross Evans Paulson, *Women's Suffrage and Prohibition: A Comparative Study of Equality and Social Control* (1973), discusses suffragists' early disappointment in Massachusetts. Ellen Carol DuBois, "Working Women, Class Relations, and Suffrage Militance: Harriot Stanton Blatch and the New York Woman Suffrage Movement, 1894–1909," *The Journal of American History* 74 (June 1987): 34–58, analyzes the efforts of the second generation of suffragists to reach out to working-class women. Mary Jo Buhle, *Women and American Socialism 1870–1920* (1981), examines the role of socialist women in the suffrage campaign. On racism in the suffrage campaign see Giddings, *When and Where I Enter*; Angela Y. Davis, *Women, Race, and Class* (1981); and Roslyn Terborg-Penn, "Afro-Americans in the Struggle for Woman Suffrage," Ph.D. dissertation, Howard University, 1977. On new tactics in the suffrage campaign see Sharon Hartman Strom, "Leadership and Tactics in the American Woman Suffrage Movement: A New Perspective from Massachusetts," *The Journal of American History* 62 (September 1975): 296–315. Davis, *American Heroine*; Davis, *Spearheads for Reform*; and Costin, *Two Sisters*, describe the social reformers' moment of triumph in the Progressive Party.

3. Claiming the Rights of Men: 1912–29

Nancy Cott, *The Grounding of Modern Feminism* (1987), is the best source for the evolution of the meaning of "feminism" in the U.S.

between 1910 and 1930. For more on Heterodoxy see Judith Schwartz, *Radical Feminists of Heterodoxy: Greenwich Village, 1912–1940* (1982), and Rheta Childe Dorr, *A Woman of Fifty* (1924). Rosenberg, *Beyond Separate Spheres*, discusses feminist work in the social sciences. June Sochen, *The New Woman: Feminism in Greenwich Village, 1910–1920* (1972), is good on Henrietta Rodman. On Belle Moskowitz and sexual attitudes among middle-class urban youth in the teens see Lewis A. Erenberg, *Steppin' Out: New York Nightlife and the Transformation of American Culture, 1890–1930* (1981). Alix Kates Shulman, ed., *Red Emma Speaks: An Emma Goldman Reader* (1983), gives the best introduction to Goldman. On Ellen Key's influence on American feminists see Floyd Dell, *Women as World Builders: Studies in Modern Feminism* (1913). Cook, ed., *Crystal Eastman*, includes Eastman's thoughts on the challenge to feminists of dealing with motherhood.

In addition to the general histories of suffrage listed above, one should consult the following for the final years of the campaign: Christine A. Lunardini, *From Equal Suffrage to Equal Rights: Alice Paul and the National Woman's Party, 1910–1928* (1986); Robert Booth Fowler, *Carrie Catt: Feminist Politician* (1986); Jacqueline Van Voris, *Carrie Chapman Catt: A Public Life* (1987); and Doris Stevens, *Jailed for Freedom* (1920). On women and World War I see Maurine Greenwood, *Women, War, and Work* (1980). Mary Louise Degan, *The History of the Woman's Peace Party* (1939), describes women's efforts to forestall war.

On the rise and decline of women's influence on politics in the 1920s see J. Stanley Lemons, *The Woman Citizen: Social Feminism in the 1920s* (1973), and Chafe, *Paradox of Change*. Anne Firor Scott discusses women's reform efforts in the South in "After Suffrage: Southern Women in the Twenties," *Journal of Southern History* 30 (August 1964): 298–315. Lois Scharf and Joan M. Jensen, *Decades of Discontent: The Women's Movement, 1920–1940* (1983), includes several essays on women's political efforts in the 1920s. Rothman, *Woman's Proper Place*, and Costin, *Two Sisters*, are especially good on the Sheppard-Towner Act. Lemons, *Woman Citizen*, tells the story of the "spider's web." Susan D. Becker, *The Origins of the Equal Rights Amendment: American Feminism Between the Wars* (1981), discusses the early debates surrounding the ERA.

On Margaret Sanger see Ellen Chesler, *Woman of Valor: Margaret Sanger and the Birth Control Movement in America* (1992). Gordon, *Woman's Body, Woman's Right*, is an excellent history of the birth control movement since the nineteenth century. David Kennedy, *Birth Control in America: The Career of Margaret Sanger* (1970), is especially useful on the history of medicine, law, and religion in relation to birth control. On the eugenics movement in America see Daniel J. Kevles, *In the Name of Eugenics: Genetics and the Use of Human Heredity* (1985). Margaret Sanger published two autobiographies, *My Fight for Birth Control* (1931) and *An Autobiography* (1938), as well as a number of books on birth control, including *Women and the New Race* (1920), *The Pivot of Civilization* (1922), *Happiness in Marriage* (1926), and *Womanhood in Bondage* (1928). On Katharine Hepburn see Christopher Andersen, *Young Kate: The Remarkable Hepburns and the Childhood That Shaped an American Legend* (1988).

On the "new feminists" of the 1920s see Elaine Showalter, ed., *These Modern Women: Autobiographical Essays from the Twenties* (1978); Dorothy Dunbar Bromley, "Feminist—New Style," *Harper's* 155 (October 1927): 552–60; and Estelle Freedman, "The New Woman: Changing Views of Women in the 1920s," *Journal of American History* 61 (September 1974): 372–93. For the quickening pace of change among the young see Paula Fass, *The Damned and the Beautiful: American Youth in the 1920s* (1977); Helen Lefkowitz Horowitz, *Campus Life: Undergraduate Cultures from the End of the Eighteenth Century to the Present* (1987); Beth Bailey, *From Front Porch to Back Seat: Courtship in Twentieth-Century America* (1988); Robert Lynd and Helen Lynd, *Middletown: A Study in Modern American Culture* (1929); Alfred Kinsey et al., *Sexual Behavior in the Human Female* (1953); and Davis, *Factors in the Sex Life*.

Cott, *The Grounding of Modern Feminism*, chapter 3, discusses women's work as volunteers in the 1920s and 1930s and their shifting work patterns. For more on married women's work-force participation see Winifred Wandersee, *Women's Work and Family Values, 1920–1940* (1981); Frank Stricker, "Affluence for Whom? Another Look at Prosperity and the Working Classes in the 1920s," *Labor History* 24 (Winter 1984): 5–33; Maurine Weiner Greenwald, "Working-Class Feminism and the Family Wage Ideal: The Seattle Debate on Married Women's Right to Work, 1914–1920," *Journal of American History* 76 (June 1989): 118–49; and Lynd and Lynd, *Middletown*. For professional women see Frank Stricker, "Cookbooks and Law Books: The Hidden History of Career Women in Twentieth-Century America," in Nancy Cott and Elizabeth Pleck, eds., *A Heritage of Her Own* (1979). On Margaret Mead see Rosenberg, *Beyond Separate Spheres*; Margaret Mead, *Blackberry Winter: My Earlier Years* (1970); and Jane Howard, *Margaret Mead: A Life* (1984). On black married women workers in the North see Jones, *Labor of Love, Labor of Sorrow*. Lois Scharf, *To Work and to Wed: Female Employment, Feminism, and the Depres-*

sion (1980), discusses the barriers to employment for professional women in the 1920s and 1930s. Sicherman, ed., *Alice Hamilton*, discusses Hamilton's career at Harvard. On the issue of nepotism and other barriers to women in academia see Rosenberg, "The Limits of Access," in Faragher and Howe, ed., *Women and Higher Education*. The reference to Virginia Gildersleeve is based on the Gildersleeve Papers, Columbia University; I am grateful to Caroline Niemczyk, who is writing a biography of Gildersleeve, for bringing this material to my attention. Regina Morantz-Sanchez, *Sympathy and Science*, analyzes the meaning of *Arrowsmith* in the context of the declining fortunes of women public-health advocates. On women in government see Lemons, *Woman Citizen*, and Scharf, *To Work and to Wed*. On changing patterns in housework and motherhood see Cowan, *More Work for Mother*. Sara Alpern, *Freda Kirchwey: A Woman of The Nation* (1987), describes Kirchwey's efforts to combine motherhood and editorial work. Crystal Eastman's "Birth Control in the Feminist Program," "Now We Can Begin," and "Marriage Under Two Roofs," in Cook, ed., *Crystal Eastman*, covers Eastman's views on feminism and marriage. On Ethel Puffer Howe see Elizabeth Scarborough and Laurel Furumoto, *Untold Lives: The First Generation of American Women Psychologists* (1987). Frederic C. Howe, *The Confessions of a Reformer* (1925), reveals this male reformer's double standard of equality. Peter Filene describes Dorothy Thompson's tempestuous marriage to Sinclair Lewis in *Him/Her/Self*. See also Kurth, *American Cassandra*.

4. Crisis Years: 1929–45

Susan Ware, *Holding Their Own: American Women in the 1930s* (1982), provides a fine overview of women in the Great Depression. Scharf and Jensen, eds., *Decades of Discontent*, includes several essays on the Depression. For general background on the Depression see Robert S. McElvaine, *The Great Depression: America 1929–1941* (1984). Scharf, *To Work and to Wed*, charts the decline of women's professional opportunities in the 1930s. Mirra Komarovsky, *The Unemployed Man and His Family: The Effects of Underemployment Upon the Status of Men in Fifty-nine Families* (1940), reports opposition to working wives even among unemployed husbands. Ruth Milkman, *Gender at Work: The Dynamics of Job Segregation by Sex During World War II* (1987), devotes the first chapter to a discussion of women in the electrical and automotive industries during the Depression. Wandersee, *Women's Work and Family Values*, reports that some businesses were more accepting of married women workers than others. Claudia Goldin,

Understanding the Gender Gap, explains the wage gap. Ruth Milkman, "Women's Work and the Economic Crisis: Some Lessons from the Great Depression," in Cott and Pleck, eds., *A Heritage of Her Own* (1979), analyzes the ways in which the sex segregation of the work force offered women a certain degree of protection from unemployment. Jones, *Labor of Love, Labor of Sorrow*, discusses the impact of the Depression on black women, as well as on Mexican women. The Women's Bureau conducted an extensive investigation of business hiring practices around the country during the 1930s; the records are available at the National Archives. Susan Ware, *Holding Their Own*, chapter 7, is very good on popular heroines of the 1930s. On women in sport see Ellen Gerber, *The American Woman in Sport* (1976). On women in the movies see Molly Haskell, *From Reverence to Rape: The Treatment of Women in the Movies* (1974), and Marjorie Rosen, *Popcorn Venus: Women, Movies, and the American Dream* (1973).

Jeane Westin, *Making Do: How Women Survived the 1930s* (1976), and Robert Lynd and Helen Lynd, *Middletown in Transition: A Study in Cultural Conflicts* (1937), describe the various ways housewives coped with falling incomes. Margaret Hagood, *Mothers of the South: Portraiture of the White Tenant Farm Woman* (1939), examines family life in the rural South. For firsthand accounts of life in the Depression see Studs Terkel, *Hard Times* (1970). Sociological studies provide one of the best sources on the impact of the Depression on family life. See, especially, Komarovsky, *The Unemployed Man and His Family*; Eli Ginzburg, *The Unemployed* (1943); Lynd and Lynd, *Middletown in Transition*; and Powdermaker, *After Slavery*. On birth control and abortion in the 1930s see D'Emilio and Freedman, *Intimate Matters*, chapter 11; Leslie Reagan, " 'About to Meet Her Maker': Women, Doctors, Dying Declarations, and the State's Investigation of Abortion, Chicago, 1867–1940," *The Journal of American History* 77 (March 1991): 1240–64; and Chesler, *Woman of Valor*.

Joseph Lash, *Eleanor and Franklin: The Story of Their Relationship Based on Eleanor Roosevelt's Private Papers* (1971), provides the best introduction to Eleanor Roosevelt's life. See also Eleanor Roosevelt, *It's Up to the Women* (1933), and *This I Remember* (1949); Joan Hoff-Wilson and Marjorie Lightman, eds., *Without Precedent: The Life and Career of Eleanor Roosevelt* (1984); and Lois Scharf, *Eleanor Roosevelt: First Lady of American Liberalism* (1987). Susan Ware, *Beyond Suffrage: Women in the New Deal* (1981), analyzes the contribution of Eleanor Roosevelt, Molly Dewson, Frances Perkins, and other members of the "women's network" to the New Deal. On Dewson see Susan Ware, *Partner and I: Molly Dewson, Feminism, and New Deal*

Politics (1987). On Roosevelt's Secretary of Labor see George Martin, *Madame Secretary: Frances Perkins* (1976); Frances Perkins, *The Roosevelt I Knew* (1946); and the Frances Perkins Oral History Collection at Columbia University.

The history of the modern welfare state is growing rapidly. See Linda Gordon, ed., *Women, the State, and Welfare* (1990); Margaret Weir and Theda Skocpol, "State Structures and the Possibilities for 'Keynesian' Responses to the Great Depression in Sweden, Britain, and the United States," in Peter Evans et al., eds., *Bringing the State Back In* (1985); Costin, *Two Sisters*; Grace Abbott, *From Relief to Social Security: The Development of the New Public Welfare Services and Their Administration* (1941); Mimi Abramovitz, *Regulating the Lives of Women: Social Welfare Policy from Colonial Times to the Present* (1988); Lubove, *The Struggle for Social Security*; Dorothy Bradbury, *Four Decades of Action for Children: A Short History of the Children's Bureau* (1956); the Katherine Lenroot Oral History Collection at Columbia University (1956); and Edwin E. Witte, *The Development of the Social Security Act* (1962). On women in unions and radicalism consult Sharon Hartman Strom, "Challenging 'Woman's Place': Feminism, the Left, and Industrial Unionism in the 1930s," *Feminist Studies* 9 (Summer 1983): 359–86; Dolores Janiewski, *Sisterhood Denied: Race, Gender and Class in a New South Community* (1985); Milkman, *Gender at Work*; Hall et al., *Like a Family*, chapter 6; Staughton Lynd and Alice Lynd, *Rank and File: Personal Histories of Working-Class Organizers* (1973); Rosalyn Baxandall et al., eds., *America's Working Women: A Documentary History, 1600 to the Present* (1976); Vivian Gornick, *The Romance of American Communism* (1977); Carol Gelderman, *Mary McCarthy: A Life* (1988); and Milkman, ed., *Women, Work, and Protest*.

On the impact of the Depression on minority women and women's role in the civil rights movement during those years see Jones, *Labor of Love, Labor of Sorrow*; Giddings, *When and Where I Enter*; Jacquelyn Dowd Hall, *Revolt Against Chivalry: Jessie Daniel Ames and the Women's Campaign Against Lynching* (1979); Lillian Smith, *Killers of the Dream* (1949); Lerner, *Black Women in White America*; Hemenway, *Zora Neale Hurston*; Rackham Holt, *Mary McLeod Bethune: A Biography* (1964); William Chafe, "Biographical Sketch," in Hoff-Wilson and Lightman, eds., *Without Precedent*; and Alison Bernstein, "A Mixed Record: The Political Enfranchisement of American Indian Women During the Indian New Deal," *Journal of the West* 23 (July 1984): 13–20.

For an overview of women's experience in World War II one should begin with Chafe, *The American Woman* (1971; revised as *The Paradox of Change* [1991]). In 1971 Chafe argued that World War II was the pivotal event in twentieth-century women's experience, and all subsequent works on this topic have been informed by the issues he raised. See, in particular, Susan M. Hartmann, *The Home Front and Beyond: American Women in the 1940s* (1982); D'Ann Campbell, *Women at War with America* (1984); and Karen Anderson, *Wartime Women: Sex Roles, Family Relations, and the Status of Women During World War II* (1981). Sherna Berger Gluck, *Rosie the Riveter Revisited: Women, the War and Social Change* (1987), includes oral histories of women from diverse backgrounds who worked in war industries. Monica Sone, *Nisei Daughter* (1953); Takaki, *Strangers from a Different Shore*; and Roger Daniels, *Concentration Camps USA: Japanese Americans and World War II* (1971), tell the story of Japanese-American internment. On the ambivalence of the government over the issue of recruiting women workers see Leila Rupp, *Mobilizing Women for War: German and American Propaganda, 1939–1945* (1978). Alan Brinkley, "The New Deal and the Idea of the State," in Steve Fraser and Gary Gerstle, eds., *The Rise and Fall of the New Deal Order, 1930–1980* (1989), offers an important analysis of the federal government's second thoughts about the advisability of a strong, federal government during World War II. Milkman, *Gender at Work*, analyzes the role of unions and employers in maintaining sex segregation in the electrical and auto industries during the war and after. See also Kessler-Harris, *Out to Work*, chapter 10, which challenges William Chafe's thesis that World War II was a watershed for women in the work force.

5. Cold War Fears: 1945–61

Betty Friedan includes autobiographical fragments in all three of her books: *The Feminine Mystique* (1963); *It Changed My Life: Writings of the Woman's Movement* (1976); and *The Second Stage* (1981). See also Marcia Cohen, *The Sisterhood: The True Story of the Women Who Changed the World* (1988), and Paul Wilkes, "Mother Superior to Women's Lib," *The New York Times Magazine*, November 29, 1970, p. 27. Nicholas Lemann, *The Promised Land: The Great Migration and How It Changed America* (1991), tells the story of Ruby Lee Daniels.

On the importance of federal policies in the rise of the suburb see Kenneth Jackson, *Crabgrass Frontier: The Suburbanization of the United States* (1985). Dolores Hayden, *Redesigning the American Dream: The Future of Housing, Work, and Family Life* (1984), and

Gwendolyn Wright, *Building the American Dream: A Social History of Housing in America* (1981), analyze the impact of suburban growth on women's lives. Elaine Tyler May, *Homeward Bound: American Families in the Cold War Era* (1988), sets postwar domesticity within the larger context of the Cold War. A number of sociologists examined the lives of suburban dwellers after World War II. See, especially, Herbert Gans, *The Levittowners: Ways of Life and Politics in a New Suburban Community* (1967), and Bennet M. Berger, *Working-Class Suburb: A Study of Auto Workers in Suburbia* (1960). For the problems faced by African-Americans searching for housing see Lemann, *Promised Land*; "Fanny Christina Hill" in Gluck, ed., *Rosie the Riveter Revisited*; and Jones, *Labor of Love, Labor of Sorrow*.

For an overview of the demographic trends of the 1940s see Hartmann, *The Home Front and Beyond*, and Mintz and Kellogg, *Domestic Revolutions*, chapter 9. Solomon, *In the Company of Educated Women*, reports on the decline in college women's belief that family and career can be successfully combined. John Kenneth Galbraith, *The Affluent Society* (1958), and Patterson, *America's Struggle Against Poverty*, discuss economic growth in the postwar years. On how memories of the Great Depression shaped postwar women's view of family life see Glen Elder, *Children of the Great Depression: Social Change and Life Experience* (1974), and May, *Homeward Bound*. On housework see Cowan, *More Work for Mother*, chapter 7, and Joann Vanek, "Time Spent in Housework," in Cott and Pleck, eds., *A Heritage of Her Own*. On childbirth see Leavitt, *Brought to Bed*. The centrality of motherhood in most women's lives is explored in Lee Rainwater, Richard Coleman, and Gerald Handel, *Workingman's Wife: Her Personality, World, and Lifestyle* (1959); Jessie Bernard, *Marriage and Family Among Negroes* (1966); and May, *Homeward Bound*, chapter 6. On medical changes and their effect on mothering see Mintz and Kellogg, *Domestic Revolutions*, chapter 9. Nancy Weiss, "Motherhood, the Invention of Necessity: Dr. Benjamin Spock's *Baby and Child Care*," *American Quarterly* 29 (Winter 1977): 519–46, discusses changes in child-rearing advice. On "momism" see William Chafe, *Paradox of Change*. May, *Homeward Bound*, discusses emphasis on gendered themes in Cold War rhetoric. Madeline Davis and Elizabeth Lapovsky Kennedy, "Oral History and the Study of Sexuality in the Lesbian Community: Buffalo, New York, 1940–1960," *Feminist Studies* 12 (Spring 1986), reports pressure to conform to rigid roles. Chesler, *Woman of Valor*, describes Sanger's shifting rhetoric. On the obstacles faced by women in political life see Kessler-Harris, *Out to Work*, and Leila Rupp and Verta Taylor, *Survival in the Doldrums: The American*

Women's Rights Movement, 1945 to the 1960s (1987). The most influential psychoanalytic and sociological works on the "naturalness" of women's wifely subordination were Ferdinand Lundberg and Marynia Farnham, *Modern Woman: The Lost Sex* (1947); Helene Deutsch, *The Psychology of Women*, 2 vols. (1945); and Talcott Parsons, "Age and Sex in the Social Structure of the United States," *American Sociological Review* (October 1942): 604–16. Examples of writers who swam against the tide of domesticity include Mirra Komarovsky, *Women in the Modern World: Their Education and Dilemmas* (1953); Margaret Mead, *Male and Female: A Study of Sexes in a Changing World* (1949); and Clara Thompson, *On Women* (1964). The strength of the ideology of domesticity is apparent from the numerous polls taken in this period. Most notable was the Gallup Poll taken in 1961 and reported in George Gallup and Evan Hill, "The American Woman," *Saturday Evening Post* 235 (December 22, 1962): 15–32. On evidence of unhappiness amidst this cheer see Jessie Bernard, "The Paradox of the Happy Marriage," in Vivian Gornick and Barbara K. Morn, eds., *Woman in Sexist Society*, 1971.

Goldin, *Understanding the Gender Gap*, examines changing patterns in women's employment in the post–World War II era. On the particular experiences of Mexican-American women see Vicki L. Ruiz, *Cannery Women, Cannery Lives: Mexican Women, Unionization, and the California Food Processing Industry, 1939–1950* (1987), and "Margarita Salazar McSeweyn," in Gluck, *Rosie the Riveter Revisited*. Margaret K. Pai, *The Dreams of Two Yi-Min* (1989), describes the life of a Korean-American woman. For negative reaction to Friedan, *The Feminine Mystique*, see the Friedan Papers at Schlesinger Library and May, *Homeward Bound*. On demographic trends and economic changes that fueled expanding work-force participation see Susan Householder Van Horn, *Women, Work, and Fertility, 1900–1986*, chapter 9, and Clair Brown, "Consumption Norms, Work Roles, and Economic Growth, 1918–1980," in Clair Brown and Joseph Pechman, eds., *Gender in the Workplace* (1987). The National Manpower Council, *Womanpower* (1957), was the first book to alert the public to the country's squandering of its female labor pool. On Mary Bunting see Aida Press, "The Bunting Institute's Climax of Expectation," *Radcliffe Quarterly* (March 1991): 2–4. For Maria Goeppert Mayer see her oral history in the Columbia University Oral History Collection and Joan Dash, "Maria Goeppert-Mayer," in Dash, *A Life of One's Own: Three Gifted Women and the Men They Married* (1988). Sarah Lawrence Lightfoot, *Balm in Gilead: Journey of a Healer* (1988), recounts Margaret Lawrence's efforts to balance a medical career with motherhood.

On women in the civil rights movement consult Pauli Murray, *Pauli Murray: The Autobiography of a Black Activist, Feminist, Lawyer, Priest, and Poet* (1987), and Murray's papers at the Schlesinger Library; Taylor Branch, *Parting the Waters: America in the King Years, 1954–63* (1988); Hollinger F. Bernard, ed., *Outside the Magic Circle: The Autobiography of Virginia Foster Durr* (1985); Jo Ann Robinson, *The Montgomery Boycott and the Women Who Made It*, edited by David Garrow (1987); Ellen Cantarow, "Ella Baker," in Cantarow, ed., *Moving the Mountain: Women Working for Social Change* (1980); Susan Kling, "Fannie Lou Hamer: Baptism by Fire," in Pam McAllister, ed., *Reweaving the Web of Life: Feminism and Nonviolence* (1982); Anne Moody, *Coming of Age in Mississippi* (1965); and Vicki Crawford, Jacqueline Anne Rouse, and Barbara Woods, eds., *Women in the Civil Rights Movement: Trailblazers and Torchbearers, 1941–1965* (1990).

6. Feminism Reborn: 1961–73

On the rebirth of feminism see Jo Freeman, *The Politics of Women's Liberation* (1975); Judith Hole and Ellen Levine, *Rebirth of Feminism* (1971); Cohen, *The Sisterhood*; and Susan M. Hartmann, *From Margin to Mainstream: American Women and Politics Since 1960* (1989). Rupp and Taylor, *Survival in the Doldrums*, and Cynthia Harrison, *On Account of Sex: The Politics of Women's Issues, 1945–1968* (1988), analyze the four-decade-long impasse over the Equal Rights Amendment and the creation of a Presidential Commission on the Status of Women. The report of the commission, with an introduction by Margaret Mead, was published as *American Women: The Report of the President's Commission on the Status of Women and Other Publications of the Commission* (1965). Pauli Murray discusses her work for the PCSW in her autobiography, *Pauli Murray*. The story of *White* v. *Crook* appears in Charles Morgan, Jr., *One Man, One Voice* (1979). Carl M. Brauer, "Women Activists, Southern Conservatives, and the Prohibition of Sex Discrimination in Title VII of the 1964 Civil Rights Act," *Journal of Southern History* 49 (1983): 37–56, recounts the byzantine tale of how "sex" came to be part of Title VII. For the founding and early activities of NOW see the surveys listed above and Friedan, *It Changed My Life*.

Robin Morgan, *Going Too Far: The Personal Chronicle of a Feminist* (1977), and Cohen, *The Sisterhood*, tell the story of the 1968 Miss America protest. For the origins of radical feminism see Sara Evans, *Personal Politics: The Roots of Women's Liberation in the Civil Rights Movement and the New Left* (1980), and Alice Echols, *Daring to Be Bad: Radical Feminism in America, 1967–1975* (1989). Mary King,

Freedom Song: A Personal Story of the 1960s Civil Rights Movement (1987), reflects on the sexual tensions in SNCC in 1964. On the relationship of minority women to feminism see Friedan, *It Changed My Life*, and Ellen Cantarow, "Jessie Lopez De La Cruz: The Battle for Farmworkers' Rights," in Cantarow, ed., *Moving the Mountain*. John Modell, *Into One's Own: From Youth to Adulthood in the United States, 1920–1975* (1989), maps the sexual revolution of the 1960s and 1970s. See also Paul Robinson, *The Modernization of Sex: Havelock Ellis, Alfred Kinsey, William Masters and Virginia Johnson* (1966), and Helen Gurley Brown, *Sex and the Single Girl* (1962). Key books and collections of articles by radical feminists include Kate Millett, *Sexual Politics* (1970); Shulamith Firestone, *The Dialectics of Sex: The Case for Feminist Revolution* (1970); Robin Morgan, ed., *Sisterhood Is Powerful* (1970); Shulamith Firestone and Anne Koedt, eds., *Notes from the Second Year: Major Writings of the Radical Feminists* (1970); Boston Women's Health Collective, *Our Bodies, Ourselves* (1971); Gornick and Moran, eds., *Woman in Sexist Society*; Germaine Greer, *The Female Eunuch*, (1972); Anne Koedt et al., eds., *Radical Feminism* (1973); and Susan Brownmiller, *Against Our Will: Men, Women, and Rape*, (1975). On Gloria Steinem and the founding of *Ms.* magazine see Steinem, *Outrageous Acts and Everyday Rebellions* (1983), and Cohen, *The Sisterhood*. For the accomplishments of feminism in the 1970s see Winifred Wandersee, *On the Move: American Women in the 1970s* (1988). Leo Kanowitz, *Sex Roles in Law and Society: Cases and Materials* (1973), evaluates judicial treatment of protective labor legislation and the labor movement's abandonment of hours limitation as a goal. See also Kenneth M. Davidson et al., *Sex-based Discrimination: Text, Cases, and Materials* (1974). Mitchel Ostrer, "A Profile of Ruth Bader Ginsburg," *Juris Doctor* (October 1977): 34–38, provides a brief biography and description of the ACLU strategy on winning women equal rights under the Fourteenth Amendment. I am grateful to Ruth Bader Ginsburg for taking the time to discuss her work with me in an interview. On *Roe* v. *Wade* see Rosalind Rosenberg, "The Abortion Case: *Roe* v. *Wade*," in John Garraty, ed., *Quarrels That Shaped the Constitution*, 2nd ed. (1988). Phyllis A. Wallace, ed., *Equal Opportunity and the AT&T Case* (1976), and Freeman, *The Politics of Women's Liberation*, analyze the AT&T case. On the impact of feminism on women's lives see Wandersee, *On the Move*, and Evans, *Born for Liberty*.

7. *The Family Claim Revisited: 1973–91*

The best overview of the political battles of the 1970s can be found in Wandersee, *On the Move*. For the rise of the right-wing to political prominence see Rebecca E. Klatch, *Women of the New Right* (1987); Jonathan Rieder, "The Rise of the 'Silent Majority,' " in Fraser and Gerstle, eds., *The Rise and Fall of the New Deal Order*; and Woloch, *Women and the American Experience*, chapter 20. On resistance to the image of the liberated women among many housewives and working-class employed women see Susan Estabrook Kennedy, *If All We Did Was to Weep at Home: A History of White Working-Class Women in America* (1979), chapter 11, and Barbara Mikulski, "We Can Begin to Move Toward Sisterhood," in Seller, *Immigrant Women*. Carol Felsenthal, *The Sweetheart of the Silent Majority: The Biography of Phyllis Schlafly* (1981), is a fine account of the life and career of the leader of Stop ERA. For the battle over the ERA see Jane Mansbridge, *Why We Lost the ERA* (1986); Janet Boles, *The Politics of the Equal Rights Amendment: Conflict and the Decision Process* (1979); Joan Hoff-Wilson, ed., *Rights of Passage: The Past and Future of the ERA* (1986); Myra Marx Ferree and Beth B. Hess, *Controversy and Coalition: The New Feminist Movement* (1985); and Sylvia Ann Hewlett, *A Lesser Life: The Myth of Women's Liberation in America* (1986). On the abortion struggle see Kristin Luker, *Abortion and the Politics of Motherhood* (1984); Rosalind Petchesky, *Abortion and Woman's Choice: The State, Sexuality, and Reproductive Freedom* (1984); and Faye D. Ginsburg, *Contested Lives: The Abortion Debate in an American Community* (1989).

The conservative backlash against the welfare state is treated in Abramovitz, *Regulating the Lives of Women*, chapter 11; Edward Berkowitz, *America's Welfare State: From Roosevelt to Reagan* (1991); Patterson, *America's Struggle Against Poverty*, Part IV; and Ruth Sidel, *Women and Children Last: The Plight of Poor Women in Affluent America* (1986). On Ruby Lee Daniels Haynes see Lemann, *The Promised Land*.

On the trend in feminism toward emphasizing women's differences from men see Echols, *Daring to Be Bad*, and Cohen, *The Sisterhood*. For examples of academic works that stress the theme of difference see Carroll Smith-Rosenberg, *Disorderly Conduct: Visions of Gender in Victorian America* (1985); Carol Gilligan, *In a Different Voice: Women's Conception of the Self and Morality* (1982); Alice Jardine, "Prelude: The Future of Difference," in Hester Eisenstein and Alice

Jardine, eds., *The Future of Difference* (1980); and Catharine Mac-Kinnon, *Toward a Feminist Theory of the State* (1989). Minority women's contributions to the analysis of gender and cultural differences include Alice Walker, *The Color Purple* (1982); Toni Morrison, *Beloved* (1987); Davis, *Women, Race, and Class*; Audre Lorde, *Zami: A New Spelling of My Name* (1982); Maxine Hong Kingston, *The Woman Warrior: Memoirs of a Girlhood Among Ghosts* (1976); Amy Tan, *The Joy Luck Club* (1989); Mary Crow Dog, *Lakota Woman* (1990); and Ruiz, *Cannery Women.*

On the wage gap, sex segregation, and comparable worth see Paul Weiler, "The Wages of Sex: The Uses and Limits of Comparable Worth," *Harvard Law Review* 99 (1986): 1728–1807; Goldin, *Understanding the Gender Gap*; Barbara Reskin and Heidi Hartmann, eds., *Women's Work, Men's Work: Sex Segregation on the Job* (1986); Linda Blum, *Between Feminism and Labor: The Significance of the Comparable Worth Movement* (1991); and Sara M. Evans and Barbara J. Nelson, *Wage Justice: Comparable Worth and the Paradox of Technocratic Reform* (1989). On maternity/parental leaves and child care see Sheila B. Kamerman, Alfred J. Kahn, and Paul Kingston, *Maternity Policies and Working Women* (1983); Sylvia Ann Hewlett, *A Lesser Life*, and Hewlett, *When the Bough Breaks: The Cost of Neglecting Our Children* (1991); Friedan, *It Changed My Life*; and Fern Marx and Michelle Seligson, "Child Care in the United States," in Sara E. Rix, ed., *The American Woman, 1990–91*. On divorce reform see Friedan, *It Changed My Life*; Leonore Weitzman, *The Divorce Revolution: The Unexpected Social and Economic Consequences for Women and Children in America* (1985); and Stephen Sugarman and Herma Hill Kay, *Divorce Reform at the Crossroads* (1990).

Epilogue: Toward the Year 2000

For an overview of American women at the end of the century see Rix, ed., *The American Woman: 1990–91*, and Steven McLaughlin, ed., *The Changing Lives of American Women* (1988). Victor R. Fuchs, *Women's Quest for Economic Equality* (1988), analyzes long-term trends in women's economic well-being. Nicholas Lemann, "Four Generations in the Projects," *The New York Times Magazine*, January 13, 1991, pp. 17–21, 36–38, 49, describes the life of Connie Haynes. Arlene Hochschild, *Second Shift: Working Parents and the Revolution at Home* (1989), explores the women's double burden of domestic and paid labor. On the continuing constraints women suffer in the world of work see Ruth Sidel, *On Her Own: Growing Up in the Shadow of the American Dream* (1990), and Perri Klass, *A Not Entirely Benign Procedure* (1987). For women's progress in politics and academics see Hartman, *From Margin to Mainstream*, and Mariam Chamberlain, ed., *Women in Academe: Progress and Prospects* (1988).

Index

Abbott, Edith, 31, 73
Abbott, Grace, 27, 29, 60, 88, 116, 117
abortion, 223, 246; in 1900, 15, 17; in 1912–29, 90; in 1929–45, 109–10; in 1963–71, 191, 204–6, 209, 210, 212, 216; in 1973–91, 227–30, 242
Abramowitz, Bessie, 42
Abzug, Bella, 209, 213
Addams, Jane, 3, 23, 25–35, 38, 39, 41, 48, 51, 56–57, 60–62, 65, 69, 71, 72, 76, 81, 146, 160; *Democracy and Social Ethics*, 31
Adkins v. *Children's Hospital*, 75
affirmative action, 190–91, 218, 233, 235–36, 237
agriculture, 4, 245; in 1900, 4, 6, 7–8, 19; in 1929–45, 104, 106, 108, 117; in 1945–61, 160; in 1961–73, 184; in 1973–91, 236
Aid to Dependent Children (ADC), 116, 117–18
Aid to Families with Dependent Children (AFDC), 230–32
Alabama, 5–6, 118, 128, 171–75, 183–84, 215–16, 220
alcohol, 9–10, 32, 55, 58
Allen, Florence, 115
Alpert, Jane, 233–34
Amalgamated Clothing Workers Union, 181

American Association of University Women, 181
American Birth Control League, 87, 118
American Civil Liberties Union (ACLU), 183–84, 214–15
American Federation of Business and Professional Women, 180–81
American Federation of Labor (AFL), 41, 42, 46, 119, 181
American Home Economics Association, 76, 93
American Medical Association (AMA), 77, 88, 90, 116
American Revolution, 3–4
American Telephone & Telegraph (AT&T), 217–18
Ames, Jessie Daniel, 125
Anderson, Marian, 107
Anderson, Mary, 42, 78, 80, 119
Andrews, Julie, 148
Anthony, Susan B., 56
antibiotics, 149, 160
Arizona, 156
Arkansas, 224
armed forces, women in, 126, 128, 185, 226, 246
Association of Southern Women for the Prevention of Lynching (ASWPL), 125
Atkinson, Ti-Grace, 203–4

Atlanta University, 173
automobiles, 92, 103, 119–20, 133, 135, 140, 141
Avery, Nina Horton, 187

Baker, Ella, 175–78, 196
Baker, Josephine, 64, 74–75
Baker, Russell, *Growing Up*, 108
Baltimore, 128, 129, 164, 206
Barnard, Otto T., 52–53
Barnard College, 57, 95, 97, 123, 156
Baruch, Bernard, 132
Baum, L. Frank, 18
Beard, Mary, 52, 80
Beauvoir, Simone de, *The Second Sex*, 203
Bell, Robert, 149
Belmont, Alva, 44, 69, 70
Benedict, Ruth, 122, 123, 126; *Patterns of Culture*, 122
Berkman, Alexander, 67
Bethune, Mary McLeod, 124, 126, 129
Beyer, Clara, 115
birth control, 65, 246; in 1900, 8, 15, 16–17; in 1912–29, 68, 77, 82–91; in 1929–45, 109–10, 118; in 1945–61, 152, 159–60; in 1961–73, 191, 201–6, 216; in 1973–91, 227–30
birth control pill, 201
Birth Control Review (journal), 86
blacks, 4, 37, 246–49; in 1900, 4–10, 12, 13, 14, 19, 22–23, 27, 30, 31; in 1901–12, 43, 51, 58, 59–60, 61; in 1912–29, 73, 77, 90, 95–96; in 1929–45, 105–6, 107, 110, 112, 117, 121–26, 129–30; in 1945–61, 139–41, 145–48, 149, 159, 164–66, 167–79; in 1961–73, 183–84, 195–200, 206, 209, 212; in 1973–91, 230–33, 235, 236
Blair, Emily, 115
Blanchard, Phyllis, 91
Blatch, Harriot Stanton, 58, 79
Blum, Marion, 241

Boston, 45, 127, 199, 204, 206, 236
bra-burning, 192
Brandeis, Louis, 50
Brandeis Brief, 50
Breckenridge, Sophinisba, 31
Brill, A. A., 64
Bromley, Dorothy Dunbar, 91, 95
Brown, Helen Gurley, 201
Brownmiller, Susan, 200–3, 209, 212
Brownsville clinic, 87–88
Brown v. *Board of Education of Topeka, Kansas*, 170, 171
Bunting, Mary, 163, 166, 182
Burns, Lucy, 69
Burroughs, Nannie, 59, 106
Bush, George, 240
Butler, Elizabeth, 19

Cable Act (1922), 74
California, 60, 73, 128, 143–44, 158, 206, 213, 238, 240
California Federal Savings and Loan v. *Guerra*, 240
cancer, 13
Carmichael, Stokely, 198
Catt, Carrie Chapman, 70–72, 76, 80, 86
Chicago, 23, 25, 29–35, 39, 41, 46, 60, 61, 73, 108, 109, 127, 139–41, 146–47, 164, 194, 199, 206, 231, 236, 248
childbearing and childrearing, 5, 245, 247–55; future of, 247–55; in 1900, 4–5, 7, 8, 10, 15, 16–17, 24; in 1901–12, 38–39, 46–54, 58; in 1912–29, 67–68, 74–75, 77, 82–91, 95, 98–101; in 1929–45, 105, 109–10, 116–18, 130–32, 149; in 1945–61, 138–42, 144, 147–67; in 1961–73, 184, 185, 186, 190, 203, 204, 212, 214; in 1973–91, 220–33, 234, 239–44
Child Development Act, 212, 242
child labor, 40; in 1901–12; 46–49, 61; in 1912–29, 74, 75, 83, 94

Children's Bureau, 48–49, 74, 79, 88, 98, 116, 132, 150
Chisholm, Shirley, 209
Civil Rights Act (1964), 212, 213, 227
civil rights movement, 167–79, 183–84, 186–87, 189, 194, 196–200, 212, 220
Civil War, 13, 37
Civil Works Administration, 114
Clark, Septima, 176–78
clerical workers, 161, 237; in 1900, 22, 28; in 1929–45, 105, 127, 129; in 1973–91, 236, 237
Coalition of Labor Union Women, 236
Cold War, 142–43, 148, 151–53, 162, 166–67, 171–72, 195
colleges, 54, 245–46, 251–52, 253–54; in 1900, 25–28, 29, 33, 34; in 1901–12, 57; in 1912–29, 65, 92, 94, 95, 96–97, 100, 123; in 1929–45, 124, 127, 138, 168–69, 223; in 1945–61, 143, 147, 154, 156, 161, 163–67, 168–70, 172–73, 178; in 1961–73, 201–2, 209, 214, 218; in 1973–91, 225, 226
colonial America, 3–4
Colorado, 15, 54
Committee on Civil and Political Rights, 182–83
Communism, 76, 120, 142–43, 148, 151–53, 172, 177, 223
Comprehensive Child Development Bill, 221
Comstock, Anthony, 15
condoms, 16, 17, 90, 91, 109
Congress, U.S., 15, 37, 48, 70, 72–75, 103, 117–23, 126, 136–37, 143, 152–53, 166, 180–81, 184–86, 188, 209, 212–13, 220, 224, 226, 227, 229, 238, 240, 243, 253; *see also specific legislation*
Congressional Union (CU), 69–70
Congress of Industrial Organizations (CIO), 119–20, 133
consciousness-raising groups, 200–6
Constitution, U.S., 15, 47, 71;

Fourteenth Amendment, 75, 170, 175, 183–84, 214, 216, 227; Nineteenth Amendment, 72–73, 77, 126; *see also* Equal Rights Amendment
Converse, Florence, 34
Cosmopolitan magazine, 201

Daly, Mary, 234
dances: in 1900, 6, 22, 23; in 1912–29, 68
dating: in 1900, 22–24;' in 1912–29, 92–93
Daughters of the American Revolution (DAR), 74, 77, 224
Davis, Angela, 235
Davis, Bette, 106
Davis, Katharine Bement, 34, 93
day care, 253, 255; in 1929–45, 132–33; in 1945–61, 144; in 1961–73, 185, 204, 212; in 1973–91, 221, 232, 241–42
de la Cruz, Jesse Lopez, 196, 199
Democratic Party, 69, 70, 72, 73, 111–15, 118, 121, 125, 152, 153, 171, 178, 182, 187–88, 231
Depression, 102–26, 130, 131, 139, 148, 168, 171
Detroit, 95, 128, 129, 134
Deutsch, Helene, 153
Dewson, Molly W., 114–15, 171
diaphragms, 89–91, 109
Dickinson, Robert Latou, 89–90
Didrikson Babe, 108
Dietrich, Marlene, 106
discrimination: in 1900, 15–16, 28; in 1901–12, 59–61; in 1912–29, 63, 97–98; in 1929–45, 103–5, 107, 110, 117, 127, 129; in 1945–61, 145–47, 161, 168–79; in 1961–73, 183–219; in 1973–91, 239
disease, 36, 37; in 1900, 5, 8, 10, 12–13, 18, 19, 24, 30; in 1901–12, 37, 50–51, 58; in 1929–45, 128; in 1945–61, 149–50, 160; in 1973–91, 241
divorce, 39, 56, 246, 248, 254; in

divorce (*cont.*)
  1900, 14, 32; in 1901–12, 53; in
  1912–29, 93; in 1929–45, 103,
  110; in 1945–61, 146, 157; in
  1973–91, 225, 226, 232, 233,
  242–44
Dodge, Mabel, 64, 83
domestic service: in 1900, 4, 13,
  18, 19, 20, 22, 32–33; in 1912–
  29, 65–66, 96; in 1929–45, 104,
  106, 108, 127, 129, 131; in 1945–
  61, 159, 160; in 1961–73, 184; in
  1973–91, 236, 237
Dorr, Rheta Childe, 64, 65, 68,
  76
Douglas, Helen Gahagan, 152
Dreier, Mary, 42
Du Bois, W.E.B., 59, 146
Durr, Virginia, 171–74, 178

Earhart, Amelia, 81
East, Catherine, 185, 189, 217
Eastland, James, 172
Eastman, Crystal, 54, 64, 68, 69,
  71, 72, 77, 82, 85–86, 99–100
Eastman, Max, 64
Eastwood, Mary, 185
economy, 245, 247, 253, 254;
  nineteenth-century, 3; in 1900,
  3–4, 7–8, 14, 16, 18–25; in
  1901–12, 36–54; in 1912–29, 65–
  68, 80–81, 84, 92, 95, 100; in
  1929–45, 120–37; in 1945–61,
  140–67; in 1961–73, 183, 186,
  188, 191, 192, 194, 195, 200,
  202; in 1973–91, 221, 225,
  230–44
Edelsberg, Herman, 188, 191
education, 56, 245–54; in 1900, 9,
  18, 19, 20, 21–22, 25–29, 33, 34;
  in 1901–12, 37, 46, 47, 48, 52,
  54, 56, 57; in 1912–29, 65, 66–
  67, 74, 92, 94, 95, 96–98, 100,
  123; in 1929–45, 115, 117, 124,
  127, 129, 138, 168–69, 223; in
  1945–61, 138, 139, 143, 147,
  154, 156, 159–67, 168–70, 172–
  73, 176–78; in 1961–73, 194,
  201–2, 209, 212, 214, 218; in

  1973–91, 221, 225, 226, 231,
  233, 235–39, 241, 245–46
Ellis, Havelock, 64, 84–85, 87
employment, *see* labor force
entertainment: in 1900, 12, 22–23;
  in 1919–29, 68, 92; in 1929–45,
  105, 106–7; in 1961–73, 212
Ephron, Nora, 212
Equal Employment Opportunity
  Act (1972), 218
Equal Employment Opportunity
  Commission (EEOC), 188–91,
  216–18
Equal Pay Act (1963), 184–85, 238
Equal Rights Amendment (ERA),
  79–82, 85, 88, 91, 113, 121, 136,
  137, 179, 180–92, 199, 212–13,
  220–27, 233, 242
Esquire magazine, 210
ethnicity: in 1900, 8, 19; in 1901–
  12, 39, 40–41, 43; in 1912–29,
  93–94; in 1929–45, 105–6, 121–
  26, 130; in 1945–61, 157; in
  1973–91, 230, 235

factory workers: in 1900, 4, 14, 18,
  19–21; in 1901–12, 39, 41–50,
  54, 61, 84; in 1929–45, 104, 105,
  119–21, 127–36; in 1945–61,
  160; in 1973–91, 225–26
Fair Employment Practices Commission, 129
Fair Labor Standards Act (FLSA),
  121, 136, 181
family, 245; future of, 245–55; in
  1900, 3–35; in 1901–12, 40, 41,
  46–54, 55; in 1912–29, 65, 74,
  79, 82–91, 93–101; in 1929–45,
  102–37; in 1945–61, 138–67; in
  1961–73, 184, 185, 190, 196, 199,
  200–14; in 1973–91, 220–44
Family Support Act (1988), 243
Farm Security Administration, 118
Farnham, Marynia, 153–54, 155
fashion: in 1912–29, 68; in 1945–
  61, 152
Federal Communications Commission, 172, 217
Federal Economy Act, 103

Federal Emergency Relief Association (FERA), 114, 115
Federal Housing Act (1949), 146
Federal Housing Authority, 144, 145
feminism, *see* women's rights
Feminist Alliance, 66–67
Feminists, The, 204
Firestone, Shulamith, *The Dialectics of Sex*, 204
Fitzgerald, Ella, 107
Florida, 4–5, 8–9, 118, 124
Flynn, Elizabeth Gurley, 46, 64
food, 246; in 1900, 8, 9–10, 12, 30; in 1901–12, 58; in 1912–29, 98, 99; in 1929–45, 107, 108, 128, 129
Fortune magazine, 130
France, 52, 144
Franklin, Butler, 187
Freud, Sigmund, 64, 153, 155, 207.
Frick, Henry Clay, 67
Friedan, Betty, 138–39, 140, 148, 157, 158–59, 162, 189, 191, 192, 194, 199, 202–8, 210, 216, 242, 243; *The Feminine Mystique*, 138, 157, 158
friendship: in 1900, 33–34; in 1912–29, 93
Fries, Amos, 76, 91
Frontiero v. *Richardson*, 215–16
Frowne, Sadie, 18–25

Garbo, Greta, 106
garment industry: in 1900, 14, 18, 19, 20–21; in 1901–12, 42–46, 47, 58; in 1912–29, 84, 94; in 1929–45, 119; in 1973–91, 237
Gay Liberation Movement, 206–7
gender roles, 36–37, 247–50; future of, 245–55; in 1900, 3–33; in 1901–12, 36–62; in 1912–29, 65–101; in 1929–45, 102–37; in 1945–61, 138–79; in 1961–73, 180–219; in 1973–91, 220–24
General Federation of Women's Clubs (GFWC), 30, 46, 57, 76, 100, 136

Georgia, 74, 118, 172, 177, 224, 225
Germany, 52, 101, 144, 164
GI Bill of Rights, 143, 166, 167
Gilligan, Carol, 234
Gilman, Charlotte Perkins, 32–33, 64–68, 71, 86, 100, 201; *Women and Economics*, 32–33
Ginsburg, Ruth Bader, 214–16, 227
Ginzburg, Eli, 110
Glasgow, Maude, 51
Goldman, Emma, 64, 67–68, 83–85, 202
Goldmark, Josephine, 50
Goldwater, Barry, 222
government jobs, 253; in 1912–29, 97–98; in 1929–45, 114–21, 126, 127; in 1945–61, 152–53; in 1961–73, 185–86, 209, 212–13; in 1973–91, 238
Great Britain, 15, 36, 52, 53, 58, 60, 69, 132, 144, 146
Greenwich Village, New York, 63–65, 83, 92, 138, 205, 206, 233
Griffiths, Martha, 188, 194, 209, 213, 220
Griswold v. *Connecticut*, 216

Hale, Ruth, 64
Hall, G. Stanley, 26
Hamer, Fannie Lou, 178, 209
Hamilton, Alice, 29, 86, 96, 121
Harding, Warren, 75, 76
Harvard University, 96, 100, 127, 169, 214, 251
Hawaii, 158
Hayden, Casey, 197–98
Hayden, Tom, 195
Hayes, Helen, 181
Haynes, Connie, 248–49
Haynes, Ruby Daniels, 139–41, 146, 231–32, 248
Haywood, Big Bill, 46, 64
Hedgeman, Anna Arnold, 124–25
Hellman, Lillian, 212
Henry Street Settlement House, New York, 40, 83
Hepburn, Katharine, 106, 181

Hepburn, Katharine Houghton, 82–83, 85, 87, 97
heterodoxy, 63–68, 69, 70, 76, 82
Hewlett, Sylvia Ann, 225–26
Hickey, Margaret, 182
Highlander Folk School, 172, 176
highways, 144, 145
Hochschild, Arlene, 250–51
Holiday, Billie, 107
Hollingworth, Leta, 64, 66
Holtzman, Elizabeth, 209
Hoover, J. Edgar, 151–52
Horney, Karen, 155
House Un-American Activities Committee, 148
housework, 246, 249–51; in 1900, 4–20, 32–33; in 1901–12, 40, 41, 48–49, 58; in 1912–29, 65, 66–67, 94, 98–101; in 1929–45, 107, 108, 111, 131–32; in 1945–61, 140, 141, 147, 151–60; in 1961–73, 204; in 1973–91, 223, 225, 233, 244
housing: in 1945–61, 140–47; in 1973–91, 236
Howard Law School, 169, 170
Howe, Ethel Puffer, 100
Howe, Frederic C., 100
Howe, Marie Jenny, 63, 65, 100
Hull House, Chicago, 25, 29–35, 39, 41, 48, 60–61, 72
Human Rights for Women, 209
Hunter College, 168
Hurston, John, 4–10, 123
Hurston, Lucy, 4–10, 123
Hurston, Zora Neale, 5, 6, 7, 10, 18, 123, 126; *Their Eyes Were Watching God*, 7, 123
Hyde, Henry, 229

Idaho, 15, 54, 130, 215
Illinois, 25, 29, 47, 48, 53, 73, 139
immigrants: in 1900, 8, 11, 17, 18–19, 20, 23, 24, 30–32; in 1901–12, 43, 44, 48, 51, 58; in 1912–29, 68, 85, 93–94, 96; in 1929–45, 106; in 1945–61, 139, 158; in 1973–91, 232–33
Immigration Act (1924), 93

Immigration Act (1965), 232
Independent, The, 21
Indiana, 90, 92, 94, 220
Indian Reorganization Act (1934), 123–24
Industrial Workers of the World (IWW), 46, 64, 84
industry, 37, 245; in 1900, 4, 14, 18, 19; in 1901–12, 36–50, 54, 61; in 1912–29, 74, 81, 94; in 1929–45, 104–8, 109, 111, 119–21, 127–37; in 1945–61, 144, 160; in 1961–73, 186; in 1973–91, 225–26, 236–39
Infant Care (1914 pamphlet), 48–49
infant mortality, 37, 65; in 1900, 5, 30; in 1901–12, 48–49, 58; in 1912–29, 74–75, 99
International Ladies Garment Workers Union, 119
Iowa, 45, 104
Irwin, Inez Haynes, 70

Janeway, Elizabeth, 255
Jardine, Alice, 234
Jews: in 1900, 17, 18–19; in 1901–12, 40, 43; in 1912–29, 67, 85; in 1929–45, 105; in 1945–61, 138–39, 145
Johnson, Grace Nail, 64
Johnson, Lyndon Baines, 186, 190, 222
Jones, Mary Harris (Mother), 47
Jordan, Barbara, 209

Kanowitz, Leo, 213–14
Kansas, 97
Kassenbaum, Nancy, 253
Kearney, Belle, 59–60
Kelley, Florence, 39–41, 48, 50, 56–57, 75, 76, 77–78, 81, 114
Kennedy, Flo, 193, 204
Kennedy, John F., 178, 181–86
Kenney, Mary, 41
Key, Ellen, *Century of the Child*, 68
Khrushchev, Nikita, 142, 167

King, Billie Jean, 219
King, Martin Luther, Jr., 174–77
King, Mary, 197–98
Kingston, Maxine Hong, 235
Kinsey, Alfred, 152
Kirchwey, Freda, 99
Klass, Perri, 251–52
Komarovsky, Mirra, 161, 162;
  Women and the Modern World,
  154–55, 156, 158

Labor Department, 115–16, 136,
  185, 189, 209
labor force, 56, 245–55; future of,
  245–55; in 1900, 3–4, 9, 13, 14,
  16, 18–25, 27–35; in 1901–12,
  36–62; in 1912–29, 65–82, 93–
  101; in 1929–45, 102–37; in
  1945–61, 138–47, 157–79; in
  1961–73, 180–219; in 1973–91,
  220–44; *see also specific
  occupations*
labor legislation, 181; in 1901–12,
  46–52, 61; in 1912–29, 74, 75,
  77, 78–81, 85, 94; in 1929–45,
  118–21, 131, 136–37, 181; in
  1963–71, 191, 213; in 1973–91,
  225, 226, 236, 240
labor unions, 181; in 1901–12, 40–
  46, 53, 61, 84; in 1912–29,
  64, 81, 84; in 1929–45,
  118–21, 133–36; in 1961–73,
  181–82, 184; in 1973–91, 236,
  238–39
Ladies' Home Journal, 209
Lanham Act, 132, 144
Lathrop, Julia, 48, 76, 88
laundry, 12, 13, 19, 98, 100, 108,
  129, 131
Lawrence, Margaret, 165–66
Lawrence textile mill strike. 45–
  46, 84
lawyers, 28, 127, 147, 169, 178,
  193, 213, 214–16, 230, 235, 243,
  253
League for Industrial Democracy
  (LID), 195
League of Women Voters, 73, 79,
  93, 112, 136, 153

Lemlich, Clara, 43, 65
Lenroot, Katherine, 116
Leopold, Alice, 153
lesbianism, 84; in 1900, 33–34; in
  1929–45, 128; in 1945–61, 152;
  in 1961–73, 202, 206–8, 211; in
  1973–91, 228
Levitt, Alfred, 141, 144
Levitt, William, 141–42, 144, 145
Lewis, John L., 119
Lewis, Sinclair, 101; *Arrowsmith*,
  97
librarians, 28, 94, 104, 171, 238
life expectancy, 245, 248; in 1900,
  13, 17, 18; in 1901–12, 53
Lippmann, Walter, 64
literature: in 1900, 17–18; in 1912–
  29, 64, 97, 101; in 1929–45,
  122–23; in 1945–61, 150–51,
  153–56; in 1961–73, 210–11; in
  1973–91, 233–35
Lochner v. *New York*, 50
Lorde, Audre, 235
Los Angeles, 128, 129, 134, 145,
  158
Lucy Stone League, 64
Lundberg, Ferdinand, 153–54, 155
lynching, 125, 168
Lynd, Robert and Helen, 108

McCarthy, Joseph, 152–53, 172,
  194
McCarthy, Mary, 120
McCarthyism, 172, 194
McKinley, William, 37
MacKinnon, Catharine, 234
MacLean, Annie Marion, 51
Mainardi, Pat, 204
Mann Act (1910), 51–52
marriage, 246, 247, 249–50, 255;
  contract, 14; future of, 246–55;
  in 1900, 3–17, 24–25, 27, 32–34;
  in 1901–12, 39, 41, 51–54, 55; in
  1912–29, 66–67, 78, 82–91, 93–
  101; in 1929–45, 103–9, 113,
  115, 122, 128–37; in 1945–61,
  138–67; in 1961–73, 186, 190,
  193, 196, 199, 200–14; in 1973–
  91, 220–44

Massachusetts, 45–46, 47, 49, 56,
57, 73, 76, 84, 181
Masses, The (magazine), 64
Masters and Johnson, 207; *Human
Sexual Response*, 207
masturbation, 34, 84
maternal mortality, 37; in 1900, 5,
10, 17; in 1912–29, 74–75
maternity leaves, 239–41
May, Elaine, 149
Mayer, Joseph, 164
Mayer, Maria Goeppert, 164, 166
Mead, Margaret, 95, 122–23, 126,
155, 156, 181; *Coming of Age in
Samoa*, 155; *Male and Female*,
155; *Sex and Temperament*, 122,
155
media: in 1901–12, 62; in 1912–29,
92; in 1961–73, 190, 192, 193,
201, 205–6, 209–12; in 1973–91,
225–26, 230, 233
Medicaid, 231
medical care, 251–52, 255; in 1900,
4–5, 10, 12–13, 15, 17, 22, 28–
29; in 1901–12, 48–49, 51–54; in
1912–29, 74–75, 77, 78, 82–91,
97, 98, 99; in 1929–45, 107,
109–10, 116–18, 127; in 1945–
61, 143, 148, 149–51, 160, 165–
66; in 1961–73, 184, 185, 191,
204–6, 209, 210, 212; in 1973–
91, 227–33
Medical Women's National Association, 77, 97
Medicare, 231
men, 249; in 1900, 3–10, 13, 14,
16–17, 22–23, 28, 32–33; in
1901–12, 36–38, 41–46, 49–62;
in 1912–29, 63, 66, 73, 75, 81,
96–101; in 1929–45, 103–11,
120, 122–24, 131, 133–37; in
1945–61, 138–79; in 1961–73,
181–219; in 1973–91, 221–24
Merman, Ethel, 110
Meyer, Annie Nathan, 57
Meyer, Maud, 57
Michigan, 45, 74, 120
middle-class women, 246–47, 254;
in 1900, 10–17, 24, 30; in 1901–
12, 41, 46–48, 58; in 1912–29,

90, 94, 96, 98; in 1929–45, 109,
124; in 1945–61, 138–39, 143–
44, 146, 149–67, 172–73; in
1961–73, 208; in 1973–91, 221,
231–32, 235
midwives, 4–5
migrant workers: in 1900, 19; in
1929–45, 106; in 1945–61, 139,
147; in 1961–73, 196
Mikulski, Barbara, 221, 253
Millett, Kate, 201–2, 204, 207–8,
211; *Sexual Politics*, 201–2, 207
mining, 19, 119
Minnesota, 201, 202
Miss America Pageant, 192–93,
204, 211
Mississippi, 6, 107, 118, 139, 140,
178, 197, 200, 231, 232
Missouri, 6, 223, 224, 229
Mitchell, S. Weir, 29, 32
Montana, 74
Montgomery bus boycott, 173–75
Morgan, Anne, 44
Morgan, J. P., 44
Morgan, Robin, 192–93, 201, 204,
233–34
Morrison, Toni, 235
mortality rates, 37; in 1900, 5, 10,
17–18, 30; in 1901–12, 48–49; in
1912–29, 74–75, 82, 99; in 1945–
61, 174
Mosher, Clelia, 16
Moskowitz, Belle, 68
Mother Earth (magazine), 67
motherhood, *see* childbearing and
childrearing
Mott, Lucretia, 56
movies, 23, 105–7
Ms. magazine, 201, 210, 211–2,
233
Muller v. *Oregon*, 50
Murray, Pauli, 168–71, 178–79,
182–83, 186, 188, 189, 199, 214,
215, 224
music: in 1900, 6, 22–23; in 1929–
45, 107, 110–27; in 1963–71, 194

Nation, The, 99
National American Woman Suf-

frage Association (NAWSA), 54, 57, 59–60, 65, 69–73, 77
National Association for the Advancement of Colored People (NAACP), 59, 122, 168, 170–72, 175–76
National Association of Colored Women (NACW), 30, 59
National Black Feminist Organization, 209
National Committee to Stop ERA, 224–25
National Consumers' League (NCL), 40, 46, 50, 57, 63, 74, 77, 79, 111, 112, 114, 115, 136, 181
National Council for Prevention of War (NCPW), 76
National Council of Jewish Women, 241
National Defense Education Act (NDEA), 166
National Education Association, 96, 136
National Federation of Business and Professional Women, 107, 182, 185
National Federation of Republican Women, 222
National Industrial Conference Board, 104
National Labor Relations Act, 118–19
National Manpower Council, 162–63, 166, 184
National Organization for Women (NOW), 189–92, 199, 202–8, 217–18, 241–43
National Recovery Administration, 115
National Right to Life Committee, 228
National Woman's Party (NWP), 70, 72, 76, 77–81, 82, 83, 91, 113, 136, 180, 182, 186, 187
National Women's Political Caucus, 209, 230
National Youth Administration, 124, 129

Native Americans, 8, 122, 123–24, 235
Nevada, 213
New Deal, 115–21, 136, 168, 171
New Jersey, 14, 45, 108, 144, 156, 192, 193
Newman, Pauline, 80
New Mexico, 22, 122
New Orleans, 22–23
Newsweek magazine, 209
New York City, 15, 111, 252; in 1900, 15, 18–22; in 1901–12, 40–46, 54; in 1912–29; 63–68, 71, 74–75, 83, 85, 88–91, 92, 95, 99; in 1929–45, 106, 109, 119, 124–25, 168; in 1945–61, 138–39, 141–42, 148, 165, 176; in 1961–73, 194, 199, 203–6, 214, 233
New York magazine, 210–11
New York State, 10–18, 47, 57, 58, 82–83, 112, 115, 141–42, 165, 168, 206
New York Times, The, 210, 230, 249
Niebuhr, Reinhold, 172
Nixon, Richard, 142, 152, 167, 182, 212, 221, 224, 230, 232, 242
Nobel Prize, 164
nonviolent resistance, 174–75
North Carolina, 118, 168, 176
Northern women: in 1900, 10–35; in 1901–12, 40–62;' in 1912–29, 63–101; in 1929–45, 110, 111–16, 121; in 1945–61, 138–48, 165–66; in 1961–73, 196, 203–5
Norton, Eleanor Holmes, 230

Ohio, 37
oil, 37
Oregon, 132
O'Reilly, Leonora, 42, 46, 58
orphans, 17–18, 31
Ovington, Mary, 59

parental leave, 239–41
Parent Teachers Association, 76, 93, 99, 152

Parks, Rosa, 171–75, 178
Parsons, Elsie Clews, 64, 66, 85, 87
Parsons, Talcott, 154
Paul, Alice, 69–70, 71, 78–81, 88, 184, 186, 187
Pennsylvania, 11, 19–20, 45, 47, 54, 69, 78
Perkins, Frances, 115–21, 153
Peterson, Esther, 181–83, 187, 188, 194
Philadelphia, 28–29, 45, 149
Pittsburgh, 20, 54, 96, 110
Planned Parenthood, 87
Plessy v. *Ferguson*, 170
polio, 13, 149–50
politics, 3, 253; in 1900, 15; in 1901–12, 36–39, 54–62; in 1912–29, 65, 67–68, 69–91, 97–98; in 1929–45, 102–3, 111–21; in 1945–61, 151–53, 166, 167–79; in 1961–73, 181–87, 192–219; in 1973–91, 220–44
poll tax, 171
poor women, 36, 246–49; in 1900, 4–10, 13, 17, 29–35; in 1901–12, 49; in 1912–29, 91, 96, 98; in 1929–45, 102, 106, 108, 117, 120; in 1945–61, 139–41, 146, 157–58, 172–74; in 1961–73, 194; in 1973–91, 230–33, 235, 241
pornography, 234
Port Huron Statement, 195
Powdermaker, Hortense, 6
Pregnancy Discrimination Act, 240
Presidential Commission on the Status of Women (PCSW), 182–86
Progressive Era, 38, 97
Progressive Party, 60–62
property rights, 56, 141; in 1900, 7–8; in 1912–29, 79; in 1945–61, 140–47; in 1961–73, 200; in 1973–91, 236, 243
prostitution: in 1900, 13, 22, 23, 24, 30; in 1901–12, 42, 50–52, 58, 59
psychoanalysis, post-World War II, 153–57

racial issues: in 1900, 4–10, 30; in 1901–12, 39, 40–41, 58, 59–60; in 1912–29, 73, 77, 90; in 1929–45, 105–6, 107, 110, 117, 119, 120, 121–26, 129–30; in 1945–61, 138–39, 145–48, 159, 164–66, 167–79; in 1961–73, 183–84, 190, 195–200, 216; in 1973–91, 230–33, 235
radicalesbians, 207
Rainwater, Lee, 149
Rankin, Jeanette, 72
rape, 209, 234
Rawalt, Marguerite, 182
Reagan, Ronald, 229, 232
Reconstruction, 37, 121, 126
Redstockings, 204, 205, 206
Reed v. *Reed*, 215
reform, 36–37; in 1900, 29–35; in 1901–12, 36, 38–62; in 1912–29, 63–101; in 1929–45, 111–37; in 1945–61, 153–57, 176–79; in 1961–73, 180–219; in 1973–91, 220–44
religion, 6; in 1900, 10–11, 12; in 1901–12, 55; in 1945–61, 174, 175; in 1961–73, 194, 202; in 1973–91, 227, 228
Republican Party, 60, 73, 76, 113, 203, 221–24, 229
Riggs, Bobby, 219
Riis, Jacob, 19
Robinson, Jo Ann, 171, 172–73, 174, 178
Robinson, Ruby Doris Smith, 196, 198
Robinson, Spotswood, 170
Robinson, Virginia, 33
Rockefeller, John D., 37
Rockefeller, Nelson, 222
Rodman, Henrietta, 64, 66–67
Roe v. *Wade*, 216, 227–30
Roosevelt, Eleanor, 111–21, 124, 125, 126, 135, 168, 169, 172, 178; *It's Up to the Women*, 113
Roosevelt, Franklin Delano, 111–16, 118, 119, 125, 130
Roosevelt, Theodore, 15, 37–38, 47, 60–62, 111
Rosenfeld v. *Southern Pacific*, 213

Rosenwald, Julius, 139
rural women: in 1900, 4–10; in
1901–12, 38; in 1929–45, 106,
108; in 1945–61, 140, 141–47
Russell, Rosalind, 106
Rutgers University, 163, 214

salesclerks: in 1900, 21; in 1912–
29, 81; in 1929–45, 104, 121,
124–25, 127, 129, 135; in 1945–
61, 159
Salk vaccine, 149
SALT agreements, 223, 224
San Francisco, 204, 206, 250
Sanger, Margaret, 15, 64, 82–91,
109, 118, 152, 181; *Family Limitation*, 84
Sanger, William, 83, 87
sanitation, 36, 37, 58
Schlafly, Phyllis, 222–27, 228; *A
Choice, Not an Echo*, 222
Schneiderman, Rose, 21, 42, 45,
46, 53, 58–59
Schroeder, Pat, 209
scientists, 162–64, 166, 167
Scudder, Vida, 34
"The SCUM manifesto," 203
Seaman, Barbara, 205–6
segregation, 167–79
Senate, U.S., 72, 152–53, 181, 212
septicemia, 17
Serviceman's Readjustment Act
(1944), 143
settlement-house workers, 29–35,
36, 39, 40, 41, 46, 53, 60–61
sewing, 4, 12, 21, 42, 108, 114, 147
sexual harassment, 254; in 1901–
12, 42; in 1973–91, 234
sexuality, 246; in 1900, 6–7, 9–10,
15, 16–17, 22–24, 33–34; in
1901–12, 50–52, 58; in 1912–29,
64, 65–66, 67–68, 77, 81, 82–
91, 92–93; in 1929–45, 109–10,
122–23, 128; in 1945–61, 149,
151–57, 171; in 1961–73, 185,
187, 189–91, 192–93, 197–208,
210–16; in 1973–91, 227–30,
233, 234, 235

sharecropping, 4–10
Shaw, Anna Howard, 65–66, 70–
71, 75
Sheppard–Towner Act (1921), 74,
75, 77, 88, 117
Simon, Kate, 17
Slee, J. Noah, 87
Smith, Bessie, 107
Smith, Howard, 187, 188
Smith, Lillian, 125
Smith, Margaret Chase, 152
Smith, Mary Rozet, 33
Smith College, 100, 138, 157,
210
Smith-Rosenberg, Carroll, 234
social class, 246–47; in 1900, 3–
35; in 1901–12, 38–62; in 1912–
29, 87, 90, 92–101; in 1929–45,
103–37; in 1945–61, 138–79; in
1961–73, 208; in 1973–91, 230–
33, 235; *see also specific classes*
Social Security, 184, 231–32
Social Security Act, 117, 121
social welfare, 145; in 1901–12,
52–54, 61; in 1929–45, 116–21,
136; in 1945–61, 140, 145; in
1961–73, 184, 198; in 1973–91,
223, 229, 230–33
Society for the Suppression of
Vice, 15
Solanis, Valerie, 203–4
South Carolina, 14, 118
South Dakota, 235
Southern Christian Leadership
Conference (SCLC), 175–77
Southern women, 4; in 1900, 4–10,
19; in 1901–12, 47, 55, 59–60,
61; in 1912–29, 73, 74, 77, 90,
94; in 1929–45, 106, 107, 108,
117, 118, 119, 121–26; in 1945–
61, 139, 148, 165–79; in 1961–
73, 196–200; in 1973–91, 231–32
Soviet Union, 76, 120, 142, 162,
163, 167, 222
SPARs, 126
Spock, Dr. Benjamin, 138, 150–
51, 165; *Baby and Child Care*,
150–51
sports, 107, 219
Sputnik, 162

Stanton, Elizabeth Cady, 56, 58
steel, 19, 37, 67, 110, 239
Steinem, Gloria, 210–12
Stevens, Doris, 64, 70, 85
Stimson, Henry, 128
stock market crash (1929), 102,
  110
Stokes, Rose Pastor, 64, 76, 85
Student Nonviolent Coordinating
  Committee (SNCC), 177–78,
  196–200
Students for a Democratic Society
  (SDS), 195, 198–99
suburban women, in 1945–61,
  141–47, 160, 161
Supreme Court, U.S., 50, 75, 136,
  145, 170, 175, 215–16, 227–29,
  240

Taft, Jessie, 33
Taft, William Howard, 48
Tan, Amy, 235
Taylor, Robert, 146
teachers, 253–54; in 1900, 21–22,
  25–26, 27; in 1912–29, 67, 94,
  96–97; in 1929–45, 104, 114,
  129; in 1945–61, 147, 164, 173,
  176–77
temperance, 55
Tennessee, 172, 176–77
Terkel, Studs, 108
Terrell, Mary Church, 30, 59
Texas, 105, 216
Third National Conference of
  Commissions on the Status of
  Women (1966), 189
Thomas, Marlo, 212
Thompson, Clara, 155, 156
Thompson, Dorothy, 11, 16, 17,
  18, 101
Thompson, Margaret Grierson,
  10–17
Thompson, Peter, 10–17
Time magazine, 209, 211
Triangle Shirtwaist fire (1911), 42,
  44–45, 115, 221
tuberculosis, 5, 13, 18
Tuchman, Barbara, 212

United Auto Workers (UAW),
  120, 133, 189
United Electrical Workers (UE),
  133
United Farm Workers, 196
United Mine Workers, 119
United States Steel, 37
U.S. v. *One Package of Japanese
  Pessaries*, 90
upper-class women: in 1900, 25–
  35; in 1912–29, 87, 94–95, 96
urban women: in 1900, 17–35; in
  1901–12, 38–62; in 1912–29, 65–
  101; in 1929–45, 106, 119–20; in
  1945–61, 138–40, 143, 145–47,
  173–75; in 1961–73, 194, 203–6;
  in 1973–91, 232
Utah, 15, 54

Vanderbilt, William, 44
Vassar College, 26, 54, 69, 163
venereal disease, 13, 24, 50–51,
  128
Veterans Administration, 143
Vietnam War, 195, 198, 221, 226
Virginia, 74, 118, 224
volunteer work: in 1912–29, 93; in
  1929–45, 126; in 1945–61, 152–
  53, 157
voting rights, 56, 63, 111, 136, 208;
  in 1900, 15; in 1901–12, 54–62;
  in 1912–29, 63, 65–66, 68, 69–
  75, 77–78, 93; in 1929–45, 114–
  15; in 1945–61, 171–72, 176–78
Voting Rights Act, 178

Waddington, Sarah, 216
wages, 247, 254; in 1900, 9, 14, 19,
  20, 21, 22, 24; in 1901–12, 40–
  52, 54; in 1912–29, 74, 75, 78,
  79, 80, 81, 83, 94, 95, 97–98; in
  1929–45, 102–7, 117, 119, 121,
  126, 127–30, 133–35; in 1945–
  61, 140, 157–58, 159, 162, 165;
  in 1961–73, 181, 184–86, 190,
  213–14, 217, 218; in 1973–91,
  225, 226, 227, 230, 232, 235–41

Wald, Lillian, 48
Walker, Alice, 235
Wallace, George, 220–21
Ware, Caroline, 169, 178, 182
Warhol, Andy, 203
war industries, women in, 127–37, 144, 145, 162
War Manpower Commission, 131, 132, 162
Washington, Booker T., 9, 60
Washington, Margaret Murray, 60
Watson, John B., 99
Waves, 126
Weathermen, 233–34
Webster v. *Reproductive Health Services*, 229
Weeks, John W., 73, 76
Weitzman, Leonore, 242–43
Wells, H. G., 87
Wells-Barnett, Ida, 59, 73, 125, 146, 168
West, Mae, 106
white-collar jobs, 247; in 1900, 22; in 1929–45, 104–5, 127, 130; in 1945–61, 160; in 1961–73, 180–81; in 1973–91, 236–39
White House Conference on the Emergency Needs of Women (1933), 113–14
white slave trade, 51–52
White v. *Crook*, 183
wife-beating, 9–10, 31, 56, 209
Wilson, Paul, 115
Wilson, Woodrow, 69, 70, 72, 73, 129
Wisconsin, 74, 78
WITCH, 204–5
Wobblies, 46, 64, 83, 84, 119
Womanpower (1951 study), 162–67
Woman Rebel (journal), 84
Woman's Peace Party, 71

Women's Army Corps, 126
Women's Bureau, 74, 79, 80, 98, 105, 116, 119, 121, 129, 134, 153, 166, 181, 182, 183, 185
Women's Emergency Brigade, 119–20
Women's Equity Action League, 191, 209
Women's Joint Congressional Committee, 73
Women's Political Council, 173, 174
Women's Political Union, 58
women's rights, 56, 167; future of, 245–55; in 1900, 29–35; in 1901–12, 38–62; in 1912–29, 63–101; in 1929–45, 102–37; in 1945–61, 138–39, 152–57, 162, 167–79; in 1961–73, 180–219; in 1973–91, 220–44
Women's Trade Union League (WTUL), 21, 41–46, 57, 65–66, 76, 79, 80, 112, 134, 136, 153
Wood, Elizabeth, 108, 146
Woodward, Ellen, 114, 115
Woolley, Helen Thompson, 66
workmen's compensation laws, 53–54
World War I, 71–72, 76, 77, 85, 92, 93, 132, 136
World War II, 126–37, 139, 140, 143, 144, 148, 151, 162, 167, 168
writers, 28, 32, 94, 127, 148, 162, 194, 210–11, 235
Wyoming, 15, 54

Yale Law School, 178
Yoshimura, Fumio, 202, 207
Young Women's Christian Association (YWCA), 93, 124–25, 181